UNDOCUMENTED

UNDOCUMENTED

How Immigration Became Illegal

AVIVA CHOMSKY

BEACON PRESS
BOSTON

49996°3

BEACON PRESS
Boston, Massachusetts
www.beacon.org

Beacon Press books
are published under the auspices of
the Unitarian Universalist Association of Congregations.

17 16 15 14   8 7 6 5 4 3 2 1

This book is printed on acid-free paper that meets the uncoated paper
ANSI/NISO specifications for permanence as revised in 1992.

Text design and composition by Kim Arney

Library of Congress Cataloging-in-Publication Data
Chomsky, Aviva.
Undocumented : how immigration became illegal / Aviva Chomsky.
pages   cm
Includes bibliographical references and index.
ISBN 978-0-8070-0167-7 (paperback)
ISBN 978-0-8070-0168-4 (ebook)
1. Illegal aliens—United States. 2. United States—Emigration
and immigration. 3. United States—Emigration and
immigration—Government policy. 4. United States—Emigration
and immigration—Social aspects. 5. United States—Emigration
and immigration—Economic aspects. 6. Mexico—Emigration and
immigration. 7. Central America—Emigration and immigration.
8. Guatemala—Emigration and immigration. I. Title.
JV6465.C46 2014
364.1'370973—dc23
2013041931

To people
without papers
everywhere

Contents

Preface

As I began to give interviews and talks about my book *"They Take Our Jobs!" And 20 Other Myths about Immigration*, published in 2007, I became more and more convinced that a key, central issue that's hampering those of us who support immigrant rights is the absence of a basic, fundamental ability to say "immigrant rights are human rights." Immigration simply should not be illegal. No politician or talk-show commentator is going to risk saying this, but we have to.

I stand by my arguments about the myths I deconstruct in the book (Immigrants DON'T take American jobs! Immigrants DO pay taxes! Immigrants ARE learning English!), but I also, deep down, think these arguments miss the point. Immigrants are human beings who have arbitrarily been classified as having a different legal status from the rest of the United States' inhabitants. The only thing that makes immigrants different from anybody else is the fact that they are denied the basic rights that the rest of us have. There is simply no humanly acceptable reason to define a group of people as different and deny them rights.

How can we claim to oppose discrimination based on national origin when our entire body of citizenship and immigration law is founded on discrimination based on national origin? When people ask me, "Why don't they just apply for citizenship?" or "Why don't they just come here legally?" they are betraying a fundamental ignorance of our immigration and citizenship laws. People don't apply for citizenship or don't obtain proper documents to come here, because the law forbids it. That's right: the law forbids them to come to the United States or to apply for citizenship. US immigration law is based on a system of quotas and preferences. If you don't happen to be one of the lucky few who falls into a quota or preference category, there is basically no way to obtain legal permission to immigrate. If you are already in the United States without proper documentation, you will never, ever be allowed to apply for citizenship.

Given the choice, nobody would risk his or her life walking through the desert to enter the country illegally, and nobody would risk the constant fear, discrimination, and threat of deportation that comes from being undocumented. Of course, everybody who comes to the United States would rather enter the country legally, and everybody who is undocumented would rather be documented. If only the law allowed them to do it!

The purpose of this book is to denaturalize illegality. I want to show it as the social construction that it is. I want to show when, why, and how it came to be, and how it came to be socially accepted as a fact. I want to show how it works and what purpose it serves. Or maybe whose purposes it serves. My goal is to unveil the complex, inconsistent, and sometimes perverse nature of US immigration law that makes some people illegal.

Introduction

When people say, "What part of 'illegal' don't you understand?" they imply that they, in fact, understand everything about it. They take illegality to be self-evident: there's a law, you break the law, that's illegal. Obvious, right?

Actually, illegality is a lot more complicated than that. Laws are made and enforced by humans, in historical contexts, and for reasons. They change over time, and they are often created and modified to serve the interests of some groups—generally the powerful and privileged—over others.

Most of the citizens who brag that their ancestors came here "the right way" are making assumptions based on ignorance. They assume that their ancestors "went through the process" and obtained visas, as people are required to do today. In fact, most of them came before any legal process existed—before the concept of "illegality" existed.

THE INVENTION OF ILLEGALITY

Illegality as we know it today came into existence after 1965. In the decades before 1965, the media rarely depicted immigration in negative terms. Nor did the public or Congress consider it a problem in need of legislation. By the 1970s, though, the demonization of immigrants—in particular, Mexican and other

Latino immigrants—and the issue of "illegal immigration" were turning into hot-button issues.[1]

There are some particular historical reasons for these changes. Some are economic. The global and the domestic economies underwent some fundamental structural changes in the late twentieth century, changes we sometimes refer to as "globalization."

Some analysts argued that globalization was making the world "flat," and that with the spread of connection, technology, and communication, old inequalities would melt away.[2] Others believed that new inequalities were becoming entrenched—that a "global apartheid" being imposed, separating the Global North from the Global South, the rich from the poor, the winners in the new global economy from the losers.[3] I'll go more into depth about these changes and show how they contributed to a *need* for illegality to sustain the new world order.

The second set of changes is ideological and cultural. Like the big economic shifts, ideological and cultural changes are a process; they can't necessarily be pinpointed to a particular date or year. I use 1965 as a convenience, because that's when some major changes were enacted in US immigration law that contributed to creating illegality. But those changes responded to, and contributed to, the more long-term economic and ideological shifts that were occurring.

In the cultural realm, overt racism was going out of fashion. Civil rights movements at home and anti-colonial movements abroad undercut the legitimacy of racial exclusion and discrimination. While apartheid continued in South Africa through the 1980s, even that lost its international legitimacy. In the United States, the Jim Crow regime was dismantled and new laws and programs were aimed at creating racial equality, at least on paper. By the new century, people were beginning to talk about the United States as a "postracial" society. At the same time, though, new laws hardened immigration regimes and discrimination against immigrants in the United States and elsewhere.

TRUE REFUGEES OF THE BORDER WARS

Before deeply delving into the dizzying and sometimes irrational nature of immigration law, it's helpful to consider what's actually happening on the ground. I had the opportunity to see firsthand the human tragedy that's resulted from the new immigration regime in March 2010, when I participated in a weeklong humanitarian delegation with the organization No More Deaths, one of several that take direct action on the US-Mexico border.

Volunteers from these organizations attempt to provide humanitarian aid to migrants by leaving water at stations along migrant trails and offering basic first-aid at camps in the desert, among other things. My group, though, was taking testimonies on the Mexican side of the border from migrants who had been caught and deported.

During that week, I met several hundred deportees. They were arrested for a crime no US citizen can commit: entering the United States without official permission. Only people who are not US citizens *need* official permission to enter US territory.

Nogales, Sonora, on the US-Mexico border, has the feel of a war zone. Every few hours, a bus from the Wackenhut private security service arrives on the US side of the border filled with would-be migrants, mostly from Mexico's poor southern regions. Most of them were captured by the Border Patrol somewhere in the Arizona desert. "They used to try to capture us near the border," one migrant told me wearily. "Now, they patrol two or three days' walk north of the border. They want to find us when we're dehydrated, exhausted, blistered, so we can't run away."

First, the drivers unload their belongings from underneath the bus—a few backpacks, but mostly clear plastic Homeland Security bags supplied by the Border Patrol. After about half an hour, the migrants descend from the bus in small groups. Under armed guard, the lucky ones retrieve their packages and shuffle back across the border to be processed by Mexican authorities. Many have lost everything on their trek through the desert, when they were attacked by robbers, became separated from their group, got lost, or fled from the Border Patrol.

Processing takes about fifteen minutes. The migrants receive a slip of paper attesting to the fact that they are deportees. The paper confirms their eligibility for the fragmentary social services that the Mexican government and several Catholic church organizations offer to migrants in Nogales: one phone call, a half-fare bus ride home, three nights in a shelter, and, most generously, fifteen days of free meals twice a day at the *comedor*, or soup kitchen, run by the Proyecto Kino, supported by both the Mexican and several US archdioceses of the Catholic church.

After processing, the migrants emerge on the Mexican side of the border. Taxi drivers and food vendors accost them as they stumble out, dazed and bewildered. "Everybody wants to pretend to be a migrant, to get services," one provider told me. "You have to look at their shoes. If they have shoelaces, they're not migrants. Homeland Security takes their shoelaces so they won't . . ." He gestured slitting his throat and laughed conspiratorially. So the migrants stumble because their feet are raw and torn from walking through the desert, and because they have no shoelaces in their tattered shoes.

If they're lucky, one of the first people they'll encounter is Sal, with the Transportes Fronterizos (Border Transport) company, contracted by the Mexican government to provide transportation services for deportees. Sal is a deportee himself. In his twenties, he speaks English with a perfect Chicano lilt. That's not surprising: he came to the United States with his parents when he was three and grew up and graduated from high school in Arizona. "How did you get deported?" I asked him, quickly realizing that we should communicate in his preferred English, rather than Spanish. "You don't want to know," he grimaced. "Jaywalking." Was it racial profiling? The police stopped him for crossing a street where there was no crosswalk, asked him for his documents, and arrested him. In Arizona, local police are empowered to enforce immigration laws.

Sal can tell migrants where to find free food and shelter, and how to access the transportation services offered by Grupo Beta, the Mexican government agency charged with removing migrants from the border to prevent them from attempting to recross. He keeps his booth open from 10 a.m. until 6 p.m., when the last bus leaves for the shelter. Migrants who get deported after that have to sleep on the streets.

Most migrants leave their homes in Mexico with identification papers, money, and family members or other traveling companions. Most are deported alone and can spend days or weeks trying to determine the whereabouts of husbands, wives, children, or cousins. Many have also lost their documents and their cash. The buses arrive every few hours, all day and night. The migrants who are dumped and wander the streets of Nogales are the true refugees of the border wars.

At the door of the Proyecto Kino soup kitchen, the long line for breakfast starts forming around 8:30 a.m. Some migrants arrive by bus from the shelters, others by foot after spending the night on the street or in the cemetery. The hundred or so men line up on the right, and the ten to twenty women and children, who get served first, on the left. To get in when the *comedor* opens at 9 a.m. for the first breakfast shift, all of them have to show their deportation document. The paper that proves that they were hunted, captured, and deported for not having the proper documents to enter the United States now becomes their ticket to a free meal.

The services available to migrants are paltry compared to their needs. "My wife, my grown daughters, and our two adopted grandchildren are in California," one man in his fifties told me despairingly. He showed me the adoption papers. His daughter's children, aged two and three and both US citizens, were taken by Child Protective Services when the daughter became a drug user. He and his wife became their foster parents and then adopted them. "I had to promise that I'd support them and care for them. How can I do that if I can't get back to them?" He asked to use my cell phone to call his wife and then thrust the phone into my hand. "Talk to her," he urged me. "Tell her I'm here. Tell her I'm trying to get back."

A young man spent three days waiting outside the exit port. He and his wife were separated during the deportation process. "Her name is Brenda. She was wearing gray sweatpants and a green T-shirt," he told everyone who would listen. As each bus arrived, he stood waiting with a desperate hopelessness, watching the deportees slowly trickle out, searching for her familiar face.

As part of No More Deaths, I could offer these people only a few tokens of aid: a phone to call their relatives, donated clothes and socks, a granola bar or rehydration drink. I could beg them to share their stories with us, so that we could tell them back in the United States and try to change our immigration policies. At the end of the day, we'd walk back to Nogales, Arizona, stepping lightly across the border that had destroyed and divided their lives.

THE COURTS PLAY THEIR ROLE

In Tucson, Arizona, the Federal Court processes seventy migrants a day through the Operation Streamline program. About 4 percent of migrants who are captured are sent to Streamline, which began functioning in Tucson in 2008 after beginning in Texas as a pilot program in 2005. Between Tucson and Yuma, the other Arizona district using the program, some thirty thousand migrants are "Streamlined" every year.

Unlike most deportees, Streamlined migrants are charged with a criminal offense and imprisoned. The daily hearings fall somewhere between a kangaroo court and a slave auction. The migrants are shackled hand, foot, and waist, and sit in rows taking up about half of the courtroom. The judge calls them up in groups of ten or so, and their harassed lawyers, who represent four or five defendants a day, scramble to accompany them.[4] Almost all of these migrants were captured in the desert, and are blistered, exhausted, disoriented, and dehydrated when they are placed in cells. They describe being stripped of their belongings and their jackets and left to shiver in T-shirts under the air conditioning, being placed seventy or eighty people deep in cells designed for four or five. There is no room even to sit, much less lie down; they receive only a small juice box and a packet of cheese crackers in two days.

Ten migrants stand before the judge in their shackles, while dozens of others look on. The lawyers hover beside their clients. The judge asks: "Mr. ___, do you understand the charge against you and the maximum penalty? Do you understand your right to a trial? Are you willing to give up that right and plead guilty? Of what country are you a citizen? On or about March 18 of this year, did you enter into Southern Arizona from Mexico? Did you come to a port of entry?"

Most answer that they are citizens of Mexico, though on the day I attended the hearing, there were several Hondurans and Ecuadorians. A court interpreter repeats the questions in Spanish simultaneously, and the defendants listen through headphones that they can't touch because their hands are shackled to their waists. Their lawyers prompt them if they falter in their responses. Mostly, they answer *sí* to everything, which the interpreter dutifully translates as yes, except to the port-of-entry question, to which they are supposed to answer no. Some answer dully, staring at the ground; some respond in strong voices, looking up at the judge. A few are dismissed because they don't speak Spanish, and the court has no interpreters for the indigenous languages of Mexico. A few scorn the headphones and answer in English.

Occasionally, a defendant breaks the pattern. One answered yes when asked if he came to a port of entry. The judge was visibly unnerved. "You came to a port of entry?" she asked. "Let me ask the question again. Did you come to a port of entry?" Again, the defendant answered yes. She asked several more times before the lawyer convinced his client to answer no. Another defendant became agitated when the judge began to question him. "I'm guilty! I'm guilty!" he exclaimed. "I know you're guilty," responded the judge impatiently. "But I still have to ask you these questions, and you have to answer them."

"How do you plead to illegal entry, guilty or not guilty?" was the judge's last question. Every prisoner answered dutifully, *culpable*—guilty. Most were sentenced to time served and prepared to be deported to Nogales, Mexico. They will leave the country that they sacrificed so much to get to with a criminal record and the threat of up to twenty years in jail if they enter again. They will be among those arriving in Nogales, penniless, lost, and bewildered.

What we saw was only part of the picture. The trip to the border can be as dangerous as the crossing and passage through the US side. Every year, many thousands of migrants are kidnapped as they travel through Mexico. Gangs and drug smugglers see migrants as easy targets and count on the fact that the friends or relatives in the United States who raised the thousands of dollars to fund their trip will be able to generate more to pay for their ransom. As violence in the border region increased, migrants made up many of the victims. If a ransom was not paid, or if migrants refused to work for the gang, they might be killed, sometimes in massacres that claimed the lives of dozens.

SOME BACKGROUND

The many competing interests at stake in the development of law, policy, and ideology surrounding undocumentedness have led to a perplexing and constantly shifting landscape. To understand the changes of the late twentieth century, we need to understand how the system worked before that. From the eighteenth and, especially, the nineteenth centuries on, the United States benefited from its place in the global industrial economy, and white people in the United States benefited from their place in the racial order. A *dual labor market* developed in which some workers began to become upwardly mobile and enjoy the benefits of industrial society, while others were legally and structurally stuck at the bottom.

This dual system was reproduced both domestically and internationally, and race played a big role in it. Legal systems were created to justify and sustain it. Globally, the system was expressed through colonialism. Europeans colonized people of color around the world and benefited from their forced labor and their resources. In the United States, slavery played a big role in sustaining a dual labor system, where whites could move up, but blacks could not.

The United States took some colonies, too, at the end of the nineteenth century, like the Philippines, Cuba, and Puerto Rico. But US companies and citizens also benefited from the dual labor system when American companies like United Fruit established plantations in Central America and produced bananas using cheap labor there. They benefited when Brazilian slaveholders or German coffee planters in Guatemala used forced labor in those countries to supply cheap coffee for US markets.

Mexico played a big role in the dual labor market in the United States, both domestically and internationally. US mining companies operated in both countries from the late 1800s, and in both, they employed an explicit dual wage system. Mexicans received a lower, "Mexican" wage, while white US citizens received a so-called gold or US wage.[5]

Inside the United States, Mexicans were welcomed as migrant workers as American investment in the southwest grew after the territory was taken from Mexico in 1848 and 1853. A reliance on Mexican workers who contribute their labor to US economic enterprises—but are denied access to the benefits that US law affords its citizens—has underpinned the economy for over a century. Over the course of time, different legal and structural mechanisms have been used to maintain this system. Early on, it was done by legally distinguishing immigrants from workers. Immigrants were the Europeans who came to Ellis Island; workers were the Mexicans and Chinese who built the railroads and planted the food that sustained white settlement in the newly conquered west of the country. They were not expected to settle, stay, or become citizens. Citizenship, after all, was reserved for people defined as white until after the Civil War.

US immigration law thus treated Mexicans not as potential immigrants but as sojourners, temporary migrants who entered the country to work, rather than as immigrants who intended to stay. Anti-immigrant sentiment was directed against newly arrived Europeans, not against Mexicans. Anti-Mexican racism was also common, but it was directed against the supposed racial category of Mexicans rather than their status or citizenship.

Until 1924, the new border between the United States and Mexico was virtually unpoliced, and migration flowed openly. Mexicans were exempted from the immigration restrictions passed into law before 1965. Because they were not considered immigrants, Mexicans were also permanently deportable and were, in fact, singled out for mass deportations in the 1930s and 1950s. The nonimmigrant status of Mexican workers over time underlies the apparent paradox between the United States as a so-called country of immigrants and its xenophobia and restrictive immigration policies.

The creation of citizenship by birth through the Fourteenth Amendment was aimed at remedying the historic exclusion of African Americans. But it also created the apparent paradox that other nonwhites—like the Chinese—could become citizens through birth. Congress quickly moved to remedy this by restricting the entry of Chinese women in 1873 and all Chinese with the Chinese Exclusion Act in 1882. California's farms then became even more dependent on Mexicans who, unlike the Chinese, could still be counted on to leave after the harvest rather than remain in the country and eventually become citizens.

In 1928, the *Saturday Evening Post* reported that there were some 136,000 farmers in California, 100,000 with farms of under 100 acres, and 83,000 farming fewer than 40 acres. These small farmers did not use hired labor during most of the year, but during the harvest, required some 10 to 50 additional workers. "Fluid, casual labor is for them a factor determining profits or ruin," the *Post* explained.

"Mexican labor fits the requirements of the California farm as no other labor has done in the past. The Mexican can withstand the high temperatures of the Imperial and San Joaquin valleys. He is adapted to field conditions. He moves from one locality to another as the rotation of the seasonal crops progresses. He does heavy field work—particularly in the so-called 'stoop crops' and 'knee crops' of vegetable and cantaloupe production—which white labor refuses to do and is constitutionally unsuited to perform." Mexican labor, the author estimated, comprised from 70 to 80 percent of "casual" or seasonal farm labor.[6]

This informal system of rotating labor prevailed until the 1940s, when it was supplemented by a government-run system that continued until the mid-1960s, the Bracero Program. The Bracero Program, which brought in over 4 million workers between 1942 and 1964, was terminated in the context of civil rights organizing that highlighted the discriminatory treatment of these guest workers. But the economic structures that relied on these workers didn't disappear, and neither did the workers; they just returned to the old, informal system.

But, suddenly, the old system became illegal. The 1965 immigration law, which coincided with the termination of the

Bracero Program, responded to the domestic and international movements for racial equality by getting rid of the racial and national quota system that had prevailed until then. It gave every country an equal quota. And it included the countries of the Western Hemisphere for the first time, considering Mexicans as potential immigrants rather than just exploitable workers.

Given the structural realities of Mexican migrant labor, treating Mexicans equally under the new law was actually a way to keep exploiting them, but now, by calling them "illegal." From 1965 on, new laws made them more and more illegal and took more and more rights away from them.

Although it may seem contradictory, restrictive immigration laws actually contributed to a rise in both legal and "illegal" immigration. Two immigration scholars point to a synergy between the way the 1965 law privileged family members of US citizens and legal residents—in many cases, exempting them from the new quotas—and the barrage of laws after 1965 that progressively restricted the rights of noncitizens. It wasn't the new quota that led to increased Mexican legal immigration after 1965, since the quota drastically reduced the number of Mexicans allowed to immigrate. Instead, it was the punitive aspects of that and subsequent laws that increased the numbers of those who decided to become immigrants, rather than sojourners.[7] In other words, workers decided to stay, bring their families, and become immigrants because the earlier, seasonal pattern was becoming increasingly criminalized.

Some of the very organizations that were pushing to expand legal and social rights in the United States in the 1960s continued to draw a line at the border. The United Farm Workers union campaigned against "illegal" workers in the 1970s.[8] California Rural Legal Assistance and the UFW supported the nation's first employer sanctions law—making it illegal for employers to hire undocumented workers—in 1971.[9] The first attempt to implement such sanctions at the national level was in 1973, at the initiative of the AFL-CIO and the NAACP.[10] (By the 1990s, all of these organizations had changed their positions and opposed the employer sanctions that were created by the 1986 Immigration Reform and Control Act.) But employer sanctions turned out to be just one more way to maintain a large, exploitable pool of workers to fill agriculture's most backbreaking jobs. The sanctions could be suspended, as they were after Hurricane Katrina, when federal contractors desperately needed migrant laborers to clean up and rebuild the city of New Orleans.

Agriculture continues to employ large numbers of undocumented workers in the twenty-first century, as farmers and their organizations throughout the United States have publicly acknowledged. Larry Wooten, the president of the North Carolina Farm Bureau, explained at an agricultural summit in Atlanta in 2012 that "agricultural employers who advertise jobs—as is required for those who are part of the federal guest worker program—for nearly two months get little to no response. 'We have no choice,' Wooten said. 'We must use immigrants.'"[11]

Since the 1980s, economic restructuring in the United States has created some huge new demands for extra-legal workers who will contribute to the economy for low wages and few benefits. Many undocumented people today work at jobs that have been in-sourced. While most of us are familiar with out-sourcing—when jobs, from manufacturing to call centers, are shifted overseas—in-sourcing is less well known. The phrase can refer to a company's decision to carry out internally those tasks that were previously contracted out, or it can mean that a company brings back a job that had been outsourced abroad. Here, though, I'm referring to a particular kind of in-sourcing: when a company closes down an operation in order to move it somewhere else inside the United States where it will have access to cheaper (often immigrant) workers, lower taxes, fewer environmental or health and safety regulations, or other financial incentives.

Almost everybody in the United States benefits from that labor in one way or another, because it underlies almost all of the goods and services we use. Whether they work in agriculture or in-sourced industries like meatpacking, or whether they work in landscaping, newspaper delivery, or cleanup after environmental disasters, the invisible labor of undocumented workers sustains the economy. Moreover, the presence of these migrants also serves to create more jobs. By living in the United States, by spending money and consuming goods and services themselves, they sustain the jobs of other workers.

The work that undocumented migrants do is essential to the functioning of the economy and to the comfort of citizens. The system is also, however, fundamentally unjust. By creating a necessarily subordinate workforce without legal status, we maintain a system of legalized inequality. It's a domestic reproduction of a global system. The border is used to rationalize the system globally; it makes it seem right and natural that exploited workers in one place should produce cheap goods and services for consumers in another place. Illegality replicates the rationale domestically: it makes it seem right and natural that a legally marginalized group of workers should produce cheap goods and services for another group defined as legally superior.

STATUS, RACE, AND THE NEW JIM CROWS

At the same time that these big economic shifts were occurring, other political, social, and cultural changes were happening globally. After World War II, overt racism and white supremacy began to lose ground. Europe slowly and painfully let go of most of its colonies, and the number of independent countries proliferated. Almost all of the new independent countries were run by people of color. In the United States, civil rights movements fought to dismantle legalized discrimination. South Africa became an international pariah and finally ended apartheid.

In an important book published in 2010, though, Michelle Alexander argues that the racial caste system that United States has maintained since the days of slavery did not end with the passage of civil rights legislation in the 1950s and '60s. Rather, a new system of legalized discrimination developed to replace the old Jim Crow system. The new system, she writes, is mass incarceration. Black people—and, as I argue here, Mexicans and other Latin Americans as well—were systematically criminalized. Although, on the surface, the system is color-blind, in fact, it targets people of color. But it works better in this supposedly postracial age, because it never uses race directly to discriminate. Instead, it criminalizes people of color and then discriminates on the basis of their criminal status.

Most citizens who rail against the undocumented insist that their opposition is based solely on technical, legal grounds: they oppose people who broke the law. But becoming undocumented is a highly racialized crime. Nationality itself has its origins in racial thinking and still bases itself on birth and origin in ways that echo racialism. The categories "Mexican" and "Latino" have been racialized in the United States, and the category of illegality is heavily associated with the category "Mexican," whether this is understood as a nationality, an ethnicity, or a race. In 2011, 93 percent of federal immigration crimes were committed by noncitizens, and 89.3 percent of them were committed by Hispanics.[12]

Another way to look at the racialized nature of undocumentedness is to compare the criminalization of immigrants (especially Latino immigrants) in the post–civil rights era with the criminalization of blacks. Alexander argues that laws passed and implemented in the aftermath of the civil rights movement and legislation that accompanied it effectively countered the gains made in the 1950s and '60s. "We have not ended racial caste in America," she writes, "we have merely redesigned it."[13] The new system, mass incarceration, consists of "not only . . . the criminal justice system but also . . . the larger web of laws, rules, policies, and customs that control those labeled criminals both in and out of prison." Once caught in the web, former prisoners are in it forever. They "enter a hidden underworld of legalized discrimination and permanent social exclusion. . . . The current system of control permanently locks a huge percentage of the African American community out of the mainstream society and economy."[14]

Alexander focuses not only on incarceration itself, but on what happens after release. "Once [prisoners] are released, they are often denied the right to vote, excluded from juries, and relegated to a racially segregated and subordinated existence. . . . They are legally denied the ability to obtain employment, housing, and public benefits."[15] Possession of a felony conviction, then, replicates the very legal restrictions that used to be enforced by Jim Crow.

In the ideology and culture of exclusion, as well as in the laws and mechanics of its implementation, the arguments Alexander makes about African Americans have a parallel in the situation of immigrants. Like the African Americans that Alexander studies, large portions of the Latin American immigrant population have also been permanently criminalized and legally excluded. As with African Americans, undocumented immigrants are criminalized by a system that is superficially race-blind and defended on that basis.

Just as African Americans have become stigmatized in the post–civil rights era through criminalization, so have immigrants. Before, legal discrimination could be based explicitly on race. When race-based discrimination was outlawed, a new system emerged: turn people of color into criminals. Then you can discriminate against them because of their criminality, rather than because of their race. A new legitimacy for discrimination was thus born.[16]

Alexander meticulously details the ways in which criminal status follows black people into every area of life. With minor drug charges turned into felonies and defendants urged to plea bargain, huge numbers of black men become permanent "felons":

> When a defendant pleads guilty to a minor drug offense, nobody will likely tell him that he may be permanently forfeiting his right to vote as well as his right to serve on a jury. . . . He will also be told little or nothing about the parallel universe he is about to enter, one that promises a form of punishment that is often more difficult to bear than prison time: a lifetime of shame, contempt, scorn, and exclusion. In this hidden world, discrimination is perfectly legal. . . . Commentators liken the prison label to "the mark of Cain" and characterize the perpetual nature of the sanction as "internal exile." Myriad laws, rules, and regulations operate to discriminate against ex-offenders and effectively prevent their reintegration into the mainstream society and economy. These restrictions amount to a form of "civic death" and send the unequivocal message that "they" are no longer part of "us."[17]

Like convicted felons—mostly African Americans—the undocumented live in a strange world of internal exile or civic death. While physically present, they are legally excluded by an official status that has been ascribed to them. They can't vote, serve on a jury, work, live in public housing, or receive public benefits. These exclusions apply equally to those, mostly blacks, with a criminal record and those, mostly Mexican, who are undocumented. Stigmatization and exclusion create a vicious circle of further stigmatization and exclusion.

"In the era of colorblindness," Alexander writes, "it is no longer permissible to hate blacks, but we can hate criminals."[18] The same argument could be made for Mexicans and criminalized immigrants. Anti-immigrant blogs, commentaries, and general opinion frequently emphasize the legalistic nature of their anti-immigrant sentiment: "They broke the law!" But it's a law that, in design and in fact, is aimed at one, racially defined, sector of society.

Another aspect that links the criminalization of blacks and of Hispanics is the enormous rise in detention and what some have termed the "prison-industrial complex."[19] The Supreme Court commented in 2010 on the dramatic changes in federal immigration law over the previous ninety years. "While once there was only a narrow class of deportable offenses and judges wielded broad discretionary authority to prevent deportation, immigration reforms over time have expanded the class of deportable offenses and limited the authority of judges to alleviate the harsh consequences of deportation." As criminal convictions of people of color for minor offenses have risen, so have the consequences of these convictions. Now, even legal permanent residents can be deported for minor convictions, well after the fact.[20]

PUTTING IT ALL TOGETHER

This new criminalization of African Americans and Latinos relates to their different places in a changing labor market. Alexander points out that earlier racial caste systems (slavery and Jim Crow) served to keep African Americans as an exploitable labor force. Now, the criminalization of African Americans has coincided with their removal from the labor force. With the collapse of the urban manufacturing sector, their labor was no longer necessary. They have become a surplus population, to be warehoused in the prison system.

The criminalization of Mexican immigrants, however, underlies their increasingly important role in the economy. The language and ideology are similar: fear, marginalization, and exclusion are based upon the supposed criminality of the objects of hatred and justified with repeated invocations of the color-blind nature of modern US society. But in the case of immigrants, the criminalization *justifies* their location in the lowest ranks of the labor force.

Like Alexander, Nicholas De Genova argues that changes in the law deliberately criminalized a group that could no longer be legally defined by race. Illegality, he writes, is not "a mere fact of life, the presumably transparent consequence of unauthorized border crossing or some other violation of immigration law." Instead, he argues, laws themselves were written with the express purpose of creating this new status of illegality, because it served the purpose of keeping workers exploitable.[21]

At an even deeper level, anti-undocumented sentiment plays into deeply held beliefs and fears about the state, the nation, and sovereignty. The world's wealthy nations have created islands of prosperity and privilege, and those who live in these islands have an interest in preserving them—and in justifying their own access to them. Illegality is the flip side of inequality. It serves to preserve the privileged spaces for those deemed citizens and justify their privilege by creating a legal apparatus to sustain it. Heightened panic about "illegality" coincides with growing global inequality and the dependence of the privileged on the labor of the excluded.

The idea that countries are such discrete entities is inherently flawed. As every Mexican is aware, the contemporary US-Mexico border is an arbitrary product of the US invasion of Mexico from 1846 to 1848, and the subsequent demand that a huge segment of Mexico's territory be ceded to the United States. As the descendants of the Mexican population living in what is now the southwestern United States like to remind us, "We didn't cross the border; the border crossed us."

Even since the creation of this new border, in the case of the United States, Mexico, and Central America, the histories, economies, politics, and militaries of these countries are so deeply intermeshed that each would be totally different without its relationship with the others. Without Mexican and Central American labor, and the consumer goods and profits that come from that labor, US prosperity would look entirely different.

And without US military, political, and economic intervention, Mexico and Central America would be quite different as well. A person might be a citizen of, and live inside the borders of, a single country. But the social and economic systems that structure our lives go well beyond the borders of any country.

Also worth considering, for a moment, is what it means to criminalize movement or presence. While we are accustomed to a global order in which nation-states define their sovereignty in part by their ability to control movement in and out of their territories, we should also be capable of critiquing this equation and imagining different definitions of sovereignty. Is it necessary to rely on a legal order that forces people to remain inside the political unit into which they were born and makes unlawful their presence outside of that political unit? With a bit of critical distance, the notion appears more and more absurd.

OUTLINE OF THE BOOK

The first chapter of this book, "Where Did Illegality Come From?" seeks to unveil the beliefs and assumptions that have led us to accept discrimination on the basis of a human invention that we call "citizenship." It places illegality in a long historical trajectory of different ways that people—and, since 1492, especially Europeans—have created an unequal world of privilege and marginalization.

The second chapter, "Choosing to Be Undocumented," looks at the origins of undocumented people and the different paths to undocumented status. It looks on the ground at sending communities in Mexico and Guatemala, and the historical and social forces that lead people to migrate and lead them into undocumentedness.

Chapter 3, "Becoming Illegal," looks at the different ways that people enter the United States without authorization or lose authorization after entering legally. Some enter the country with legal permission but fall out of that status, while others pay thousands of dollars to coyotes (smugglers) to make a dangerous and sometimes fatal trip across the desert. This chapter also discusses how Operation Gatekeeper and other US border policy choices have affected people's lives and choices.

Chapter 4, "What Part of 'Illegal' Do You Understand?" explores what exactly is considered illegal about people without documents. It looks at what is actually prosecuted and how this has changed over time, and at who is deported and why. It also examines the contradictory and shifting legal landscape that structures migrants' lives.

Chapters 5 and 6 look at the world of work. What kinds of work are undocumented people doing in the United States? How does their work support the United States and the global economy? Who benefits, and who is harmed, by the existence of undocumented status? These chapters look into the jobs and the working conditions of the undocumented, and how their status affects their rights in the workplace and the functioning of the US economy as a whole.

Chapter 7 focuses on children and families. As the undocumented population grew, its profile also changed. In earlier years, the undocumented were primarily single, working-age men. By the late twentieth century, large numbers of children were undocumented or had undocumented parents. How does status affect the lives of children and families? What kinds of organizations have these youth formed, and what are the prospects for their future?

The last chapter looks at solutions. If we do not want to live in a society divided by status, with large numbers of "illegal" people, what can we do to change the situation? I outline some of the so-called solutions that have been attempted, ranging from deportation to border patrols to legalizations. I argue that current immigration reform proposals do not address the problem of being undocumented in a realistic way, and that only by challenging the contradictions inherent in the category itself—that is, by declaring that no human being is illegal—can the law adequately address human rights and human needs.

When people ask me what I think we should do about immigration reform, I tell them that I think the immigrant rights movement had it right back in the 1980s when we insisted that "no human being is illegal." If discrimination on the basis of national origin is illegal, then we need to acknowledge that our immigration laws are illegal. Human rights—including the right to be recognized as a person equal to other people—apply to everyone: no exceptions. Let's admit that our discriminatory laws are unjustifiable. Let's abolish the category "illegal" and give everyone the right to exist. We would solve the problem of illegal immigration with the stroke of a pen.

But I also understand that a lot of political and cultural change is going to have to occur before such a policy change could enter the realm of possibility. Thus, while we insist on unveiling and challenging the roots of injustice and inequality, we need to also, pragmatically and simultaneously, work to relieve its excesses where we can, even if our larger goals seem distant. It's important, though, to keep sight of the larger goals as well and not adopt short-term campaigns that work at cross-purposes to what we really believe and seek to change.

If we accept the argument that changes in the law deliberately created illegality, and did so for the purpose of keeping Mexican workers available, cheap, and deportable, then it should not be unimaginable to propose drastically changing the law. Likewise, if we understand that, with respect to Mexico, restrictive immigration legislation has had virtually no effect on migration patterns, we must be able to question the value of such legislation even in achieving its avowed purpose. I hope that this book will contribute to opening a new debate that goes well beyond so-called comprehensive immigration reform to challenge the very concept of undocumentedness or illegality in our society.

CHAPTER 1

Where Did Illegality Come From?

Most of us think that we know what the word illegal means and why some people fall into this category. It seems right and natural to us that people should be divided by citizenship, and by documents, into different categories with differential rights.

We assume that the world is naturally divided into countries and that every human being somehow belongs in one country or another. People are supposed to stay in the country that they were born in, unless they can get special permission to enter another. Each country expresses its sovereignty by deciding who is allowed to enter into its territory and who is allowed access to citizenship. So we rarely question the idea that countries should be able to decide who can cross their borders and treat people differently under the law depending on statuses that these same countries assign them.

But there is nothing natural about this state of affairs. Countries, sovereignty, citizenship, and laws are all social constructions: abstractions invented by humans. What's more, they are all fairly recent inventions. Today, we use them to justify differences in legal status. In this chapter, I will call into question the contemporary concept of illegality by looking at how we came to accept this particular kind of status difference as legitimate, even as we have rejected other historical rationales for laws that inscribe inequality.

We assume that these social constructions have some kind of independent reality or existence, but in fact they don't: people invented them to serve their own interests. There were historical reasons that people created them, and it's important to understand those reasons in order to think critically about them.

Our current system of organizing the world into sovereign countries made up of citizens (and, in almost all cases, noncitizens) has roots in past ideas and categories, which have evolved over hundreds of years. The laws that make some immigration—and thus, some people—"illegal" are recent creations, though they grow out of older ideas. Once we carefully examine the history of these concepts, they start to look more and more untenable. Rather than the question we often hear, "What part of illegal don't you understand?" perhaps we need to ask, "What part of illegal *do* you understand?"

There are several concepts that can help us to trace the roots of illegality. First, we'll look at ideologies of European domination that spurred the continent's expansion after 1492. Ideas about *mobility*, and who has the right to move where, played an important role in the ideologies of European superiority that justified conquests and colonization.

Connected to ideas about mobility are ideas about the law. In 1894, French novelist Anatole France noted with irony "the majestic equality of the laws, which forbid rich and poor alike to sleep under the bridges, to beg in the streets, and to steal their bread."[1] Even if a law looks like it treats everybody equally, laws only exist in social contexts. If the social context is unequal or unfair, even a law that purports to be equal might serve to cover up, or even reinforce, existing inequalities. Recently, the discipline of critical legal studies has developed this perspective, arguing that despite its pretensions, the law is never neutral, but rather reflects power relationships in society. As we talk about mobility, we'll look at how Europeans used laws to assert their superiority and their right to move, and to deny others the right to freedom of movement, all the while asserting that the rule of law must be held sacred.

We'll also look at how, over the past one thousand years, Europeans have used religion, race, and nationality—that is, countries and citizenship—as organizing principles to divide people into categories or castes. Each has been used hierarchically to justify social inequalities and differential legal treatment of different groups. Once status is inscribed in the law, this becomes an automatic justification for inequality: "it's the law!"

Status has been used historically to justify forcing people defined as inferior or outsiders to work for those defined as superior or insiders. Low-status people are forced to work in society's dirtiest, hardest, and most dangerous jobs.

In today's world, the connection of status to work is different. Until recently, one of the main purposes of status was to create a subject labor force through enslavement and other systems of forced labor. In the twenty-first century, laws are still used keep certain people working in low-wage, undesirable jobs. But the way status is used to enforce labor has changed. Force became more subtle, and work itself became redefined as a privilege. As twentieth-century economic changes in the United States and abroad made it more and more difficult for people to produce their own subsistence, overt force became less and less necessary as a way of making people work. Now, people work out of need.

Along with these structural changes came ideological changes. In today's ideology, work is a privilege reserved for those of superior status, rather than a burden imposed on those of inferior status. Of course, those of inferior status still work, and they still do the worst jobs. But the system is upheld by laws that claim to *prevent* people of inferior status from working. But the laws are only actually enforced in more desirable sectors of the labor market; thus, people labeled inferior are once again relegated to the worst jobs. Still, it's notable that the late twentieth century was the first time that laws have claimed to try to reserve jobs for the privileged, rather than force them upon the unprivileged.

These issues are interrelated in many ways. While we'll address them one by one, the discussion will also build an argument about the arbitrary and historically specific nature of illegality and the role it serves in the modern world.

DOMINATION AND MOBILITY

Some of the unspoken foundations that support the idea of illegality today come to us thanks to Christopher Columbus and the European expansion that followed in his wake. It might surprise readers to hear that many of the structures that have led to the current ways that people are moving around the planet— or prevented from this movement—date back to that same colonial expansion.

The "age of exploration" sent Europeans around the globe with the aim of settling and ruling distant lands and peoples. They developed an ideology to justify this exploration: an ideology that granted full humanity, free will, intellect, and strength to white Christians. To those who did not fall into that category, the Europeans (who did not at that time think of themselves as Europeans or even as white but rather primarily as Christians) attributed irrationality, brutality, stupidity, and barbarity.[2]

Along with these ideologies went ideas about movement: who belonged where. Europeans, apparently, belonged everywhere. Christians needed to spread their religion to heathens, European governments needed to expand their realms and bestow the benefits of their government to others, and settlers needed to fulfill their pioneering spirit and manifest destiny by applying their will and their capital to new lands and peoples.

And they created countries, governments, and laws to authorize themselves to do these things.

In the mind frame undergirding European exploration, non-Europeans were not capable, nor had they the right, to make their own decisions about residence or movement. It was up to Europeans to forcibly relocate them to where they could best serve European needs. Native Americans and Africans were both subject to transportation—Native Americans to mines and haciendas (in Spanish America) or simply off of lands that Europeans desired (in British America), and Africans to those same lands, to work for Europeans.

In the New Imperialism of the nineteenth century, Europeans (who by now identified explicitly with that term) once more demonstrated their will to move, to rule, and to displace. In the Scramble for Africa, Britain, France, and Germany laid their claims to the continent. The new United States followed its Manifest Destiny and displaced Native Americans westward and onto reservations, and then went on to appropriate colonies like Puerto Rico, Cuba, and the Philippines from the declining Spanish empire. After abolishing slavery, the United States established legal systems of segregation to prohibit African Americans from whites-only spaces. Meanwhile, the new imperial powers transported indentured Africans, East Indians, and Chinese to the Caribbean and the American continent to work on their plantations, railroads, and other enterprises.

In the intellectual spirit of the time, King Leopold of Belgium offered a pseudoscientific justification for this European control of migrations, explaining that "the races inhabiting [the southern continents] are captives in the bonds of all powerful nature; they will never break down the fences that sunder them from us. It is for us, the favored races, to go to them."[3] Go to them, and then confine them. As one white settler in Arizona proposed, the United States should "[p]lace the Indians on reservations . . . establish military posts along their limits, and shoot every Indian found off the reservations."[4]

From apartheid South Africa to the Jim Crow South, white Europeans during the twentieth century made it clear that the right to decide who could move where was inherent to domination. In 1917, the United States created the Asiatic Barred Zone prohibiting immigration by "Asiatics," who were defined as "aliens ineligible to citizenship" because of their race. Meanwhile, US forces were demanding the opening of China and Japan to US migration, trade, and business enterprise and, indeed, demanding the right of extraterritoriality for its citizens there. As Woodrow Wilson declared in 1907 (before he became president), "The doors of the nations which are closed . . . must be battered down. Concessions obtained by financiers must be safeguarded by ministers of state, even if the sovereignty of unwilling nations be outraged in the process. Colonies must be obtained or planted in order that no useful corner of the world may be overlooked or left unused."[5] Although China was not a colony, with the Treaty of Wanghia in 1844, the United States insisted on American access to Chinese ports and, moreover, that US citizens in China would be subject to US rather than Chinese law. In the words of Teemu Ruskola, not only were Americans guaranteed the right to enter China, but "when Americans entered China, American law traveled with them, effectively attaching to their very bodies."[6]

Americans and Europeans currently assume that freedom to travel is their birthright. "Over much of the world today citizens of many countries can travel freely," Jared Diamond asserts confidently. "To cross the border into another country, either we arrive unannounced and just show our passport, or else we have to obtain a visa in advance but can then travel without restrictions."[7] What he really means is that citizens of the former colonial powers (and also, generally, postcolonial elites) can travel freely. These same countries routinely deny entry to people, especially poor people, from their former colonies. Freedom to travel, then, is still a privilege reserved for those in control.

Americans and Europeans also rarely question their right to send troops and establish governments in their former colonies. Iraq and Afghanistan, they implicitly believe (like Puerto Rico, Cuba, Nicaragua, Haiti, the Dominican Republic, Vietnam, and so on), simply can't govern themselves without a US and European presence. People from all of those former colonies, however, also need to have their mobility severely restricted. Countries like the United States established themselves by driving out nonwhites or non-Europeans or non-Christians, and establishing rule over nonwhites, non-Europeans, and non-Christians in the Global South. Now, they argue, they need to erect militarized borders to prevent the descendants of those nonwhites from infiltrating, at the same time that they continue to send their citizens to those countries as occupying armies, aid workers, investors, tourists, or students.

FROM RELIGION TO RACE

Columbus and those who traveled with and after him were heirs to a medieval Spanish tradition that used religion as the main principle for organizing and categorizing people. Muslim Spain, from 711 to 1492, like many other medieval and earlier (and some later) empires, was based on the idea of *convivencia*, or religious tolerance, among Muslim, Christian, and Jewish communities. Not so Christian Spain. The *reconquista*, or reconquest, of the Iberian peninsula by Christians drew on the spirit of the Crusades: to drive out and destroy the infidels.

Spanish Christian ideas about religion were much more essentialist than the way most people think about religion today. Religion was thought to be defined by blood. The Spanish developed elaborate theories of lineage based on what was called Christians' purity of blood. Jews' and Muslims' blood was considered to be stained. Even if they converted to Christianity, they would continue to bear the stain of their non-Christian ancestry. So-called New Christians were viewed with suspicion and periodically repressed or expelled.

Ideas about mobility—who belonged where—were based on religion. The Spanish conquest in the Americas began the same year—1492—that the last Muslims and Jews were driven out of the Iberian Peninsula, and the Spaniards took their ideologies with them. Spanish Christians were already transporting and enslaving Africans with the rationale that they were not Christian. They debated the humanity of the native peoples of the Americas, in the end deciding that they were, in theory, capable of being converted to Christianity and, therefore, not to be enslaved.

Capable of being converted or not, though, the indigenous inhabitants clearly did not have pure blood. In the Americas, Christian Spaniards' struggle to assert, define, and justify their so-called purity of blood began to take on a more racial cast. The term purity came to mean the absence of African or indigenous ancestry.

In the elaborate legal hierarchy of Spanish America, racialized castes proliferated by the eighteenth century. Spaniards born in Spain were the purest, because there was no chance that their ancestry could have been compromised with indigenous or African admixture. People of (supposedly) 100 percent Spanish ancestry born in the New World occupied a space on a rung lower, and from there, the ranks descended all the way down to enslaved Africans and tributary Indians, with multiple mixtures in between.

Emerging ideas about race were also part of an elaborate system of legal status and access—or lack of access—to rights in society. People defined as belonging to the lower races were prohibited from spaces reserved for the privileged and subject to special taxes and forced labor. Purity of blood could also be purchased. Suspicious or inferior ancestry could be erased for a fee, thus strengthening the relationship between race and social status.[8]

British colonizers in North America were heirs to some of the same broad European cultural mores as the Spanish, but their colonial enterprise was also infused with a form of Protestant, northern European ethno-nationalism exemplified in the "Black Legend." Promoted by British and Dutch thinkers and artists like Theodore de Bry, the Black Legend depicted the cruelties of Spanish conquest and attributed them to Spanish Catholicism and the Spanish racialized character. British and Dutch colonialism, in contrast, was conceived as a benign project.[9]

Religion was a key factor for the British in defining who they were as a people and justifying their right to conquer, dominate, and exclude. Legal scholar Aziz Rana argues that, for the British, the original "savages" were the Catholic Irish. The conquest of Ireland served as a "test case" or "rehearsal" for subsequent British conquest in the Americas. In Ireland, the British refined their rationale for land expropriation. If the natives didn't cultivate the land according to British standards or did not accept British religious dictates, they lost their rights to the land itself.[10]

In the American colonies, British ideas about race grew from and eventually came to supersede those about religion. In King Philip's War (1675), colonists slaughtered Native Americans, Christianized or not.[11] By the 1700s, white indentured servants were moving off the plantations and being replaced by African slaves. As whites took advantage of the economic rewards of freedom, they also began to impose laws that protected their privileges and their access to slave labor—the first racial laws that targeted free blacks solely on the basis of race. Thus, by the 1700s, free blacks had become "a segregated and separate caste" in American society.[12]

Just as religion became a palimpsest for race in the first centuries of European colonialism, the race/religion complex likewise became a palimpsest for what came to be called the nation. New ideas evolved from, and were shaped by, what came before. When the United States declared itself an independent nation, race was the key factor in determining who belonged to the polity. Emerging European nation-states, too, based their legitimacy on what Benedict Anderson called "imagined communities" of peoples connected primordially, ethnically—essentially, racially or by blood.[13]

FROM RACE TO NATION

Racially based ideas held considerable sway well into the twentieth century, even as policies and ideologies came to replace race with nation as the prime rationale for legal domination, discrimination, and restrictions on mobility. The abolition of racially based slavery, most analysts now agree, led to an upsurge in racially exclusive and repressive policies and attitudes throughout the Americas. Not until the late twentieth century, with Europe's rejection of Nazism and the dismantling of the racial regime in the United States, did overtly racialist thought lose its legitimacy. Precisely in this recent period, the use of nationality as an excuse for discrimination and persecution rose to new prominence. It was not a new concept or justification, but it emerged, perhaps, in full ideological flower, after generations of germination.

What we think of as countries today—also known as nation-states—first emerged in Europe several centuries ago. The idea of the nation-state was that the country was the manifestation of a historical unity or essence of the people that lived there—the nation. Older, multicultural empires like the Russian, Austro-Hungarian, and Ottoman gave way by the twentieth century to a proliferation of countries or states, each claiming to represent a people or nation.

In the United States, rights and access that used to be assigned on the basis of religion or race were gradually transferred to citizenship status. Racial restrictions on immigration and citizenship were replaced by national restrictions. Historian John Torpey wrote that gaining a monopoly over "legitimate means of movement" was precisely how emerging nation-states established their claims to sovereignty.[14]

To examine the different components of this second shift—from race to nation—let us look for a moment at the evolution of controls on mobility in the United States. In the nineteenth-century United States, private individuals and subnational localities held the right to control freedom of movement, especially that of enslaved and even free blacks. National membership was overtly based on race: until 1868, citizenship was restricted to whites. The Dred Scott decision in 1857 reiterated the primacy of race as a justification for deprivation of rights, but also of individual rights to control mobility. Until the civil rights acts of the 1960s, racial controls on physical access and individual, local, or institutional controls on access prevailed. School and bus segregation may be the best-known examples, but sundown towns, in which blacks were allowed to work but not remain after sunset, also hung on until 1968.[15]

Explicitly *national* manifestations of control of movement emerged in the late nineteenth century, imbued with racial ideas. The first restrictive immigration laws in the United States conflated race and nation. Chinese exclusion in 1882 was based on race: as "racially ineligible to citizenship," the Chinese should be excluded from entering the country as well. The quota system that restricted southern and eastern European immigration—and virtually proscribed non-European immigration—starting in 1921, likewise relied on racialized notions of nationality: Italian was as much a race as an official citizenship status.

Even as national citizenship became more important in the early twentieth century, race continued to play an important role in determining status and access to rights. Hiroshi Motomura uses the term "intending citizenship" to explain the privileges granted to white immigrants in the nineteenth century. Although not formally citizens, by virtue of their race they were accorded privileges of access to the benefits of society, including the right to vote and virtually automatic naturalization. Aziz Rana elaborates by distinguishing formal citizenship from "free citizenship"—the latter available only to whites. Mexicans, after 1848, and blacks, after 1868, were accorded formal citizenship, but still denied the right to vote, to own land, and to move freely.[16] New immigrants from Europe—Motomura's "intended" citizens—were accorded all of those rights, even when they were not yet formally citizens. Thus, race frequently trumped nationality in determining access to rights.

As the twentieth century progressed, national citizenship more and more joined race as a primordial legal identification and determinant of status. For example, voting laws were changed to prohibit noncitizens from voting. Instead of being considered automatically part of the country on the basis of their whiteness, European immigrants came to be considered foreign because of their immigrant status.[17] For the first time, white Europeans were treated as legally other and subordinate, the way conquered and racially differentiated peoples—African and Indian—had been since the first days of British settlement. Noncitizens were also told that, like Africans and Indians, they were no longer in charge of their own mobility. State authorities now had the right to exclude or deport them.[18]

The 1924 immigration legislation illustrates some of the ways that national citizenship was coming to stand in for race. Asians were excluded as "aliens ineligible to citizenship" based on the same legal ideas that had previously excluded African Americans. The new legal category of national origins was invented for Europeans.[19] They were defined as implicitly belonging to the white race, but having so-called nationalities or ethnicities that did not preclude assimilation into the United States. Mexican and Chinese nationalities, though, became legally defined as nonwhite. So while race and nationality were separated for European Americans (i.e., a person could be both white and Italian), they became one for Asians and Mexicans; their nationalities were essentially legislated to be nonwhite races.[20]

These legal changes complicated racial categories by overlaying them with nation. If Chinese and Mexican became races, the very meaning of race was changing fundamentally, its power giving way to nation. If Congress and the courts had to resort more and more to nationality as a pretext for the denial of rights, it was precisely because racial justifications were being chipped away, at least in the legal sphere.

During most of the twentieth century, legal subjection by race and by immigration or citizenship status coexisted. By the end of the twentieth century, though, differential legal treatment on the basis of race had fallen from international favor. Formal abolition of racial discrimination may not have created actual racial equality, but it did dismantle and delegitimize legal structures of discrimination, including racialized restrictions on freedom of movement. Facilities formerly justified as separate-but-equal were abolished, along with sundown towns. Federal antidiscrimination law prohibited long-standing practices that denied access to jobs, spaces, and benefits on the basis of race.

But just as the first round of antiracialist legislation after the Civil War led to a surge in anti-immigrant legislation—aimed at racially defined unwanteds—so did the second round after World War II. If citizenship were to be granted to all by birth, as per the Fourteenth Amendment, then race could no longer be explicitly used to deny citizenship. So nationality stood in for it, and citizens of countries like China lost their right to immigrate. If formal citizenship was to be made real—if citizens could no longer be excluded from jobs, landownership, voting, and other rights on the basis of race—nationality could once again be mobilized as a method of exclusion. In 1965, numerical immigration restrictions were applied for the first time to the Western Hemisphere. Mexicans could no longer be discriminated against for belonging to the Mexican race; now they would be discriminated against for their nationality, their Mexican citizenship, their lack of US citizenship, or their illegality.

The status of illegality and its concomitant legal exclusion affected more individuals by the early 2000s than did the Jim Crow system in the US South at its height.[21] Just as Jim Crow had imposed discrimination on the basis of race, new legislation in the late twentieth century increased discrimination against noncitizens and especially those who challenged their exclusion from the country by nonviolent direct action—that is, entering "illegally" or overstaying a visa. A study of Hispanic immigrants in rural North Carolina found that they felt that their lack of citizenship status, rather than their ambiguous place in the black-white racial hierarchy, was the main factor causing the discrimination they experienced.[22]

Recently, political scientist Jacqueline Stevens has suggested that discrimination on the basis of citizenship is incompatible with the notion of a liberal, egalitarian society, as much so as earlier laws and institutions that discriminated on the basis of religion or race. "The history of the United States, as for all countries, is one of a struggle between the voices on behalf of rationality and equality, on the one hand, and those urging the imposition of rigid distinctions based on ancestry and religion," she writes.[23] The idea of birthright citizenship—that people belong and should have rights only in the place they happen to be born—is the epitome of a "rigid distinction based on ancestry." An immigration system that attempts to force people to reside inside the national territory in which they were born is in fact one of "global apartheid," she insists.[24]

Restricting freedom of movement, as in apartheid, is a way of enforcing domination and maintaining inequality. This is true whether the restriction is based on something defined as religion, race, or the arbitrary fact of birthplace. On a global level, patrolled borders prevent the poor of the world from escaping the poverty they were born into and gaining access to the jobs, education, and health and welfare that are reserved for those fortunate enough to be born in the wealthy countries that border them. Global apartheid is enforced with walls, stadium lights, and guns. And global apartheid never talks about race, only nationality.

THE USES OF ILLEGALITY

Throughout most of human history, both states and economic enterprises have struggled to incorporate people into their projects.[25] A strikingly different characteristic of the contemporary era is the extent to which access to states and to the right to work has come to be seen as a privilege. In some ways, this change reflects very real shifts in the functioning of states and economies, but in other ways, the differences are more apparent than real.

People have always needed to work for their subsistence. Until well into the twentieth century—and in some regions, into the twenty-first—this has meant, primarily, that they have needed access to land. Most people worked for themselves. Labor for others generally happened as a result of force: when one group conquered another, took control of land, or took prisoners of war, those conquered could be forced to work for their conquerors, often as slaves. "The use of socially marginalized communities for menial tasks helped maintain a higher standard of living and greater property ownership for settlers," Rana wrote of the early United States.[26] While creating privilege for settlers was characteristic of settler colonial societies, the creation and use of the socially marginalized for labor was pretty much a universal of civilization.

Would-be employers initially had to rely on state power to force people into working for them. Gradually, though, direct force was no longer required. In the nineteenth century, industrialization and colonialism separated more and more people worldwide from their lands and left them no option except wage labor. As access to land diminished, people started voluntarily moving to cities and seeking to work for others. Some sectors of the labor force gained access to the privileges and benefits of consumer society. Other sectors remained marginalized, creating what sociologists have termed a segmented or dual labor market. Even in the marginalized sectors, though, a lack of alternatives rather than force became the prime motivation for workers. Work, in fact, had become a privilege.

In her study of mass incarceration, Michelle Alexander notes that coerced labor has given way to mass unemployment among black men. First slavery and then Jim Crow were designed to make blacks work for the white-dominated economy. The dismantling of Jim Crow, she argues, coincided with the collapse of the American manufacturing sector and loss of the jobs that sustained African American communities. She cites sociologist Loïc Wacquant, who "emphasizes that the one thing that makes the current penal apparatus strikingly different from previous racial caste systems is that 'it does not carry out the positive economic mission of recruitment and disciplining of the workforce.' Instead it serves only to warehouse poor black and brown people for increasingly lengthy periods of time, often until old age. The new system does not seek primarily to benefit unfairly from black labor, as earlier caste systems have, but instead views African Americans as largely irrelevant and unnecessary to the newly structured economy."[27]

The newly structured economy may not need to benefit unfairly from black labor, but it still needs to benefit unfairly from the labor of *some* socially marginalized community. In the late twentieth century, African Americans became less "cheap" because they gained legal rights, gained access to social services, and organized unions. Simultaneously, the sectors like manufacturing and government that had employed them collapsed, contributing to high unemployment among African Americans. But other sectors—"downgraded manufacturing and expanded service sectors," in Nicolas De Genova's study of Chicago—began to massively employ immigrant and, especially, undocumented immigrant workers.[28] (Chapters 5 and 6, on the topic of working, go into more detail about the kinds of work undocumented people do.)

Here, however, I'd like to emphasize how useful illegality has been in the late twentieth-century reconfiguration of work from an obligation to a privilege. Illegality is a way to enforce a dual labor market and keep some labor cheap, in a supposedly postracial era. Illegality uses lack of citizenship—that is, being born in the wrong place—to make workers more exploitable. Once naturalized, the status neatly hides the human agency that forces workers into this marginalized status. It is not just coincidence that illegality has burgeoned in the postindustrial societies of the Global North at the end of the twentieth century. It serves a crucial role in their economies and ideologies.

Choosing to Be Undocumented

US citizens often wonder why immigrants in the United States don't "do it the right way" and obtain proper documents to authorize their entry and presence in the country.[1] They believe—usually erroneously—that their own ancestors obtained proper visas prior to coming to the United States and also know that if they intended to travel or move to another country, they would assemble their documents before attempting to travel.

When you get your US passport in the mail, it comes with a flyer that says "With Your US Passport, the World Is Yours!" Holders of the US passport are accustomed to simply arriving at the border of another country, showing their passport, and easily crossing. Rarely, they have to apply for a visa in advance. If they pay the fee and fill out the application correctly, the visa is routinely granted. Holders of US passports tend to believe that freedom to travel is their birthright, a view reinforced by the literature that comes with their passports. For the cost of a plane ticket, and occasionally a small visa fee, they can leave the country they were born in any time they want.

For most of the world's population, though, freedom to travel is a distant dream. They can't leave the country of their birth because, instead of that magical ownership of the world that comes with a US passport, they are citizens of countries in Africa, Latin America, or most of Asia. Many of them are also poor and people of color. They can't leave their countries because no other country will let them in. Least of all, the United States. In today's global apartheid, whole countries—almost all of them in the First World—shut themselves off to travelers, while assuming that their own citizens have the right to travel anywhere they choose. Meanwhile, the citizens of other countries—mostly in the Third World—are imprisoned in the country they are born in, because of the restrictions established by those richer and more powerful.

From the comfort of their First World homes, many citizens of the United States assume that anyone can get a visa to travel legally to any country. If someone comes to and/or lives in the United States without proper documentation, they assume it must be because they simply failed to follow the correct procedure. If only there were such a procedure to follow.

I've even heard a Massachusetts state legislator express this assumption in a hearing on the question of allowing undocumented students to be considered state residents for the purpose of paying in-state tuition rates at public colleges and universities. He interrogated a panel of students, members of the Student Immigrant Movement who had come to testify in favor of the bill. All were undocumented, and each one explained how and why he or she had ended up with that status.

"What's your status now?" the legislator asked them. "I'm undocumented," one Brazilian student answered, bewildered. "Why don't you start the process to become a citizen?" he continued. "I can't," she explained. "Why not?" he asked, revealing his profound ignorance of immigration law. Just as the law forbids most residents of the Third World to travel here—by requiring visas, but refusing to grant them—it also forbids virtually all people who are undocumented to regularize their status.

SOME HISTORY

Structural factors, mostly related to the economy and labor needs, have shaped migrations for centuries. Some of the largest sources of out-migration to the United States today were recipients of in-migration only a few generations ago. The Caribbean islands in particular fall into this category. Other places that now send large numbers of migrants to the United States have long histories of temporary, seasonal, and permanent out-migration. Mexico stands out in this regard.

Since the nineteenth century, nation-states have increasingly attempted to regulate migration and control freedom of movement across often newly established borders. US immigration policies have changed frequently, creating a mesh of regulations and statuses that even immigration lawyers and scholars find confusing.

Until 1890, there was no national immigration system or agency in the United States. Individual states enforced existing immigration laws until the establishment of the federally operated immigration inspection station at Ellis Island in 1892. Certain categories of people became excludable starting in 1875, and in 1891 the law provided for deportation of an immigrant who became a public charge within a year of arrival or was found to belong to a prohibited or excluded group—like Chinese contract workers, prostitutes, convicted criminals. After a year, though, those who had entered "illegally"—that is, in violation of the laws that excluded them—could no longer be deported. The 1903 Immigration Act extended these periods of potential deportability to two years for becoming a public charge, and three years for belonging to an excludible class. In 1917, this was extended to five years.[2]

It's important to note that so-called illegal entry, up until this time, referred to entry by persons belonging to a *class* of people who were unilaterally denied entry: it had nothing to do with the way a person entered. It was the 1907 Immigration

Act that first made entering without inspection itself a violation of the law. The 1907 act formalized the inspection procedure, requiring every would-be immigrant *coming in by sea* to pass through inspection, and made it a misdemeanor for a ship owner to bring in anybody belonging to an excluded class.[3] The act did not apply to Mexicans. Inspection was for immigrants, and immigrants were defined as people who arrived by sea, not Mexicans, who crossed the southern border to work. Likewise, Mexicans were exempted from the literacy requirement and head tax imposed on immigrants in 1917, as long as they were coming to work in agriculture. Mexicans weren't even required to enter through an official port or inspection point until 1919.

For Europeans, a passport was first required for entry in 1918, but even then, it was only for identification. Would-be immigrants did not need to obtain prior permission in their home countries before traveling to the United States, and they couldn't be deported for entering without inspection until 1924.[4] In 1929, entry without inspection became a misdemeanor, punishable with fines and jail time.[5] But there were still exceptions for Europeans.

A new process called registry for noncitizens who had entered without inspection prior to this time allowed them—if they were otherwise (i.e., racially) eligible to citizenship—to regularize their status if they could demonstrate "that they had resided in the country continuously since 1921, were not otherwise subject to deportation, and were of 'good moral character.'"[6] In practice, the registry helped Europeans who had evaded the 1919 inspection requirement. The registry system set a precedent—that a period of residence outweighed the technicalities of inspection, or lack of inspection, upon entry. Later laws like the 1986 Immigration Reform and Control Act and the twenty-first-century proposals for a path to citizenship would revive that idea.

The 1924 Immigration Act created what was called the "quota system," putting numerical limits on immigration (still conceived as European immigration) for the first time. Immigrants from Europe now had to comply with quotas established based on the proportion of immigrants from that country already present in the United States. Non-Europeans didn't get quotas. The Bureau of Labor Statistics explained the intent of the law: "Immigrants of New World countries or their descendants, aliens ineligible to citizenship or their descendants, the descendants of slave immigrants, and the descendants of American aborigines were specifically excluded from the national-origins plan. In a broad sense, therefore, the problem was to find the extent to which the various countries of Europe, as now constituted, had contributed to the white population of the country."[7] For the first time, Europeans could be excluded, not on the basis of their individual characteristics, but because of the country they came from. Somewhat paradoxically from today's perspective, Mexican labor migration was unaffected by the restrictive law.

Most Europeans who arrived in the United States prior to 1924 did pretty much what immigrants from Mexico and Central America did a few decades later: they gathered their families and their belongings, put together the money they needed for the trip, and embarked on their journey. They didn't "do it the right way," wait in line, or follow a legal process, because there was no line or process.

The records of Ellis Island are filled with the stories of individuals like Irving Berlin, who went on to become an iconic American songwriter, author of "I'm Dreaming of a White Christmas" and "God Bless America." The family of Israel Baline, age five, fled their home in Russia after their village was attacked in a pogrom and their house burned to the ground. They traveled "illegally" because, in 1893, Russia (unlike most countries at the time) required a passport for travel and exit;

they "smuggled themselves from town to town and country to country" until reaching Antwerp, Belgium, where they boarded a ship bound for New York. On the ship's manifest, their last name was changed from Baline to Beilin, so they entered the United States under a false name. (The name "Irving Berlin" was introduced by a printer's error when Israel produced his first album at age nineteen.)[8] Since the United States had only minimal entry requirements for Europeans at the time, family members were given a medical inspection by the US Public Health Service to determine whether they had any infectious disease and a legal inspection to determine whether they were likely to become public charges. Only about 2 percent of would-be immigrants were rejected as a result of these inspections.

Mae Ngai argues that with so few restrictions on immigration in the nineteenth and early twentieth centuries, "there was no such thing as 'illegal immigration.' The government excluded a mere 1% of the 25 million immigrants who landed at Ellis Island before World War I, mostly for health reasons. (Chinese were the exception, excluded on grounds of 'racial unassimilability.') The statutes of limitations of one to five years meant that even those here unlawfully did not live forever with the specter of deportation."[9]

The 1924 law, in addition to establishing the quota system, created the concept of illegality by making entry without inspection illegal, and making deportability permanent by eliminating the statute of limitations. Before 1924, what made a person deportable was his or her membership in an excluded class; furthermore, after the person had been in the country for a period of time, his or her presence became legal despite prior excludability. Now, a person who entered without inspection could be, technically, "illegal."[10]

Still, there were many ways for Europeans who didn't "follow the rules" to become legal. The 1929 registry law helped those who entered before 1921. Between 1935 and the late 1950s,

European immigrants without documentation were allowed to adjust their status by reentering through Canada to obtain legal permanent residency. After 1940, immigrants who could show that their families would suffer "serious economic detriment" could have their deportation suspended. All of these provisions applied only to European immigrants, since they were the only ones allowed to immigrate under the 1924 exclusions. (Mexicans were still crossing the border easily, but they were not considered immigrants.) Some two hundred thousand Europeans without documents were able to legalize their status using these means.[11]

In 1965, the United States abandoned the differential quota system, replacing it with a new one that imposed equal quotas on all countries. This meant that, for the first time, Western Hemisphere migrants—primarily Mexicans—were classified as immigrants. This change essentially created illegal immigration from Mexico and Central America, but without all of the loopholes and exceptions that had allowed Europeans to adjust their status.[12]

Donna Gabaccia's research shows that media references to so-called illegal immigration closely followed restrictive legislation.

> The earliest references are to "illegal immigration," which referred to the movement of workers from China; they appeared immediately after passage of the 1882 Chinese exclusion. With the exclusion of all Asians and the restriction of southern and eastern European migrations in the 1920s, "illegal immigrant" became an intermittent fixture in the pages of *New York Times*, where it usually meant stowaways, persons who "jumped ship," or the "immigrant bootleggers" who supposedly smuggled in workers and "immoral" women. Only after World War II (and a brief period when most stories about "illegal immigrants" focused on European Jews entering the British mandate in

Palestine) did the term—understood by then to mean "wet-backs" crossing the Rio Grande—become attached firmly to workers from Mexico. And only after 1965 did the term become common in a wide array of writings by journalists, scholars, and Congressional representatives.[13]

Today, of course, the term "illegal immigrant" has become common currency. The rest of this chapter will look at two of the largest sources of undocumented immigrants in the United States today, Mexico and Guatemala. It will ask how people from those countries came to migrate to the United States, and how and why their migrations have become illegalized.

AN OVERVIEW OF UNDOCUMENTED MIGRATION

The undocumented population in the United States increased rapidly between 1965, when the first restrictive measures were passed against Mexican and other Latin American immigrants, and the beginning of the twenty-first century. By 1980, there were from 2 to 4 million undocumented immigrants in the country, rising to 8.5 million in 2000 and reaching a peak of almost 12 million in 2007.[14]

Notably, over half of those undocumented in 2011 had arrived between 1995 and 2004, with only 14 percent arriving between 2005 and 2011.[15] Thus, most undocumented people have been in the country for quite a while. The rise in the undocumented coincided with an even greater rise in the overall Hispanic population in the second half of the twentieth century. In 1970, the 9.6 million Hispanics in the United States made up 4.7 percent of the population. Four decades later, the Hispanic population had jumped to 50.5 million or 16 percent of the population.[16]

Most of these have consistently been Mexicans. Estimates for the undocumented Mexican population rose from 1.13 million in 1980 to 2.04 million in 1990 and 4.68 million in 2000, rising to a high of 7.03 million in 2008 before stabilizing and declining to 6.8 million in 2011. The Central American un-documented population also rose after 1980, reaching 570,000 Salvadorans, 430,000 Guatemalans, and 300,000 Hondurans in 2008. For Central Americans, the numbers continued to increase after 2008: in 2011, there were 660,000 from El Salvador, 520,000 from Guatemala, and 380,000 from Honduras. Together, Central Americans and Mexicans made up three-quarters of the growth in the undocumented population between 1980 and 2008.[17]

Moreover, a significant proportion—over half—of Mexicans and Central Americans who are here are undocumented. Fifty-eight percent of Mexicans, 57 percent of Salvadorans, 71 percent of Guatemalans, and 77 percent of Hondurans are undocumented. "Never before have so many people been outside the law and never before have the undocumented been so concentrated within such a small number of national origins," wrote Douglas Massey and Karen Pren.[18] Mexico and Central America are thus key pieces in the puzzle of undocumentedness in the United States.

With this big picture in mind, we must start to untangle the history of undocumented migration from Mexico and Central America.

MEXICANS

The largest group of undocumented people in the United States today comes from Mexico. Many are from the central-western Mexican states that have been sending migrants northward for over a century, although increasingly migrants hail from heavily indigenous regions in the south of the country that had seen little out-migration before the 1990s. Almost 60 percent of the undocumented, over 6 million people in 2010, were Mexican. Other Latin Americans make up another 23 percent.[19] Mexicans also make up the largest foreign-born population in the United States, with about 29 percent of the foreign-born or 12 million people.[20] As noted above, over half of Mexicans in the United States are undocumented.

Surveys taken of Mexican migrants in Mexico (i.e., having returned from the United States) show another side of the story: that lots of undocumented people return home after being in the United States. The Mexican Migration Project at Princeton University and the University of Guadalajara surveyed eighty thousand return migrants from twenty-one Mexican states, as well as migrants from those communities who have settled in the United States. In Mexico, the interviews show that 83 percent had entered the United States illegally on their first trip, and 73 percent on their most recent trip. In the United States, 77 percent responded that they had entered illegally on their first trip, and 56 percent that they entered illegally on their most recent trip. (The last response may be skewed by individuals reluctant to reveal current illegal status.)[21]

To understand why and how so many Mexicans have come to be undocumented, it's crucial to examine the history.

The border that divides the United States from Mexico, and that large numbers of Mexicans and Central Americans cross each year without authorization, was established by the Treaty of Guadalupe Hidalgo in 1848 and adjusted by the Gadsden or La Mesilla Purchase of 1853. Much of the US Southwest used to be Mexico. The first Mexicans in the United States did not cross any border; rather, the border crossed them.

Until 1924, the new border between the United States and Mexico was virtually unpoliced, and migration flowed openly. Mexicans worked in the mines and railroads of the Southwest and migrated to the factories and urban centers in the Midwest. In 1908, US Bureau of Labor Statistics researcher Victor Clark reported that, while "complete statistics of those who cross the frontier are not kept," an estimated sixty thousand to one hundred thousand Mexicans crossed each year to work in the United States. "Except in Texas and California, few Mexicans become permanent residents, and even in those two states, a majority are transient laborers who seldom remain more than six months at a time in this country."[22]

The many laws that were passed to try to control immigration from the Civil War on did not apply to Mexicans, because Congress did not consider them immigrants or potential immigrants at all. In agriculture, Clark explained, "the main value of the Mexican . . . is as a temporary worker in crops where the season is short. . . . Mexicans are not likely to be employed the year round by small farmers, because they are not entertained in the family like American, German, Scandinavian, or Irish laborers of the North. Yet they do not occupy a position analogous to that of the Negro in the South. They are not permanent, do not acquire land or establish themselves in little cabin homesteads, but remain nomadic and outside of American civilization."[23]

RAILROADS AND MIGRATION

Railroads played a crucial role both in moving Mexicans to the border and into the United States and in creating a demand for Mexican labor. Mexico's nineteenth-century rail system was "designed, planned and constructed by Americans" and extended US lines into Mexico to facilitate the transport of US manufactured goods into Mexico. Thus, decisions about Mexico's economy and infrastructure were made in the United States, for the benefit of US capitalists. The railroads also helped bring Mexicans to, and across, the border.[24]

As US capital moved south, it drew southerners northward. Railroad concessions displaced over three hundred thousand peasants in Mexico's central plateau, creating one pool of potential migrants. Many of them were recruited to work in new American enterprises in the north of the country. Some went to work on the railroad itself; others in new American-owned mining and oil operations. Mexico's demographic patterns were fundamentally, and irrevocably, altered with this shift of population to the North.[25] In Arizona, as the copper mines boomed in the last decades of the nineteenth century, they sent labor contractors to scour Mexico for workers being displaced from their lands. The first Mexican mineworkers in Arizona were Sonorans who crossed the border, but they were soon joined by central Mexicans who traveled north along the new rail lines.[26]

Victor Clark described how the railroads contributed to the creation of a migrant labor force and the long-term social and cultural changes that the railroads and the migrations brought:

In Mexico railways have given both the opportunity and the inducement to emigration. Needing unskilled labor for their construction and maintenance, they drew among the agricultural population along their lines, at first for a few days or weeks of temporary service between crops and later for more extended periods. At first the true peon was averse to leaving his home, and would not work where he could not sleep under his own roof, but gradually he became bolder and more worldly-wise and could be prevailed upon to work for a month or so a hundred miles or more up and down the line. He became accustomed to having silver in his pocket occasionally and found it would exchange for things he had not heretofore thought of having for his personal use. He became attached to cash wages in about the same degree that he became detached from his home surroundings. Employers in the more primitive parts of Mexico say that at present the people will not work for money so long as they have food in their cabins. When they first leave home they will work only long enough to provide themselves with food and shelter for a few days in advance. But the railways, bringing a greater variety of wares at lower prices, have made possible the attractive shop of the railway town, and this market for money has made the latter a more desirable commodity in the eyes of the peon. . . . The railways have thus attracted labor and have held it more and more permanently from a constantly widening area along their lines. A general officer of the National Railroad of Mexico stated that his company had brought north about 1,500 laborers to work on the upper section of the road within a year, and that practically all of them had ultimately crossed over into Texas.[27]

Newcomers were met at the entry point and offered "fair wages."[28]

US aid and investment, then, directly uprooted Mexican peasants, recruited them into a migrant labor stream, and initiated the social and cultural changes that led them to leave their homes and work for cash in distant lands. It was US influence deep inside Mexico that set into motion the process of out-migration.

A TYPICAL SENDING COMMUNITY: ARANDAS, JALISCO

By 1933, economist Paul S. Taylor found that a tradition of migration had become well established in the Mexican sending community of Arandas in Jalisco. The ongoing migration, he wrote, was "but a modern and expanded phase" of a process that had begun decades before.[29]

First, the railroad arrived. The Mexico City–El Paso rail line, which passed through Jalisco, recruited workers from the adjacent countryside. Then US railroad and mining companies began to send employment agents into Mexico's interior to contract potential migrants and deployed station agents on the border to recruit arriving workers.

The earliest migrants from Arandas had heard rumors about the availability of work in the United States from former prisoners, local men who had been arrested and sent to fight in ongoing military campaigns against the Yaqui Indians in Sonora. They traveled by rail to El Paso, where an employment agency contracted them for railroad work in Independence, Kansas. On their next venture, agents in El Paso sent them to Fresno, California, again to work on the railroad.[30]

Mexican employment agents also visited Arandas to recruit laborers. One former migrant told Taylor that a railroad construction recruiter offered him free passage to the border.[31] "In 1913, an agent [Mexican] from the Santa Fé railroad came to Arandas and took three or four of us by auto to the railroad, and north. I did not pay anything to go to the frontier; they paid all," one source from the village told Taylor, adding that "American *contratistas*, representing railroads and mines, had been all through the region twenty-odd years ago."[32]

Taylor emphasizes that the migration was spurred by US actions. When Congress passed the Literacy Act for immigrants in 1917, railroad, agricultural, and mining corporations raised a howl of protest and insisted that an open border was essential in order to obtain the labor they needed.[33] In response, Congress quickly exempted Mexicans from the literacy requirement. Migration ebbed and flowed directly in response to employment demands in the United States.[34] When they needed workers, employers turned to Mexico. When they didn't—as in 1929, when Depression-era unemployment began to rise—the State Department instructed consular officers to increase their enforcement of the "likely to become a public charge" restriction on would-be immigrants and refuse to grant entry visas to Mexicans unlikely to find work.[35]

Emigrants from the small community of Arandas worked in twenty-four states in the United States by the 1930s, and in a wide variety of industries ranging from automobile factories to agriculture to coal mining, though the railroad was by far the largest employer.[36] Most came to the border without papers and were automatically granted entry. After 1928, the American consular service began to encourage prospective migrants to obtain permits from a consulate before arriving at the border, though this was still not required.[37]

Some also crossed without inspection, either paying a small sum to a professional or simply wading across the river at a spot distant from any border post. By 1931, though, the word had spread that the consular service was not granting papers, that deportations were rising and employment contracting.[38]

BORDER PATROL AND SEGREGATION

Although the 1924 law did not include any restrictions on immigration from the Western Hemisphere, it did create a new border police force, the Border Patrol. In the early years, according to historian Aristide Zolberg, "its mission was to prevent the entry of alcohol rather than people, so that in effect, the border remained an informal affair."[39] The force also sought to deter prohibited Chinese attempting to enter through Mexico.

Was it a paradox that the Border Patrol was created in the 1920s, just when agribusiness, with its need for migrant labor, was rapidly expanding in the Southwest? Several scholars argue that in fact the system worked well for farmers who needed migrant workers. Mexican workers could still cross the border easily, but because they became more deportable, the new laws also made them more exploitable. "Agribusinessmen kicked, winked, screamed, lobbied, and cajoled for border patrol practices that allowed unrestricted access to Mexican workers while promoting effective discipline over the region's Mexicano workforce."[40] Deportability was part of that discipline. Local officials served farmers' interests by carrying out deportation raids in cases of union organizing or, sometimes, just before payday.[41]

The need to patrol the border was mitigated in some ways by the fact that the (mostly) men who crossed into the United States carried the border with them, even before the Border Patrol was created. Many had worked under segregated conditions for US enterprises inside Mexico. In Mexico, workers did "Mexican work" and received a "Mexican wage"; they lived in segregated housing.[42]

These segregated conditions were replicated in the United States. "Recruited laborers whether destined for northern Mexico or for the United States, travel in parties, under a boss, or 'cabo' who holds the tickets," wrote Victor Clark in 1908. Then, after "crossing a virtual open border, Mexican workers were again housed in company towns, confined to 'Mexican work,' treated to dual wages, and segregated socially . . . the workers' experiences in Mexico continued in the United States."[43]

Thus, the most important border was the internal or racial one that kept Mexicans and Americans socially separated from each other, even as they labored in a single, integrated economy on both sides of the political boundary that separated the countries. Gilbert González concludes that "rather than interpreting segregation as a means of keeping people out of the 'mainstream' or of 'marginalizing' them to the social and economic periphery, segregation was the method of integrating Mexican immigrants and their families into the heart of the American economy. . . . Segregated settlements brought a variation of the border to the employers' doorsteps."[44]

Mexican workers' theoretical deportability became real in 1929, as the country entered the Great Depression. On the pretext that they were likely to "become a public charge" as employment opportunities evaporated, both Mexicans and Mexican Americans were rounded up for deportation. A "frenzy of anti-Mexican hysteria" justified roundups of entire Mexican neighborhoods and hundreds of thousands were deported with little attention to legal niceties.[45]

THE BRACERO PROGRAM

With the ending of the Depression and the coming of World War II, agricultural interests confronted a new labor shortage. The US government responded with the Bracero Program, administered jointly by the US and Mexican governments from 1942 to 1964, which recruited millions of Mexicans to migrate north for a season or more.[46] Over the period, 4.5 million contracts were signed, representing some 2 million workers (many went more than once). The program cemented US agribusiness's reliance on migratory Mexican workers to the present day.

The four central-western states of Jalisco, Guanajuato, Michoacán, and Zacatecas comprised 45 percent of the participants. "Here," argues historian Michael Snodgrass, "is where a culture of Mexican migration first took root in the early twentieth century." Because of demand from both would-be migrants and local officials, the Mexican government established its processing centers in Guanajuato and Jalisco. Workers from "depressed mining villages and drought-stricken farm towns" flocked to the program.[47]

Alongside Bracero migrants, others from the same region migrated on their own, undocumented, but not unwelcome. "It was easy then," Snodgrass explains. "When he headed north for the first time in 1955, the first English expression that Gerardo López learned was 'go ahead,' the words a Border Patrol agent spoke while encouraging his entry."[48] Aristide Zolberg, who was stationed in El Paso for military service in the mid-1950s, commented that "informality" prevailed regarding border crossings. "You were more likely to be stopped crossing the Juarez Bridge if you looked like an American in military service than like a Mexican seeking work."[49]

Former migrants from the highlands of Jalisco recalled that the program resurrected networks that had been established in the 1920s, only to be temporarily interrupted in the 1930s. Other parts of Jalisco, like the sugar region, had no prior history of migration. Now, though, union leaders began to demand Bracero contracts for their members during the *tiempo muerto* from May to December, which conveniently coincided with California's harvest season. Thus, new areas were drawn into the "culture of migration."[50] Remittances became Mexico's third-largest source of foreign exchange by the 1950s. While renewing old flows and creating new ones, the Bracero Program also redefined the destinations of Mexican migrants: now almost all of them were recruited directly into farm labor.[51]

The program also deepened the structures and culture of migration, including extralegal migration, in western Mexico.[52] A whole industry of smugglers or "coyotes" emerged, who worked with US-based labor contractors to supply undocumented workers to farmers.[53] Some famers preferred to avoid the bureaucracy and protections involved with the official system. Others lived in states like Texas that the Mexican government blacklisted from the program because of labor violations. By the time the program ended in 1964, it had outlived its demand because the extralegal system that had grown alongside it had grown large and strong enough to fulfill the country's farm labor demand.[54]

Legal scholar Daniel Kanstroom argues that the program legitimized "a particularly instrumentalist view of Mexican immigrant workers." Employers, the law, and the population in general had long seen Mexicans as different from other immigrants—as essentially temporary and disposable. The Bracero Program institutionalized this position for the post–World War II period. Mexicans in the United States were automatically assumed to be temporary and perhaps without papers. In other words, Mexicans' status was inherently "legally tenuous."[55]

The Bracero Program was also accompanied by a "massive bilateral deportation policy" that increased deportations to some seven hundred thousand by the early 1950s. "The wetback is a person of legal disability who is under jeopardy of immediate deportation if caught. He is told that if he leaves the farm, he will be reported to the [Immigration and Naturalization Service (INS), which] will surely find him if he ventures into town or out onto the roads," reported the President's Commission on Migratory Labor in 1951.[56]

Still, both farmers and government tacitly admitted that the line between legality and illegality was a fine one, and that "wetbacks" were an essential component of the system.[57] In one incident in early 1954, as workers massed on the border seeking to cross in Mexicali, the INS urged them to the edge of town, where they crossed "illegally." "Instead of sending them back to Mexico, however, US Border Patrol officials trotted them to the US side of the official crossing and directed them to touch a toe onto the Mexican side. . . . When this was done, US Labor Department officials gave the migrants contracts to sign, which completed their transformation from illegal immigrants to guestworkers."[58]

Just a few months later, the Eisenhower administration initiated Operation Wetback, a massive, military-style sweep of Mexican and Mexican American neighborhoods aimed at deporting en masse those deemed to be in the country "illegally." Over a million were deported. Like the deportations of the 1930s, Operation Wetback snared many individuals, including US citizens, simply for being ethnically Mexican.

Attorney General Herbert Brownell distinguished between "the illegal Mexican migrants known as 'wetbacks,' and the legal Mexican nationals known as 'braceros.' . . . The illegals, who cross the border furtively in violation of the laws and regulations of both the United States and Mexico cause serious social and economic problems for the United States."[59] Yet the operation illustrated the symbiotic relationship between the Bracero Program and undocumented workers. Even as it was being carried out, Bracero recruitment continued unabated, and the INS offered numerous methods for farmers to legalize the workers they needed, a process termed "drying out the wetbacks."[60] As Kanstroom points out, "The remarkably symmetrical relationship between labor recruitment and the deportation system is illustrated by the fact that, up to 1964, the number of braceros, nearly 5 million, was almost exactly the same as the number of deportees."[61]

After Operation Wetback, deportations dropped again as the number of Bracero-contracted workers grew alongside the number of work-permitted or green-card entrants. The green card had its origins in the Alien Registration Act of 1940 in the context of World War II, requiring all noncitizens to register at a local post office, which would then mail them the card. The Security Act of 1950 created the green card as we know it today. Still, for Mexicans, since there were no numerical restrictions, "obtaining residency [i.e., the green card] required little more than a letter verifying employment and a trip to a US consulate."[62] During the 1960s and early 1970s, some forty thousand Mexicans living south of the border held green cards that enabled them to commute to work in the United States.

THE 1965 IMMIGRATION LAW
AND THE INVENTION OF ILLEGALITY

During the two major waves of deportation/repatriation of Mexicans before 1965—during the Depression of the 1930s and in the mid-1950s—undocumentedness as we know it today was not the rationale used to justify deportation. As entry to the country was restricted on the grounds of indigence or the probability of becoming a public charge, the vague "likely to become a public charge" accusation was harnessed to justify the deportations of Mexicans during the Depression.[63] During the 1950s, many people mounted arguments against both illegal immigrants—then accorded the insulting moniker wetback—and the Bracero Program, regardless of the fact that one was technically legal and the other illegal. Even as Operation Wetback targeted the supposedly illegal, the INS offered multiple methods for legalization. Mexican American organizations like LULAC and the American GI Forum campaigned equally against both the Bracero Program and the "wetback tide," both of which they believed to be harmful to the efforts of Mexican Americans to assimilate into white US society.[64]

The Immigration and Nationality Act of 1965 for the first time ever placed numerical limits on Mexican migration, just as the Bracero Program was being shut down. Suddenly, legal migration for Mexicans, after so many years of being encouraged, was closed off. But the demand for Mexican labor, and Mexican workers' need for jobs, continued. A smaller guest-worker program, the H-2 program, remained and was expanded over the following decades, but came nowhere near to filling the demand.

The abolition of the Bracero Program was supposed to create better, more equal treatment for Mexicans in the United States, in keeping with the civil rights movements of the era, including a growing farm-worker movement. It failed miserably. Unlike the European countries, which legalized their guest workers when they ended similar programs around the same time, the United States simply illegalized its Mexican workers. "In essence, in 1965 the United States shifted from a de jure guestworker program based on the circulation of bracero migrants to a de facto program based on the circulation of undocumented migrants."[65]

The visa cap for Mexicans was far below the number who had been migrating as braceros in previous years. Thus, the law "intensified the institutional framework that further enabled the codification of Mexicans as 'illegals.'" And the newly created problem of illegality became the rationale for a huge increase in apprehensions and deportations.[66] The number of Mexican migrants who lacked the green card and were therefore deportable rose from 88,823 in 1961 to over a million a year by the mid-1970s.[67]

Still, writes Oscar Martínez, "because of leniency on the part of US authorities at the time, undocumented commuters found it rather easy to cross the border."[68] As the Mexican government pointed out, many of the undocumented were part of a "seasonal, temporary, and circular" migration.[69] With the "relatively open" border between 1965 and 1985, "85 percent of undocumented entries were offset by departures, yielding a relatively modest net increment to the US population."[70] Still, Douglas Massey wrote that "never before have so many immigrants been placed in such a vulnerable position and subject to such high levels of official exclusion and discrimination."[71]

The US government acknowledged the contradictions of this new situation in 1986, when the Immigration Reform and Control Act (IRCA) allowed Mexicans in the country illegally to regularize their status. The concept was not new; earlier European immigrants became exempt from deportation and were allowed to become citizens after they had established roots in the country. Some 2.3 million Mexican immigrants (and 700,000 non-Mexicans) were able to become legal under the IRCA's provisions.[72] To do so, though, they needed documents: documents proving their continuous presence in the country since 1982, or documents demonstrating that they had been involved in seasonal agricultural work. A small industry grew manufacturing false documents. The ever-fuzzy line between legal and illegal remained, as many were able to legalize illegally with fraudulent documents.

When the IRCA was passed, the Department of Agriculture estimated that some 350,000 undocumented migrants were working in agriculture and would be eligible for Seasonal Agricultural Worker (SAW) status. However, some 1.3 million applied—almost as many as applied for status under the four-years-of-continuous-residence provisions. In California, with an estimated two hundred thousand undocumented agricultural workers, some seven hundred thousand applied. By early 1992, the INS had approved 88 percent of these applications, or over a million nationwide.[73] But independent studies carried out in Mexico, among migrants who had applied for the SAW provision, showed that only 60–70 percent of those who applied were actually eligible.[74]

Thus, the IRCA contributed to what could perhaps be called illegal legalizations—people using false documents attesting to their status as agricultural workers to apply for, and obtain, legal status in the United States—and what Philip Martin called "documented illegal aliens." In an article in the *New York Times*, Robert Suro claimed there had been "fraud on a huge scale."[75] Yet fraud or no fraud, people became officially legal. Moreover, the whole process may have actually spurred further undocumented immigration by "spreading work authorization documents and knowledge about them to very poor and unsophisticated rural Mexicans and Central Americans, encouraging first-time entrants from these areas."[76]

The 1986 law also for the first time made it illegal to employ a worker without proper documents. Employer sanctions created an enormous and costly illegal infrastructure that migrants had to navigate to obtain false documents in order to work, but did little to reduce the numbers of undocumented workers. Moreover, the law left employers virtually immune to prosecution, and with even greater ability to exploit their now more legally vulnerable workers.[77]

The 1986 IRCA was ostensibly aimed at ending illegality by legalizing many resident Mexicans and discouraging new arrivals through increased border controls and employer sanctions that criminalized work. However, it had exactly the opposite effect. Mexicans who obtained legal status under the amnesty were able to leave the more marginalized sectors of the labor market. But these traditional sectors, like agriculture, plus newly emerging sectors (discussed in Chapters 5 and 6) only increased their demand for workers. Some developed new strategies of subcontracting to evade the law. Meanwhile undocumented migrants, once in the country, began to extend their stays and send for their families, since the long-standing circular migration patterns were disrupted by the border militarization.[78]

Until the 1990s, what migration scholars call the "traditional" or central-west region of Mexico, including Jalisco, had been the source of the majority of migrants.[79] Since the 1990s, the proportion from that region has shrunk considerably and that from the south-southeast region has increased. Migrants from the traditional sending regions were primarily Spanish-speaking *mestizos*.[80] Since the 1980s, though, a series of blows, including the 1982 peso crisis, the debt crisis that followed it, and neoliberal restructuring in the 1990s and components of the North American Free Trade Agreement in 1994, have severely affected indigenous communities in southern Mexico. Over a million families lost their land as a result of these changes. The result was that new areas started their own massive out-migration to the North, greatly diversifying the Mexican population in the United States.[81]

CASE STUDY: THE HERNÁNDEZ CRUZ FAMILY

One family's story can illustrate the various and contradictory ways that people become illegal in the contemporary United States. Consider the case of the Hernández Cruz family of Irapuato, Mexico. The father, Juan Miguel Hernández Pérez, began the family's migration tradition in the middle of the century, when he was recruited to work in the Bracero Program. But if the program created a legal means to initiate a migrant stream from 1942 to 1964, the termination of the program did not end either the demand for migrants' labor nor their desire to work in the United States. When Juan Miguel's son Juan Hernández Cruz left Irapuato to work in the fields of California in 1981, "he was following his father's footsteps but, unlike his father, who had been a registered worker under the Bracero Program, Juan would be crossing as an unauthorized migrant."[82]

Juan Hernández Cruz's younger sister, Samantha, followed her brother in 1988, bringing their seriously ill mother with her. First they tried to enter without inspection, crossing "through the back hills of San Ysidro many times without success." Finally, "the coyote suggested they get false papers instead. . . . By using someone else's papers, altered to include their photos, they found it easy to cross via the San Ysidro US Port of Entry."

Meanwhile, Juan was working to regularize his and his sister's status using the Seasonal Agricultural Worker provision of the 1986 IRCA. "Through friends, they were connected with a farmer in the United States who signed all the documents they required for $800 each. They both received a letter that they had worked on a farm for the required number of years and were both granted permanent residency."[83] Legally, but on the basis of false documents.

The ins and outs of this family's immigration history are more typical than unusual for Mexican migrants. Their story, and the long history behind it, helps to explain why Mexicans supposedly choose to come to the United States "illegally." From the railroads, to the various maneuvers in US immigration policy over the past century, to the current neoliberal regime in Mexico, structural factors have created what is today called Mexican illegality.[84]

GUATEMALAN MAYANS: A HISTORY OF MIGRATION

Central Americans, coming primarily from Honduras, El Salvador, and Guatemala, comprise the second-largest group of undocumented people in the United States. My focus here is on one group of Central Americans, indigenous rural Mayans from Guatemala's highlands. The history of today's Mayan migration to the United States began over five hundred years ago.

While we have little evidence about Mayan migration patterns prior to the Spanish conquest in the 1500s, patterns of coerced and voluntary migration clearly characterized the colonial period. The Spanish concentrated the indigenous in new communities to better implement political, religious, and economic control. They imposed various systems of coerced labor that forced people out of their communities for weeks or months at a time to work in colonial mines, plantations, and factories. Mayans also fled from their communities to avoid forced labor demands.[85]

The coffee plantation system that grew in Guatemala after independence led to new forced labor demands and displacements. Historians have documented the fearful violence involved with dispossessing large numbers of indigenous peoples from their lands and forcing them into labor on the new plantations. They estimate that one in five of the highland Indian population migrated seasonally to work in the coffee fields in the 1880s.[86] The numbers increased after the overthrow of the brief revolutionary experiment in the 1950s: Christopher Lutz and George Lovell calculate some two hundred thousand Mayan labor migrants a year in the 1950s, three hundred thousand in the 1960s, and five hundred thousand in the 1970s.[87]

Guatemalan Indian activist Rigoberta Menchu described her initiation into migration to coffee and cotton plantations as a child. Migration to work was simply a fact of life, not to be questioned.

> From when I was very tiny, my mother used to take me down to the *finca,* wrapped in a shawl on her back. She told me that when I was about two I had to be carried screaming into the lorry because I didn't want to go. . . . It sometimes took two nights and a day from my village to the coast. . . . By the time we got to the *finca* we were totally stupefied; we were like chickens coming out of a pot. We were in such a state, we could hardly walk to the *finca.* I made many trips from the *altiplano* to the coast, but I never saw the countryside we passed through. . . . I saw the wonderful scenery and places for the first time when we were thrown out of the *finca* and had to pay our own way back on the bus. . . .
>
> I remember that from when I was about eight to when I was about ten, we worked in the coffee crop. And after that we worked on the cotton plantations further down the coast, where

it was very, very hot. . . . That was our world. I felt that it would always be the same, always the same. It hadn't ever changed. . . .

The lorries belonged to the *fincas*, but they were driven by the recruiting agents, the *caporales*. These *caporales* are in charge of about forty people, or more or less what the lorry holds. When they get to the *finca*, the *caporal* becomes the overseer of this group. . . . The overseers stay on the *fincas*. . . . They are in charge. When you're working, for example, and take a little rest, he comes and insults you. . . . They also punish the slow workers. . . .[88]

Every *finca* in Guatemala has a *cantina*, owned by the landowner, where the workers get drunk on alcohol and all kinds of *guaro*, and pile up debts. They often spend most of their wages. They drink to get happy and to forget the bitterness they feel at having to leave their villages in the *Altiplano* and come and work so brutally hard on the *fincas* for so little.[89]

Menchu's testimony suggests that, like the Mexican peasants described earlier, Guatemalan highlanders were not seeking to leave their homes to work for pay. It took generations of forced recruitment to create this migration tradition.

Interestingly, human rights advocate Daniel Wilkinson found that the Mayan descendants who live on the plantations today know little of the violence that went into the making of this history. "People knew where their families had come from, but they didn't know—or didn't care to recall—much more about what had brought them to the plantations."[90] Wilkinson, like others who study Guatemala, emphasizes the silences that surround people's understanding of their realities. Decades— or centuries—of genocide and terror have shaped the culture of Guatemala's highland indigenous communities. People may have few tools to understand the forces behind their oppression, and they have learned over and over that trying to protest or change their situation only invites further repression.

The civil war—or more accurately, dirty war—against highland Maya communities during the 1970s and '80s was one result of people in the highlands trying to challenge their poverty and dispossession. It led to the destruction of hundreds of villages, and perhaps a million internally displaced and one hundred thousand to two hundred thousand refugees who fled the country, many across the border to Mexico. Others were forced from their homes into model villages under army control.

Thus, historians of the Maya have argued that migration has been a "ubiquitous feature of Maya life" that became central to Mayan history and identity. Ever since the arrival of the Spanish conquerors, and in accelerated ways since the 1800s, political, legal, military, and economic structures have directly enforced migration or simply made it impossible to survive without it.[91]

"An absent community or family member may be in one of several places: on the coast picking coffee (returning home within a month, with wages); in the capital working as a domestic, merchant, or worker (sending money home to the family, returning periodically or permanently, such as after a stint or a marriage proposal from home); in another *municipio* selling firewood, animals, or agricultural products (returning once or twice a month for business and domestic activities); and, increasingly, *allá lejos* (in the United States), sending US dollars home on a regular basis."[92] Both in its structural aspects and in its cultural aspects, today's migration is just a new phase in a process that is rooted in hundreds of years of history.[93]

CASE STUDY: GUATEMALANS IN PROVIDENCE

Among the undocumented Mayans of Providence, Rhode Island, Patricia Foxen found a very different conception than what most citizens understand about illegality. Rather than imagining themselves as autonomous individuals making a decision to break the law, they, like Rigoberta Menchu, understand their migration as a requirement imposed upon them by outsiders, which they have no right or opportunity to question.

The coyotes that offer to take them across the border may be considered smugglers under US law, but to the Mayans Foxen studied, they were no different from the labor contractors who had been forcibly recruiting them—legally—for generations. Instead of going to the Pacific coast to work on plantations, now they were being sent to *la costa del Norte* to work in jewelry factories. One woman told Foxen that "the *coyote* is the same as the *contratista* (labor contractor) on the coast: he should know when there is work over there, and should not be sending people if there is no work." Others told her that they went to Providence "because that is where the *coyotes* sent them."[94] In many cases, *contratistas* themselves became coyotes, relying on their existing networks and standing and just expanding their geographic scope.[95] "As did their forefathers centuries ago," Lutz and Lovell write, "Guatemalan Mayas continue to migrate in order to survive."[96]

Once in the United States, understandings and worldviews shaped by their history in Guatemala continue to inform immigrants' understanding of their current realities. One Mayan in Providence explained to Foxen that "the *migra* here, it is like, as they said, the guerrillas over there. . . . If *la migra* is looking for one of us, we all run, run escaping, it is like the guerrilla." Likewise in Guatemala, one *campesino* (peasant farmer) told her that "he had heard that the INS had not yet arrived in Providence, though they were said to be close (thus likening them to the army or guerrillas)."[97]

Foxen also notes a "total confusion surrounding understandings about the legality and illegality of different types of documentation" that stems from the population's long history of the law being used against them.[98] Some of her informants had paid hundreds of dollars to a *notario* for a temporary work permit. These *notarios* often had no legal credentials, but played on a semantic confusion, since in Latin America the term often refers to a lawyer. The *notarios* would file a fraudulent asylum application, which would nonetheless entitle the migrant to a temporary, legal work permit, until their asylum hearing, which would generally result in deportation. Foxen encountered frequent references to people obtaining "*papeles legalmente falsificados*"—legally falsified documents—a further example of the impenetrable character of the law from the perspective of the immigrants.[99]

Describing his experience as a court interpreter for Guatemalan migrants after an immigration raid at a meatpacking plant in Postville, Iowa, Erik Camayd-Freixas explained that workers there had simply followed recruiters' and employers' instructions, and had not knowingly chosen to break any law.

"Do you know what this number is?" asked the lawyer, pointing to the social security number on his I-9 employment form. "I don't know," said the man. "Who put it there?" "At the plant, they helped me fill out the papers 'cause I can't read or write Spanish, much less English." "Do you know what a social security number is?" the lawyer insisted. "No," said the man. "Do you know what a social security card is?" "No." "Do you know what it's used for?" "I don't know any of that. I'm new in this country," said the man, visibly embarrassed.[100]

Like their ancestors and their contemporaries, these migrants had simply gone where the recruiters had taken them to work.

A *New York Times* reporter interviewed Guatemalan and other Central American migrants on Mexico's southern border in early 2013. "Few had even heard about the debate to overhaul immigration laws and possibly open a pathway to citizenship for immigrants living illegally in the United States," he commented. "Instead, the prevailing force seems to be deteriorating conditions at home."[101]

For at least five hundred years, Guatemala's highland Mayan populations have been buffeted, or coerced, by the winds of the global economy. They have been slaughtered, displaced, massacred, and enslaved. They have had to leave their homes and their families to do the hardest, dirtiest, and lowest work for the benefit of others. They have been discriminated against socially and legally. For centuries, they have been forced to migrate and suffered poor working conditions and legalized discrimination. Their migration to the United States is only the latest phase of this long history. Their technical illegality in the United States is but a small part of a system that has worked to control their movement and their labor for hundreds of years.

CHAPTER 3

Becoming Illegal

There are two main ways to become undocumented in the United States. About half of the undocumented population enters without inspection. They may have attempted to obtain a visa and been denied. More likely, they either knew that such an attempt was hopeless or did not even know that such a process existed and didn't try at all. So they crossed somehow, usually by land but sometimes by sea, through a border that may have been unmarked, invisible, or at least unpatrolled. Thus, they were not inspected by any official from Immigration and Customs Enforcement (ICE) when they entered. This means that while they may have many kinds of identification documents, they have none that specifically authorizes their entry into the United States.

The other portion of the undocumented population entered *with* inspection, usually with a visa of some sort or with a Border Crossing Card. One US government estimate calculates that between 30 percent and 60 percent of the undocumented became so through visa overstays, meaning that though they were initially authorized entry, they neglected to leave in the designated time frame.[1]

Millions of Mexicans obtain tourist visas every year, and the number has been rising steadily, from about 4 million a year at the beginning of the 2000s to almost 13 million in 2010.[2] However, the vast majority of Mexicans who obtain tourist visas do not overstay their visas and become "illegal." Most Mexicans who are undocumented became so by crossing the border without inspection, and most people who become undocumented through visa overstays are not Mexican.

Under today's immigration laws, citizens of most countries must request a visa in their home country before traveling to the United States. Europeans, as always, are privileged: the Visa Waiver Program allows most of them to enter as tourists (but not to work) without a visa. Some Mexicans are eligible for Border Crossing Cards that allow them to travel for a specified period of time in the border region. Border Crossing Cards are like tourist or visitors' visas: they authorize *entry* into the United States, but they don't authorize the holder to work. People who enter with these kinds of permission can become undocumented if they either overstay their visa or violate its terms in some other way, including, for Border Card holders, leaving the twenty-five-mile border zone. Because nonimmigrant visas are temporary permits with specific conditions attached to them, ordinary activities that are not in themselves illegal can still constitute visa violations. In some cases, there are lies or questionable and illegal activities involved in obtaining the visa itself.

In 2011, 159 million nonimmigrant visitors entered the United States with some kind of legal permission. Thirty-three percent or 53.1 million of them were I-94 card holders, meaning that they either had obtained a nonimmigrant (temporary) visa or were admitted under the Visa Waiver Program. The largest source of I-94 admissions was Mexico, with 33 percent of the total. (The next largest source was United Kingdom, with only 8.6 percent.) Eighty-seven percent of these visa holders had visitors' or tourist visas that allowed them to travel for business or pleasure. The others held student, temporary worker, or other kinds of visas.[3] Some one hundred thousand were H-2 guest workers, some 80 percent of them Mexican. Most of the other two-thirds of inspected entries were Mexicans and Canadians with Border Crossing Cards.[4]

For all categories of nonimmigrant travel, then—as visitors or temporary workers with a visa, with a Border Crossing Card, or as undocumented entries—Mexicans constitute the largest numbers. Of the 11.5 million or so undocumented immigrants in 2006, some 4–5.5 million had entered with visitor or tourist visas, and another 250,000–500,000 entered with Border Crossing Cards. The other 6–7 million entered without inspection.[5]

ILLEGAL VISAS

Although evading ICE inspection points and the Border Patrol is a common method of illegal entry, it's not the only one. The head of Customs and Border Protection (CBP) explained to researcher Lynnaire Sheridan that before resorting to a dangerous crossing through the desert, migrants could attempt to borrow, purchase, or steal an authentic US passport or permanent resident card. Absent that possibility, they might obtain a false document or alter a document themselves by inserting their own photograph. If they could not access any documents, they might hide in a vehicle and cross at night.[6] The professional cross-border smugglers Sheridan interviewed offered a rather similar assessment. They told her that the safest way to cross was to obtain a tourist visa or, if that was not possible, to use a valid visa belonging to a family member. A bit riskier was the use of false or altered documents. The most dangerous method was to attempt to cross without being seen, generally in isolated areas with little Border Patrol presence.[7]

Sheridan interviewed many families that had crossed illegally multiple times. They corroborated this assessment. They listed their preferred options as, first, crossing with a tourist visa and overstaying it; second, using someone else's documents;

third, using false documents; and last, attempting to cross without being discovered. If the latter was the only option, they emphasized that the more isolated the area, the more dangerous the crossing.

Cost was also a factor. The safest options were the most expensive. Sometimes families would pay more to have their young children, for example, cross with false papers (perhaps accompanying adults with valid documents), while the adults would opt for a dangerous clandestine crossing.[8]

Another method of crossing the border is with a temporary work visa, generally through the H-2A (agricultural) or H-2B (nonagricultural) programs. (There are other categories of temporary work visas, but most require specific types and levels of skills and don't apply in most situations.) But with the H-2 program, as with the Bracero Program before it, paperwork and requirements are so bureaucratic and onerous that many employers and potential workers find the program not worth the effort.[9] There is also a lot of room for illegal and unfair maneuvering within the H-2 system.

US employers begin by requesting authorization to recruit H-2 workers from the Department of Labor. Once an employer receives authorization, they generally turn to a US contracting agency, which in turn contracts with a Mexican recruiting agency to find available workers. Opportunities for abuse within the system abound.

The complexity of the H-2 program and the gap between the overwhelming demand on both sides and the small number of visas actually available make the program ripe for fraud and exploitation. "Illegality" enters the system in numerous ways, as uncovered by a 2010 United States Government Accountability Office (GAO) report. In six cases that the GAO reviewed, "employers charged their H-2B workers fees that were for the benefit of the employer or charged excessive fees that brought employees' wages below the hourly federal minimum wage.

These charges included visa processing fees far above actual costs, rent in overcrowded apartments that drastically exceeded market value, and transportation charges subject to arbitrary 'late fees.' Workers left the United States in greater debt than when they arrived. In one case, these fees reduced employees' paychecks to as little as $48 for a 2-week period." In eight cases, "employers were alleged to have submitted fraudulent documentation to Labor, USCIS, and State to either exploit their H-2B employees or hire more employees than needed. Employers and recruiters misclassified employee duties on Labor certification applications to pay lower prevailing wages; used shell companies to file fraudulent labor certification applications for unneeded employees, then leased the additional employees to businesses not on the visa petitions; and preferentially hired H-2B employees over American workers in violation of federal law."[10]

Eighty percent of H-2A and H-2B visa requests in Mexico are processed at the US consulate in Monterrey. The director of the Mexican Oficina de Atención al Migrante in that city has filed complaints about "hundreds of cases of fraud" in which unscrupulous agents charge would-be migrants illicit fees in exchange for promises of access to the coveted visa.[11] "In practice, nobody can hope to obtain one of these visas if they don't use the intermediaries. Otherwise how will they find out about the opportunities that exist?"[12] From the perspective of the Mexican worker, working through the H-2 program might be almost indistinguishable from crossing without inspection to work. Both involve relying on shady networks for information, paying exorbitant fees, and working under poor conditions and at wage rates that are frequently "illegal" as well as exploitative.

In 2004, the Farm Labor Organizing Committee or FLOC, a farm-workers' union in the United States, negotiated an agreement with North Carolina growers that allowed the workers to bypass the contractors. The organization opened an office in Monterrey to monitor the recruitment process there. On September 9, 2007, the director of the FLOC office, Santiago Rafael Cruz, was found tied up, tortured, and murdered. The union suspected that local labor contractors were behind the murder. As FLOC president Baldemar Velázquez explained, "FLOC's agreement eliminated the extortion of illegal fees from workers by criminal elements. They have been unhappy with the union taking away their goldmine. We disrupted not only the recruiters working for growers in North Carolina, but all the recruiters who recruit workers for all the other states: from Florida and Georgia, through South Carolina and Virginia, all the way up to Pennsylvania and New York." Labor journalist Dan LaBotz added that "FLOC's presence in Mexico meant that the racketeers were losing hundreds of thousands of dollars in exorbitant fees and bribes."[13]

The chains reach deep into Guatemala. Some twelve hundred workers recruited by Mexican agency Job Consultoría paid from $1,000 to $3,000 for supposed access to a visa. In Amatitlán, Guatemala, 370 men and their families attacked local resident Pablo Roberto Valencia in late 2011 when they learned that the money they had given him to pay for their visas had disappeared.[14] According to the Southern Poverty Law Center, workers generally arrive in the United States with debts between $500 and $10,000 owed—illegally—to recruiters.[15]

While these workers do enter with visas that authorize their presence and permit them to work in the United States, the process that connects them with these visas violates US, Mexican, and sometimes other countries' laws. It frequently involves threats, violence, extortion, and debt peonage. These violations are generally met with impunity, however. In fact, the violations are built into the system itself; they are integral to its functioning and to the arrival of officially legal H-2 workers to the United States.

GETTING TO THE BORDER

Although the majority of uninspected border crossers are Mexican, others are Central and South Americans. Today, Central Americans often travel a perilous land journey from their homes across one or more countries and through Mexico. A century ago, excluded people like the Chinese entered through Mexico, because of the openness of that border.

While the number of Mexicans crossing illegally has declined in recent years, the number of Central Americans has been steadily increasing. The economic crisis in the United States meant that some sectors, like construction, that had traditionally attracted Mexican migrants, were not hiring. Some experts have also suggested that increased deportation rates, violence along the border, and a declining birthrate in Mexico have contributed to a slowing of Mexican crossings.[16]

In Central America, though, economic stagnation and horrific levels of violence, especially in Guatemala, El Salvador, and Honduras, have meant that the numbers crossing into the United States continue to increase. Somewhere between 150,000 (according to the Mexican government) and 400,000 (according to advocacy organizations) undocumented migrants were entering Mexico each year as of 2010, mostly from Central America.[17] In 2011, 46,997 non-Mexicans, mostly Central Americans, were detained at the border; in 2012, the figure more than doubled, to 94,532.[18] While still much fewer than the 188,467 Mexicans detained during the 2011–2012 fiscal year, the trend was clear: the number of Mexicans was decreasing, while that of Central Americans was increasing.[19]

Although in even smaller numbers, South Americans also cross the border by land, first traveling by plane to Mexico. In Montevideo, one travel agency offered a choice of a tourist visa and a ticket to New York or a ticket to Mexico and a connection to a coyote who would arrange an illegal land crossing, depending on how much the traveler was willing to pay.[20] Similarly in Brazil, travel agents sell package deals that include airfare to Mexico City, a guide to Tijuana, and a coyote for crossing the border. In New York, Maxine Margolis found that only 3 percent of Brazilians in her sample had crossed the Mexican border, but in Framingham, Massachusetts, another study found that 43 percent had. Wealthier Brazilians were more likely to be able to obtain the tourist visa, while those who were poorer and less educated were more likely to have to resort to the Mexican route.[21]

When US consulates in the Dominican Republic began to reduce the number of tourist visas they granted, informal visa brokers began to offer their clients other, more expensive routes. Migrants were sent to Puerto Rico by boat or to Mexico to cross the land border. A market sprang up in forged or false papers. Samuel Martinez noted that while Dominicans saw some modes of entry as preferable to others, the relative illegality was not their prime concern. It was just how the system worked: rich people got preferred access to visas; poor people had to pay huge sums for the same privilege. "'Legal' and 'illegal' modes of entry are viewed by Caribbean people more as bureaucratic obstacles to circumvent than as immutable law," he concluded.[22]

Eugenia Georges' research on emigration from the Dominican Republic noted the same pattern of poorer immigrants having to take more costly and dangerous routes. In the town she studied, richer residents—those who owned land or businesses—could usually get tourist visas and fly directly to the United States, since, as property owners, they could convince US consular officials that they would return home after their tourist excursions. Poorer, landless Dominicans had to resort to the more expensive, riskier, indirect route via Mexico.[23]

In the case of Central Americans, almost all of those trying to migrate are poor, and their journey through Mexico is a perilous one. In 2001, Mexico—under pressure from the Bush administration—began to implement what it called "Plan Sur" to secure its southern border, while Guatemala countered with "Venceremos 2001" to control exit traffic from its own country. The militarization of this border mirrored what had begun a decade earlier on the US-Mexico border, and the results were also similar. Official statistics showed migration numbers slowing. But migrants and human rights organizations pointed out that these statistics were deceptive. Many migrants shifted away from the newly enforced and militarized checkpoints into more remote areas. As crossing became more difficult and more dangerous, it also became more criminalized, as gangs, drug traffickers, and professional smugglers became involved.[24] Deportations also rose, but much more slowly than the migrant stream. Between January and November 2010, the Mexican National Institute of Migration (INAMI) deported 49,143 Central Americans: 19,876 Hondurans, 8,263 Salvadorans, 20,354 Guatemalans, and 646 Nicaraguans.[25] Another 40,971 Central Americans were detained in Mexico in 2012.[26]

Many Central Americans attempt to cross Mexico by stowing away on the freight trains that run from Chiapas on the Mexico-Guatemala border up to Mexico City and then on to the US border. The journey can take days or weeks, as migrants slip from train to train. Up to fifteen hundred Central Americans attempt to board *La Bestia* or the Beast—also known as "The Train of Death"—every day. Thousands have been killed or maimed in the process.[27]

Because migrants carry money for their trip and because most of them have relatives working in the United States who are helping to pay for them and can be extorted for ransom money, the kidnapping of migrants has become a regular occurrence on their trip through Mexico. In just six months between September 2008 and February 2009, the Mexican National Human Rights Commission uncovered cases of almost 10,000 migrants kidnapped.[28] From April to September 2010, the commission found 11,333 kidnapping cases. "This figure reflects the fact that there have not been sufficient government efforts to lower the rates of kidnapping affecting the migrant population," the commission declared. Most of the cases discovered by the commission were Hondurans (44.3 percent), followed by Salvadorans, Guatemalans, Mexicans, and small numbers of Cubans, Nicaraguans, Colombians, and Ecuadorians.[29]

Although various social actors—including Mexican police and other government officials—participate in kidnapping and extortion networks, their modus operandi is similar: migrants are captured and tortured to force them to reveal contacts in their home country or in the United States. The kidnappers then call these relatives or friends and demand payment, threatening to kill the migrant if they don't comply.[30] The majority of kidnappings take place along the train route or on the trains themselves.

Kidnapping is only part of the story. A Mexican church-based human rights coalition decried a broad spectrum of "human rights violations committed by public servants and federal, state, and municipal police. This criminalization of undocumented migration sets the stage for physical, psychological, and sexual aggression, and human trafficking."[31]

The emergence of the Zetas cartel in 2002 greatly worsened the situation just as the numbers of Central American migrants passing through Mexico was increasing. According to Mexico's Assistant Attorney General's Office for Special Investigations on Organized Crime, "its main activities include extortion and sale of protection services, carrying out assassinations, holding and selling drugs, piracy, gasoline sales, and the capture and ransom of hostages." According to victims, the Zetas are the main perpetrators of migrant kidnappings.[32]

> The Zetas use a strategy of displacing and taking control of small communities. They terrorize and extort the local population and co-opt individuals who belong to gangs or small local

bands, training them to carry out actions like surveillance of trains, apprehension of migrants, transferring and overseeing migrants in safe houses, making telephone calls for the purpose of extortion, and receiving the ransom. These delinquent groups, made up mostly of young people, are popularly known as the "Zetitas." In every kidnapping case they also commit serious crimes like assassination, sexual exploitation, and human trafficking. In its first two years, the Zetas cartel succeeded in establishing itself all along the routes traveled by migrants.[33]

As the flow of Central American migrants increased, so did cases of kidnapping, especially after 2007.[34] In one notorious case, in August 2010, seventy-two migrants from El Salvador, Honduras, Guatemala, Ecuador, and Brazil were victims of a massacre as they passed through Tamaulipas on their way to the border. Their captors—members of a drug gang, possibly the Zetas—demanded that they pay ransom or agree to work as couriers. When the migrants refused, they were slaughtered. A lone survivor managed to reach a nearby military base and tell the story of what had transpired. A year later, a young member of the Zetas confessed to the crime.[35] In another massacre, in May 2012, forty-nine mutilated bodies of supposed migrants were found dumped along a highway near Monterrey. "Because of the number of people, it appears that they could be passengers from a bus full of illegals; it could be a case in which organized delinquents [i.e., drug cartels] were extorting the coyote, since they have now taken over this illegal business," a Mexican government representative explained.[36]

According to the Human Rights Coalition report, "Migrants are typically captured on the trains themselves, or while waiting along the tracks. Groups of heavily armed persons approach the migrants, force them onto pickup trucks, and take them to safe houses. The kidnappings are carried out with unremitting brutality. In the 'safe houses' where they are held they suffer all kinds of tortures, cruel and inhuman treatment, and physical and psychological punishments, until their family in the United States (or in Central America) collects the money for their ransom."[37]

Mexican government officials have also been heavily implicated in these abuses. The Mexican INAMI and state security forces carry out "migration verification operations" on the trains, sometimes using electric shock instruments. They detain some migrants, leaving others in the hands of the gangs or armed groups.[38]

While it might be tempting to simply blame this violence against migrants on Mexican actors, the situation really can't be separated from its larger context: the criminalization of migrants by the United States, and its pressure on Mexico to enforce similar policies. While Mexico has publicly denounced US anti-immigrant policies, its government has also collaborated in many ways. US policies create a political context—illegality—that legitimizes abuses against migrants. The Bishop of Saltillo in northern Mexico articulated what many Mexicans and Central Americans believe: "My conclusion is that the Mexican government's migration policies are aimed at preventing migrants from crossing into the United States. It is abundantly clear that the impunity enjoyed by organized crime, like that previously enjoyed by gangs, is a policy of terror."[39] A policy of terror that thrives in and serves the climate of criminalization of immigrants in their destination.

ON THE BORDER

Crossing the US-Mexico border used to be a rather mundane affair, as described in earlier chapters. With politicians pandering to (and fanning the flames of) the rising anti-immigrant climate inside the United States in the early 1990s, the border changed dramatically. Operation Hold the Line in El Paso in 1993 and Operation Gatekeeper in California in 1994 began today's still-ongoing obsession with the border.[40] In September 1993, the Border Patrol chief of the El Paso Sector, Silvestre Reyes, launched his new policy, a "highly visible show of force along a 20-mile section of the boundary dividing El Paso from Ciudad Juárez. Inspections at official ports of entry also intensified. The strategy represented a radical departure from the prior Border Patrol strategy of pursuing and apprehending unauthorized immigrants after they had crossed the boundary into the El Paso area." Apprehensions quickly fell in this sector, not because overall border crossings declined, but because migrants simply shifted to new crossing points.[41]

Likewise, Operation Gatekeeper in California succeeded in deflecting migrant traffic away from the sixty-six-mile stretch known as the San Diego Sector of the border. Operation Gatekeeper included construction of a wall, massive deployment of Border Patrol agents along the border, stadium lighting, vehicles, sensors, and other equipment. Beginning at the Imperial Beach Station in the west and moving east, the Border Patrol hoped to bring the entire San Diego Sector "under full control" within five years.[42] As in Texas, "control" did not mean that migrants stopped coming; they simply moved to other, much more treacherous entry points.

In 2009, the American Civil Liberties Union and Mexico's National Human Rights Commission on accused the US government of causing thousands of deaths at the border. "This report is the sounding of an alarm for a humanitarian crisis that has led to the death of more than 5,000 human beings," they declared. The crisis was a direct result, they said, of US decisions: "The deaths of unauthorized migrants have been a predictable and inhumane outcome of border security policies on the US-Mexico border over the last fifteen years." The new policies implemented by Gatekeeper, militarizing the more populated San Diego Sector, "intentionally forc[ed] undocumented immigrants to extreme environments and natural barriers that the government anticipated would increase the likelihood of injury and death."[43] To reach safety, migrants had to hike for miles over treacherous desert terrain, enduring the extreme heat of the days and cold of the nights. Few were able to carry enough water. As the death rate rose precipitously, "the chief cause of death shifted . . . from traffic fatalities to deaths from hypothermia, dehydration, and drowning."[44]

The Arizona-based Coalición de Derechos Humanos has tallied the dead in the Arizona sector since 2000. Basing its figures on recovered remains, the organization noted that at least 100 to 300 have died each year, with the highest number, 282, being reached in 2006. Since many remains are not recovered, the actual death rates are considerably higher. The organization attributes the slight decline after that (down to 179 in 2011–2012) to lower numbers of total crossings.[45] A GAO investigation in 2006 found that border-crossing deaths had doubled in the past decade, to a high of 472 in 2006. Three-quarters of the increase was due to rising death rates in the Tucson sector, and most were due to heat-related exposure.[46] The Pima County, Arizona, medical examiner's office took custody of the remains of 1,915 migrants who died in the desert between 2001 and 2010.[47] The Border Patrol's own figures corroborated the high (492) in fiscal year 2005 and show that despite a slight drop after that, numbers rose again, to 483 in fiscal year 2012.[48]

Even as the total number of people crossing may have declined after 2006, the process became increasingly dangerous. The *Arizona Daily Star* noted that the ratio of known deaths per apprehensions rose from three per one hundred thousand in 1998 to thirty-nine in 2004 and eighty-eight in 2009. "That means the risk of dying is more than twice as high today compared with five years ago and nearly 30 times greater than in 1998," the newspaper reported at the end of 2009. "Border-county law enforcement, Mexican Consulate officials, Tohono O'odham tribal officials and humanitarian groups say the increase in fencing, technology and agents has caused illegal border crossers to walk longer distances in more treacherous terrain, increasing the likelihood that people will get hurt or fatigued and left behind to die."[49]

In response to the growing death rate and the outcry it provoked, the Border Patrol initiated the Border Safety Initiative in 1998 and formed BORSTAR to train agents in search, trauma, and rescue. The goal was to address the humanitarian crisis created by the United States' own new border policies. Border Patrol agents did provide life-saving aid to hundreds of migrants in the years since the program was initiated. But "while the Tucson Sector BORSTAR unit routinely provided search, rescue, and medical intervention to undocumented immigrants under harsh conditions, the number of times it responded was insignificant in comparison to the volume of Border Patrol law enforcement activities."[50] Soon, other, independent church-based and grassroots organizations began to form to try to respond to the issue.

CONCLUSION

The laws that allow or disallow entry into the United States are and have always been arbitrary and discriminatory. One set of laws, primarily for Europeans and for the wealthy, allows freedom of travel. Another set, for Latin Americans and the poor, creates a labyrinth of enticements and obstacles.

The Las Americas Premium Outlets complex on the US side the Tijuana–San Ysidro crossing just south of San Diego symbolizes the contradiction. Looming over the border, the 125 outlet stores beckon to tourists from the Mexican side, offering them a consumer mecca if they cross to shop. "The big fence surrounding the outlets and the Mexican flag [just beyond the complex, on the other side of the border] was a bit distracting," wrote one US reviewer on the popular website Yelp.com.[51] Between the mall and the flag are the imposing border wall and the security apparatus that sustains it, reminding Mexicans that their welcome is decidedly conditional.

Myriad historical and economic factors draw and sometimes force migrants from their homes into the US economy. Many of these factors are the result of deliberate decisions implemented by US employers, investors, and government. At the same time, increasingly convoluted webs of laws, restrictions, and discrimination ensure that migrants remain in a subject position, exploitable and exploited. Today, the system works by drawing or forcing them into a status deemed illegality.

The borders that divide immigrants from the United States are not just physical. Once inside the country—whether by means of a traumatic border crossing or a simple visa overstay—people without documents live behind another kind of border, a baffling and sometimes terrifying border that separates them from those around them and the country and society in which they live. These internal borders are the subject of the next chapter.

CHAPTER 4

What Part of "Illegal" Do You Understand?

Arbitrary and precarious. If life for poor people in Mexico and Central America seems to be filled with precarious status and arbitrary events to which they must simply adapt in order to survive, life in the United States continues the pattern. Why do some government agencies welcome the undocumented, while others ignore them, and still others threaten, imprison, and deport them? What really determines their status, and why does it seem to change so frequently and unpredictably? How can they plan for the future or prepare, when everything seems so capricious?

THE BLURRINESS OF CATEGORIES

In the minds of most citizens, the terms "legal" and "illegal" are clearly defined and clearly distinguished categories. In real life, though, there is a large gray area between the two ostensibly opposite poles. Most people who are undocumented live ordinary lives and are not immediately distinguishable from immigrants with documents or from citizens. Yet in some ways, hidden to the outside, documented world, their lives are very different. As Jose Antonio Vargas puts it, "Everyday life for an undocumented American means a constant search for loop-holes and back doors."[1]

Most of the approximately 11 million undocumented people in the United States have been here for quite a while. As noted earlier, only 14 percent arrived in the country after January 1, 2005, meaning that 86 percent have been in the country for over seven years.[2] While the law may consider them alien, most of them are people who have deep roots in the United States.

Mexicans are overrepresented among those deported: Mexicans make up 58 percent of the undocumented population, but 70 percent of those deported are Mexican.[3] Apparently, being Mexican makes you somehow *more* undocumented, in the eyes of society and of law enforcement, than others. Since undocumentedness is a socially imposed status, then how you are seen by those in authority is in fact what brings it into being.

Many individuals have experienced being both documented and undocumented. Laws have changed, as in 1986 when many undocumented people were offered the chance to legalize. Individuals who entered the country legally may fall out of status if they violate the terms of their visa in some way, while, more rarely, those who are undocumented may find a way to regularize their status.

The 1986 Immigration Reform and Control Act, the country's most recent attempt at some sort of supposedly comprehensive immigration reform, exemplified the arbitrary nature of immigration law. In order to qualify for legalization, migrants must have resided in the country continuously since January 1, 1982. This cutoff date meant that the large numbers of Central American immigrants who arrived later were excluded. Of the 500,000 to 850,000 Salvadorans in the country in 1986, only 146,000 qualified.[4] The *American Baptist Churches v. Thornburgh* (or ABC) Settlement Agreement in 1990 reopened thousands of political asylum cases, offering a new chance for legal residence for undocumented Salvadorans and

Guatemalans. But the process was agonizingly slow, and tens of thousands of Central Americans remained in limbo through the 1990s, renewing their work permits every eighteen months as their cases languished.

The Immigration Act of 1990 (IMMACT)—among many other provisions—created the new category of Temporary Protected Status (TPS), offering temporary protection and work authorization to immigrants from countries affected by war or natural disaster. Salvadorans were granted TPS, based on the state of civil war in the country that made it impossible for them to return. Guatemalans, despite the war in their country, were not included. TPS for Salvadorans was extended several times, but ended in 1995 after a peace agreement ended the war. At that time, some 1 million Salvadorans lived in the United States. Half of them were legal immigrants, and between 90,000 and 190,000 had been protected by TPS.[5] (Some 200,000 applied originally, but many failed to complete the repeated renewal process.)[6] When TPS ended, many Salvadorans returned to the stalled asylum process.

The 1997 Nicaraguan Adjustment and Central America Relief Act (NACARA) was an attempt to address the backlog in asylum cases by offering permanent residency to certain asylum seekers. But NACARA too left many Guatemalans and Salvadorans in limbo, as it favored Cuban and Nicaraguan petitioners and continued to be plagued with backlogs. In 2001, the INS estimated that it could take "up to 20 years" to process the pending, almost three hundred thousand Central American applications.[7] Between 1999 and 2003, the approval rate for Salvadoran and Guatemalan asylum applicants hovered between 7 percent and 11 percent, not much higher than the low rate in the 1980s that had led to the ABC lawsuit. For applicants from other countries, the rate was 33 percent to 44 percent.[8] Salvadorans and Guatemalans, in the words of Cecilia Menjívar and Leisy Abrego, "have faced being granted only temporary permits, seemingly interminable applications, re-applications, long waiting times for their applications to be processed, and the threat of imminent deportation." Neither fully legal nor illegal, they exist in a state of "permanent temporariness" or "liminal legality."[9]

Menjívar describes the experiences of many undocumented Central American immigrants:

> Occasionally they are granted temporary relief from deportation with multiple and confusing deadlines for applications and renewals of permits and convoluted application procedures (e.g., fees, forms, photos, fingerprints, proofs of residence, and innumerable caveats and conditions). Indeed, so much work is involved in preparing these applications and information is so difficult to obtain that a veritable industry has developed among document preparers, notaries, and other entrepreneurs (some of whom are not particularly well qualified) to fulfill the needs of Central Americans applying for the different dispensations. This situation creates enormous anxiety, as each deadline accentuates these immigrants' precarious situation, which for many has gone on for over two decades.[10]

Immigration law revisions have continued the pattern of creating new ways of punishing illegality, while concomitantly creating sometimes unexpected and apparently arbitrary new avenues for legalization. A new Temporary Protected Status for Salvadorans (2001) and Haitians (2011) offered undocumented people from those countries a temporary respite, but with the knowledge that it could just as easily be rescinded in the future. President Obama's June 2012 announcement of Deferred Action for Childhood Arrivals (DACA) granted some youth a similar two-year reprieve during which they could receive temporary documents, including permission to work, but with no prediction about what their status would be at the end of those two years.

Many migrants hope that someday a legal avenue will be opened for them to regularize their status, as occurred in 1986, and do everything possible to improve their chances for obtaining legal status if and when the opportunity arises. Thus, once in the United States, they are constantly torn between laws they feel they have no choice but to violate (for instance, laws that prohibit them from working) and a desire to prove themselves as law abiding and deserving of legal status.

For this reason, many thousands of undocumented immigrants apply for and receive Individual Taxpayer ID Numbers (ITINs) that allow them to file income tax returns each year. They readily appear in court when cited for traffic violations or the more serious charge of driving without a license. Yet they continue to work and drive without official authorization to do so.

SOCIAL SERVICES

The social service network is often a maze of complexity even for citizens and contributes to the arbitrariness that undocumented status entails. Undocumented immigrants are eligible for some types of benefits, while both the undocumented and temporary immigrants with legal documents are restricted from others. Since 1996, even legal permanent residents are excluded from many services. Disentangling what an immigrant is legally eligible for is a complex task. Furthermore, as people often live in mixed-status families, different services may be available to different members. Regulations for welfare, Medicaid, and other types of social services have struggled to parse the categories and decide exactly what "lawfully present" means when determining eligibility. Several pages of the 2011 edition of the United States Code are needed to explain the various legal statuses and determine which qualify a person for different types of benefits.[11]

The complexity reveals both the legal and moral difficulty of identifying individuals by status and the confusing questions

that undocumented immigrants face. Why does one government agency want to help them, while another wants to harm
them? Can they be punished for accepting services that are offered to them?

To further confuse the issue, most social service providers
are trained and eager to make sure that people obtain access to
the services for which they are eligible. Undocumented immigrants may be overwhelmed with phone calls and urgings to accept certain benefits, while finding it impossible to access others
that are even more urgently needed. (Of course, this is true for
citizens as well.) The patchwork reflects competing interests in
the passage of laws and the interests of agencies, but, like status
itself, presents a bewildering panorama to those in need.

Immigrants may learn that pregnant women are eligible for
the federal Women, Infants, and Children (WIC) food supple-
mentation program, but not for the Supplemental Nutrition
Assistance Program (SNAP). One (US-born) child might be
eligible for SNAP, while another (foreign-born) child in the
same family is not. Undocumented children can go to Head
Start and to public schools, but their eligibility for public
higher education varies by state. The Affordable Care Act explicitly excludes the undocumented from eligibility, but hospi-
tal emergency rooms are still required to provide care for them.
They are not eligible for publicly funded housing, but can live
in such housing if it's shared with a qualified family member
who is not undocumented.

Because they are ineligible for most publicly funded social
services, and because they are generally reluctant to claim even
those services for which they may be eligible, the undocumented
tend to place fewer costs on the public coffers than would be expected, given their low incomes. In a careful study of the fiscal
impact of undocumented immigration, the Center for Immigration Studies concluded that "the primary reason they create
a fiscal deficit is their low education levels and resulting low

incomes and tax payments, not their legal status or heavy use of most social services."[12]

FRAUDULENT DOCUMENTS

Almost all people who are undocumented in fact possess a spectrum of valid and fraudulent papers. They may hold a birth certificate, driver's license, or passport from their home country, but lack a visa authorizing their presence in the United States or perhaps hold an expired visa.

There are many degrees of fraudulence and many methods for trying to gain access to the documents people need for everyday life. One of the first documents an undocumented immigrant needs upon arrival in the United States is a Social Security card. A thriving underground business in false (and often poorly made) Social Security cards preys on the newly arrived. For a few hundred dollars, the forgers simply place the immigrant's name—or a false name—along with a random number on a card designed to approximate an actual card.

Since the E-Verify program has become more common in the past decade, more undocumented people are finding that they need a Social Security number with a correctly matched name. Sometimes, an immigrant can borrow a name and number from a friend or relative. Or, for a much higher fee, a forger will sell an immigrant an actual person's name and Social Security number.

Puerto Rico has been an especially lucrative source for valid birth certificates and Social Security numbers with Spanish names. A person might sell his own documents, those of a child or elder who is not working, or even those of a person who has died. Or the documents could be stolen. The buyer—often an undocumented immigrant in the continental United States—most often just wants a valid Social Security number that matches the name on the card so that he or she can work. In some cases, though, the fraud moves into more aggressive theft, where a person will use the documents to apply for social services that are available only to citizens or to obtain tax refunds, loans, or credit in the other person's name.[13]

In 2010, the Puerto Rican government responded to the situation by invalidating all Puerto Rican birth certificates and requiring everyone born in Puerto Rico to obtain a new, more secure document. Many were skeptical that this would end the problem. One Puerto Rican citizen explained drily, "Money buys everything. . . . Anyone will do anything for money."[14]

There's a big difference between using a false number and identity theft. In a case of identity theft, an individual attempts to access someone's bank account, credit card, or other property to benefit from it. Using a false Social Security number—even if it happens to belong to someone else—does not give you access to anything that actually belongs to that person. Rather, when an employer pays payroll taxes using the false number, the IRS flags the discrepancy and simply transfers the Social Security payments into its Earnings Suspense File.[15] The person to whom the number actually belongs is not affected in any way. In recognition of the ubiquity—and the harmlessness—of the use of false Social Security numbers, the Obama administration clarified that using a false Social Security number would not count against a young person applying for DACA.

Marrying for documents is another strategy that ranges from legal to illegal, with myriad shades of gray in between. Some marriages may be arranged as financial transactions between strangers solely in hopes of obtaining documents. This practice is illegal, and ICE prosecutes people who obtain legal residency through this kind of arranged marriage. But not all marriages of convenience are fraudulent. No laws govern the amount of love a person must feel in order to marry; most people who marry do so for a spectrum of reasons ranging from the emotional to the extremely practical. There is nothing illegal about marrying for security, money, prestige, or power.

DRIVING

During the 1980s and '90s, most states had no rules preventing the undocumented from obtaining a driver's license and driving legally. This changed after 9/11, when suddenly driver's licenses were turned into a matter of national security. Millions of people who had been driving legally, with legitimate licenses, found that driving had become illegal.

The REAL ID Act of 2005, passed as part of the recommendations made by the 9/11 Commission, attempted to set a national standard for driver's license issuance. Among other things, the act required a birth certificate or passport with a visa that demonstrated that the person was in the country legally. The license would then serve as an electronically readable, federally approved identification card. The Department of Homeland Security would set the standard and approve the cards, essentially turning the state-issued driver's license into a national identity card.

The act was slated to go into full effect in 2008, but full implementation was postponed several times. By the end of 2012, most states were in compliance. Once fully implemented, a driver's license from a state not in compliance would not be considered valid identification for travel, opening a bank account, applying for benefits or Social Security, or entry into federal buildings.

Driving is such a basic necessity for adult life in most of the United States that numerous methods have emerged for undocumented immigrants to obtain a license. Like a Social Security card, a false driver's license can be purchased. A new industry mushroomed, making false driver's licenses. Some people used licenses from their own countries—legal or falsified. Others traveled to New Mexico or Washington State—two states that still allowed the undocumented to obtain a license—and claimed residence there.

In Utah, the legislature created a "driver privilege card" in 2005 for those unable to obtain a driver's license because they had no Social Security card. The privilege card cannot serve as official identification, but it does certify that the holder has passed a driving test and entitles him or her to drive. Other states, concerned with the safety problems posed by the proliferation of unlicensed drivers, experimented with other kinds of driving permits that would evade the REAL ID Act. Some allowed noncitizens to use a license from their own country for a limited period of time while in the United States.

Even immigrants legally authorized to work are not always able to obtain the license they need. Part of the problem is legislators' simple ignorance of the amazing complexity of immigration law and status. The state of Texas, for example, passed legislation in 2007 requiring that, in order to obtain a commercial driver's license, an applicant must be a citizen, a legal permanent resident, an asylee, or a refugee, or else provide an I-94 form proving that they crossed the border legally. But there are many immigrants who are legally present and have work authorization but don't fit into those categories.

A large number of Central Americans in Texas have Temporary Protected Status, which authorizes their continued presence and allows them to work even if they were formerly undocumented. Other undocumented immigrants may have received authorization to work while they pursue an asylum case. These statuses do not, however, grant them a permanent status like resident, asylee, or refugee. Nor do they retroactively create an I-94 form making their initial entry legal. They give recipients *other* legal documentation. When the legislature passed the Transportation Code, however, it failed to take these other categories into account and thus made it impossible for these state residents to obtain or keep their licenses.[16]

In the case of the driver's license, a fraudulent document is not generally of much use. Police are trained and motivated to recognize a fake license, unlike employers, who are usually content to do the minimal inspection required by law. Many undocumented immigrants simply drive without one. The consequences, like so much about immigration law and enforcement, are arbitrary. Depending on the state, or even the community within a state, an undocumented, unlicensed driver who is stopped by police might receive warning or a small fine, or might lose his or her car or be imprisoned and deported. If a jurisdiction is participating in a federal program like ICE 287(g) or Secure Communities, which requires officials to share data on those arrested with ICE, a routine court appearance might end in incarceration and deportation. In 2010, the *New York Times* estimated that 4.5 million undocumented people were driving, mostly without licenses. That year, some thirty thousand of those stopped for common traffic violations—or even being involved in an accident in which they were not at fault—were deported.[17]

Some law enforcement agents support the hard-line position. Republican state senator Chip Rogers of Georgia took a get-tough attitude in promoting the draconian driving laws in that state. "There are certain things you can't do in the state of Georgia if you are an illegal immigrant," he said proudly. "One of them is, you can't drive."[18] In Los Angeles, however, the police chief joined Mayor Antonio Villaraigosa and the police commission in overturning a rule impounding the car of anyone found driving without a license. The police union protested vociferously, but the conservative city attorney backed the change.[19]

Law enforcement agencies have frequently had very mixed reactions to federal efforts to toughen immigration policies.

In Framingham, Massachusetts, the police pulled out of the 287(g) Program two years after adopting it. The police chief, Steven Carl, "said he signed up two years ago exclusively to tap into federal databases to investigate crime, and balked when federal officials wanted him to detain immigrants, transport them and even testify in immigration court. Carl said that could hurt the police's relationship in the community, where 26 percent are immigrants. 'It doesn't benefit the police department to engage in deportation and immigration enforcement,'" he explained.[20]

In contrast, when Massachusetts governor Deval Patrick announced his intention to withdraw Massachusetts from the federal Secure Communities program, the chief of police of Milford, a town not far from Framingham and, like the latter, home to large numbers of immigrants, had the opposite reaction. "It takes an important tool away from police officers, who are trying to perform a difficult job," the police chief said. "We need to make it clear to (people) who are here improperly, and those who are engaged in employing them, that we need to take this issue seriously."[21]

WHAT EXACTLY IS ILLEGAL?

It's illegal to cross the border without inspection and/or without approval from US immigration authorities. As we've seen above, about half of the undocumented population entered the country illegally (as opposed to entering with inspection and permission, but overstaying or violating the terms of their visas). Entering the country illegally is a crime, and a person who does so can be subject to up to six months in prison. Entering the country again after being deported is a more serious crime—a felony—punishable by up to two years in prison. Simply *being* in the country without authorization, though, is not in itself a crime but rather a civil violation, remedied by removal (either voluntary departure or deportation) rather than a criminal penalty. Unlawful presence becomes a criminal offense only "when an alien is found in the United States after having been formally removed or after departing the US while a removal order was outstanding."[22]

Even when a would-be immigrant is apprehended at the time of unlawful entry, neither criminal nor civil immigration charges have generally been pressed. Because the standards for criminal prosecution are much higher than for immigration proceedings, the government has every incentive to keep immigration violations out of the criminal court system. The immigration court system has a backlog of hundreds of thousands of cases, which means that an immigrant sent into that system will likely be subject to a lengthy—and expensive—detention.

Many immigrants who are apprehended are offered voluntary departure or voluntary return, meaning that the person leaves the country without being officially deported. There is no order of removal, but the person tacitly admits to removability, that is, to being present without authorization. Under voluntary departure, the person is given a time limit and permitted to arrange his or her own departure. Mexicans apprehended at the border are usually granted voluntary removal, which means that they are bused back to the border and deposited on the Mexican side.[23] For many immigrants, especially those who have little likelihood of winning an immigration case, voluntary departure is the preferred route, although many who depart voluntarily soon attempt to reenter.

Immigrants apprehended in the interior or those apprehended at the border who do not accept voluntary departure, who are accused of other crimes or infractions, or who are flagged for other reasons may instead be subject to formal (involuntary) removal or deportation. In this case, they must appear before a judge who orders their deportation.[24] Those who are removed are not deemed guilty of any crime, and removal is not considered a punishment. Once a person is formally removed, however, attempted reentry becomes a felony, and unlawful presence too becomes criminalized.

For most of the twentieth century, voluntary departures—mostly by people apprehended by the Border Patrol and returned (usually to Mexico) without an official deportation order—were far more numerous than removals. Since 2006, the number of voluntary departures has plummeted, from over a million a year down to only 323,000 in 2011, while the number of removals (mostly people apprehended in the interior) has risen steadily, surpassing 50,000 a year for the first time in 1995 and then rising quickly to almost 400,000 a year since President Obama was elected in 2008.[25]

Some attribute the decline in border apprehensions to increased enforcement. The Border Patrol, they point out, grew from nine thousand agents in 2001 to twenty thousand by the end of 2009, and twenty-one thousand by 2012, while the Customs and Border Protection budget rose from about $6 billion in 2004 to about $11 billion in 2009. (The Border Patrol accounted for about $1.4 billion of that.) The border wall grew and employed increasingly sophisticated technology. The purpose of all this so-called "enforcement" was to discourage potential border crossers from even trying. Maybe it was working, some argued. Others, though, attribute the decline to the economic downturn in the United States, arguing that fewer people are trying to cross the border, as demand for their labor has declined.[26]

Meanwhile, the number apprehended by ICE Enforcement and Removal Operations inside the country skyrocketed, principally as the result of the Obama administration's emphasis on programs for interior enforcement.[27] This meant that many more people with jobs, lives, and community ties in the United States were being uprooted and deported. Through 2005, only about 5 percent of Mexicans deported had been in the United States for over a year. In 2010, two years into President Obama's first term, over a quarter of those deported had been in the

United States for over a year; in 2011, it was almost half.[28]
Meanwhile, in 2010, ICE requested $5.5 billion in discretionary
funds for the following year, the majority of which was designated for detention and deportation.[29] Enforcing illegality was
an expensive operation.

WHO BENEFITS FROM ILLEGALITY?

Although illegality resides inherently in the realm of law, it has
significant economic implications, as discussed in the next two
chapters. Employers of low-wage labor benefit from the illegal status of some workers, as do consumers of low-cost goods
and services. State and local budgets face costs that result from
the economic marginalization of the undocumented, while
federal programs like Social Security benefit handsomely from
payments into the system by undocumented workers who will
never be eligible for benefits.

Illegality also has significant benefits for the prison system,
in particular, the new and mushrooming private prison system.
Immigration enforcement creates jobs in the prison industry,
which in 2011 employed eight hundred thousand people and
cost some $74 billion a year.[30]

But beyond the economic costs and benefits to different sectors of society, there are other, intangible benefits. Politicians
and talk-show hosts have zeroed in on the issue to whip up
audiences and support. Anti-immigrant sentiment and, especially, the demonization of the undocumented can bring votes
and attention.

What Leo Chavez calls the "Latino threat narrative" overlaps
with anti-undocumented sentiment, as "Mexican immigration,
the Mexican-origin population, and Latin American immigration in general [came] to be perceived as a national security
threat" in the 1990s.[31] The threat narrative, Chavez explains, has
been expressed so repeatedly that its components have become
culturally accepted. Mexican immigrants are "illegal aliens" or

criminals, the narrative suggests. They want to create a "Quebec" (i.e., a culturally and linguistically distinct region), invade the country, or reconquer the Southwest. They refuse to learn English or assimilate, procreate too rapidly, and threaten national security.[32]

In addition to attracting votes or increasing ratings, the Latino threat narrative serves the more subtle purpose of channeling national anxieties about social inequality; environmental crisis; economic downturn; lack of access to jobs, housing, health care, and education; deteriorating social services; and other real issues facing the US population away from their real causes. Those who benefit from the status quo would rather have people blame immigrants than fight for real social and economic change.

DETENTION

According to the American Civil Liberties Union, the detention of immigrants has reached "crisis proportions." "Over the last 15 years, the detention system more than quintupled in size, growing from less than 6,300 beds in 1996 to the current capacity of 33,400 beds. In 2010, the Department of Homeland Security (DHS) held 363,000 immigrants in detention in over 250 facilities across the country."[33] Meanwhile, ICE's detention operations budget jumped from $864 million in 2005 to over $2 billion in 2012.[34] According to Amnesty International, the use of detention for immigration violations contradicts international rights law against arbitrary detention. "Everyone has the right to liberty, freedom of movement, and the right not to be arbitrarily detained," Amnesty explained.[35]

Immigrant detention sends people into a Kafkaesque netherworld. Immigration court is a separate entity from the criminal justice system; it is an administrative court. This means that the whole body of law designed to protect those accused of crimes and guarantee them a fair trial does not apply. (An immigrant accused of a crime does receive those rights in criminal court, however.) In the immigration detention system, prisoners have few rights and often lack the means to find out what rights they do have or make use of these rights. For example, immigrants have the right to be represented by an attorney, but not at public expense. Many detainees don't know that they have the right to representation, don't know how to obtain representation, and/or can't afford it. For those who do go through deportation hearings, 84 percent lack representation.[36]

Some detained migrants will choose voluntary departure because it leaves their names clear for a legal entry sometime in the future. Many are unaware of legal provisions that might authorize them to remain in the country and have no way to find out about them, since they have no way to obtain legal counsel. Some choose voluntary departure to escape lengthy detention, even if they are convinced that their case to stay could be won if they were to finally obtain a hearing. Unlike those detained on criminal charges, immigrants have generally been ineligible to be released on bail.[37]

If they do not choose (or are not offered) voluntary departure, detainees have the right to a hearing before an immigration judge to determine whether they can obtain legal permission to remain in the country. Some detainees may be eligible for political asylum; others, for parole or prosecutorial discretion based on the lack of a criminal record, family relationships to citizens or permanent residents, hardship that would be caused to citizens or permanent residents (e.g., to their children who are citizens) by their removal, or other reasons. But without a lawyer to argue their case, immigrant detainees may have no idea what kinds of arguments could work in their favor.

Moreover, the deportation procedures for those who reject voluntary departure are often quite lengthy. While the proceedings crawl along, the petitioner remains in detention. A study by Amnesty International found that "immigrants and asylum seekers may be detained for months or even years as they go through deportation procedures that will determine whether or not they are eligible to remain in the United States." The average was ten months, but some individuals remained in detention for up to four years before a decision was reached.[38] If the judge who hears the case rules against them, they will be deported and barred from legal reentry, usually for ten years.

A new twist in this system emerged at the border in 2005 with Operation Streamline, described in the introduction, which takes migrants caught at the border out of the civil immigration system and lodges criminal border-crossing charges against them. After a criminal conviction, they are generally sentenced to time served and returned to ICE for civil removal procedures. The program has been expanded along the border, so that by 2012 every border sector participated, with some referring all of those apprehended for criminal prosecution. Tens of thousands of migrants who would have been returned to Mexico are now instead detained, tried, and incarcerated at government expense. While Streamline aims to rush dozens of cases through each court every day, the size of the program—some fifty-five thousand prosecutions a year—still means that the government requires a large amount of short-term space for incarceration.[39]

Since 2005, the federal government has spent $5.5 billion on private prison contracts for criminal immigration cases, over $1.4 billion in 2011 alone.[40] At the end of 2011 there were sixty-three thousand Streamline cases in pretrial detention and twenty-five thousand convicted and incarcerated.[41] District Court Judge Sam Sparks of the Western District of Texas protested that "[t]he expenses of prosecuting illegal entry and reentry cases (rather than deportation) on aliens without any significant criminal record is simply mind boggling. The US Attorney's policy of prosecuting all aliens presents a cost to the American taxpayer that is neither meritorious nor reasonable."[42]

Streamline and the overall increase of federal prosecution of immigration violations turned immigration cases into the top federal crime by 2011.[43] Immigration is a highly racialized crime: as immigration charges began to take up more and more of the federal criminal caseload, it meant the courts were prosecuting and convicting more and more Latinos. Hispanics made up more than half of those arrested on federal charges in 2011.[44]

Streamline and other criminal prosecutions account for only a fraction of immigration arrests. Most of the 391,953 immigrants removed were apprehended in the interior through ICE enforcement and apprehension operations, and their removal was ordered by immigration judges without any involvement of the criminal justice system. Some of those arrested by ICE enforcement operations inside the country, though, come into ICE custody with current or prior criminal charges.

The intersection of criminal law with civil immigration law creates a web of complexity in which many immigrants and their attorneys become entangled. Increasingly, criminal charges are resolved through plea bargains rather than contested in court. In a plea bargain, the accused agrees to plead guilty to a lesser but still criminal charge in exchange for receiving a lighter sentence, frequently a suspended sentence or probation rather than jail time. Strikingly, more than 96 percent of those arrested on federal charges pled guilty in 2011.[45]

For an immigrant, though, a criminal conviction on even a minor charge can render him or her deportable. Legal permanent residents (green card holders) may also find themselves in immigration detention if they are convicted of a crime. Or if they are discovered by immigration authorities to have previously been convicted of a crime that is a deportable offense. Or even if they are discovered to have been convicted of a crime that was not a deportable offense at the time, but later became one. Even decades-old minor drug-possession convictions have become grounds for deportation.

The public defenders that most poor immigrants rely on in criminal cases generally have little knowledge of immigration law or the possible implications of a guilty plea. One attorney told the American Immigration Lawyers Association (AILA): "On the one hand . . . the immigration matter should not affect the criminal case, and, from an intellectual purity standpoint, that makes a lot of sense. But [for the client], that makes no sense at all. It's part of their circumstances. . . . I have to be aware of that, and I need to give advice based upon what their circumstances are." Public defenders, AILA explained, rarely have the time or resources to research the immigration implications of their advice to their clients. Most are juggling twice as many cases as are allowed by the American Bar Association. Less than a third worked with immigration attorneys in their cases involving immigrants, even though their decisions could directly affect their clients' immigration status.[46]

RAMPING UP THE NUMBERS

In early 2010, James Chaparro, director of ICE Detention and Removal Operations (DRO), wrote an internal memo—later obtained by the *Washington Post*—noting that while the number of removals of criminals so far that year had been satisfactory, the agency's numbers in removing "non-criminal aliens" were too low. "As of February 15, 2010, DRO removed or returned 60,397 non-criminal aliens which is an average of 437 removals/returns per day. The current non-criminal removal rate projections will result in 159,740 removals at the close of the fiscal year. Coupling this with the projections in criminal removals only gives us a total of just over 310,000 overall removals—*well* under the Agency's goal of 400,000." For the first time, the agency had explicitly acknowledged having an established target.[47]

Chaparro insisted that field agents increase the average daily population in ICE detention facilities to 32,600 and "[i]ncrease the number of Tier One Non-Criminal Fugitive alien arrests along with Tier Two arrests (Re-Entry/Reinstatement) in every field office." He recommended that each office process thirty to sixty noncriminal cases per day in a "surge" aimed at meeting deportation quotas.[48] Basically, the memo instructed ICE officers to increase the detention and deportation of noncriminals and of "criminals" whose only offense was reentry into the country, in the interest of meeting the annual deportation goal.[49]

Another program that helped ICE increase its numbers in the Obama years was Secure Communities. Introduced by the Bush administration and piloted in a number of cities around the country in late 2008, Secure Communities requires law enforcement agencies in participating jurisdictions to automatically share with ICE the fingerprints of anybody arrested. If ICE flags the individual as potentially deportable, the agency issues a detainer. When the person is released, he or she is turned over to ICE. The Obama administration initially stated that participation was voluntary, but later announced that the program would be required nationwide by 2013. Eighty-three percent of those who come into ICE custody through Secure Communities are sent to ICE detention centers. Ninety-three percent are Latino.

Promoters touted the program as a way to "remove dangerous criminals from your community."[50] However, only about half of those deported through Secure Communities fit the profile of a criminal—that is, had been convicted of a crime other than a traffic or immigration violation. The only violation for 45 percent of those deported was being "present without admission"—that is, being undocumented. Only half of those deported received a hearing before an immigration judge to determine their deportability. The other half were simply deported under ICE administrative procedures or pressured into taking voluntary departure. By late 2011, 226,694 immigrants had come into ICE custody through Secure Communities.[51]

DETENTION, INC.

In addition to ICE itself, there are powerful interests supporting the detention industry, ranging from private prison companies to elected officials who see prisons as a boost to local economies. The Immigration and Naturalization Service (precursor to today's ICE) started to contract out its detainees to private prisons in the early 1980s when the detention system started to exceed its capacity of beds. By 1989, the agency was holding about two thousand people a day, with five hundred in private facilities.[52] Over the past three decades, immigration violations served as a reliably increasing source of revenue for private prisons.[53] As ICE detention rates doubled to the current rate of four hundred thousand a year in the first decade of the twenty-first century, the proportion of immigration detainees held in privately run detention facilities also rose, from one-quarter to one-half.[54] Private prisons specialize disproportionately in detaining immigrants, who tend to be young, healthy, and nonviolent, and therefore among the cheapest and the most profitable inmates to house.[55]

The first private prison company, the Corrections Corporation of America (CCA, founded in 1983), was poised to benefit from and promote the increases in criminal sentencing and immigrant detention in the 1990s. According to Travis Pratt, professor of criminology at Arizona State University, who studied the private prison industry's lobbying campaigns, "The private prisons industry has a very, very heavy lobby in most states and the federal government to increase sanctions for a number of offenses. They've been doing this for a very long time. It's a multi-million-dollar lobbying effort. . . . And they've been exceptionally successful—longer sentences for more types of offenses means more inmates, more inmates means they have to be housed somewhere, which translates to greater profits for that industry. They have a very clear agenda there, and they've been unapologetic about it. They haven't hidden that at all."[56]

Between 2002 and 2012, private prison companies had spent over $45 million in campaign contributions and lobbying.[57]

The GEO Group (founded in 1984) currently runs 109 facilities in the United States, the United Kingdom, Australia, and South Africa, with 75,000 beds in the United States; CCA has 60 in the United States that can hold 90,000 inmates, and Management and Training Corporation (MTC), founded in 1987, runs 22 prisons in the United States with 29,500 beds.[58] CCA is the fifth-largest corrections system in the country, following the federal government and three states.[59] In 2010, GEO and CCA together earned revenues of over $2.9 billion.[60] They have spent millions of dollars lobbying over the past decade.[61]

The private prison industry has a vested interest in increasing both the criminalization of immigrants and the drug wars that criminalize African Americans. "Our growth is generally dependent upon our ability to obtain new contracts to develop and manage new correctional and detention facilities," CCA explained to its shareholders. "The demand for our facilities and services could be adversely affected by . . . the decriminalization of certain activities that are currently proscribed by our criminal laws." In particular, CCA warned, "any changes with respect to drugs and controlled substances or illegal immigration could affect the number of persons arrested, convicted, and sentenced, thereby potentially reducing demand for correctional facilities to house them."[62] Company officials were optimistic, though, that ICE would continue to supply "a significant portion of our revenues."[63]

The Justice Policy Institute concluded in 2011 that "[w]hile private prison companies may try to present themselves as just meeting existing 'demand' for prison beds and responding to current 'market' conditions, in fact they have worked hard over the past decade to create markets for their product. As revenues of private prison companies have grown over the past decade, the companies have had more resources with which to build political power, and they have used this power to promote policies that lead to higher rates of incarceration."[64]

One avenue they have used is the American Legislative Exchange Council (ALEC), a "conservative, free-market orientated, limited-government group," in the words of staff director Michael Hough.[65] Legislators pay $50 a year to join, while companies pay tens of thousands of dollars for a seat at the table, giving ALEC a total budget of over $6 million a year. ALEC's main focus is on drafting model legislation. Because it does not officially lobby, it doesn't have to disclose its activities. Because it's a nonprofit, corporations can deduct their donations to the organization.[66]

"Is it lobbying when private corporations pay money to sit in a room with state lawmakers to draft legislation that they then introduce back home? [ALEC senior director of policy Michael] Bowman, a former lobbyist, says, 'No, because we're not advocating any positions. We don't tell members to take these bills. We just expose best practices. All we're really doing is developing policies that are in model bill form.'"[67]

At an ALEC meeting in late 2009, Arizona senator Russell Pearce first presented his proposal for what became the state's radical anti-immigrant Senate Bill 1070, and a draft for the model legislation was outlined. S.B. 1070 required immigrants to carry proof of their documentation at all times and required local law enforcement officials to detain immigrants unable to produce such documents. After it became law in April 2010, S.B. 1070 became the prototype for anti-immigrant legislation passed in Georgia, Alabama, Indiana, South Carolina, and Utah in the following years.

Two representatives of CCA, which clearly stood to benefit from the bill, sat at the table where the text was agreed upon. "Asked if the private companies usually get to write model bills for the legislators, Hough said, 'Yeah, that's the way it's set up. It's a public-private partnership. We believe both sides, businesses and lawmakers should be at the same table, together.'"[68]

ALEC and CCA influence was evident not only in the shaping of the legislation, but in the response among legislators: "As soon as Pearce's bill hit the Arizona statehouse floor in January . . . thirty-six co-sponsors jumped on, a number almost unheard of in the capitol. . . . Two-thirds of them either went to that December meeting or are ALEC members." Furthermore, a report continued, "thirty of the 36 co-sponsors received donations over the next six months, from prison lobbyists or prison companies—Corrections Corporation of America, Management and Training Corporation and The Geo Group." Two of Arizona governor Jan Brewer's top advisers were former lobbyists for private prison companies.[69] Referring to the passage of S.B. 1070, the president of GEO Group stated, "I can only believe the opportunities at the federal level are going to continue apace as a result of what's happening. Those people coming across the border and getting caught are going to have to be detained and that for me, at least I think, there's going to be enhanced opportunities for what we do."[70] Indeed, CCA and GEO Group doubled their revenues from the immigration detention business between 2005 and 2012.[71]

Depressed communities can see private prisons as engines of economic opportunity. One such area is Pinal County, Arizona. CCA is the largest employer in the county, where five facilities hold up to three thousand detainees a day.[72] "The expanding prison populations have allowed small towns to carry budget surpluses in a state that has otherwise been pummeled by the recession," explains journalist Chris Kirkham. "Prison communities have largely avoided the dire economic straits suffered by Arizona communities in every direction, where the housing bust and subsequent foreclosure crisis have ravaged local government coffers."

The Pinal County town of Florence, with a population of 7,800, also houses 17,000 detainees. Flush with state revenues from the prison industry—$5.2 million in 2011—the town has been able to offer services and build infrastructure like skate parks, dog parks, and sports fields. Deputy town manager Jess Knudson bragged that Florence was "one of the few towns in Arizona that has been able to stay in the black with this recession." For Florence, as well as neighboring Eloy and other Arizona communities, "boosting the prison population has emerged as a primary economic development strategy." The county too has a financial incentive—$2 per day per prisoner, which adds up to over a million dollars a year—and County Sheriff Paul Babeu has been a champion for ramped-up immigrant detentions.[73]

In rural Irwin County in Georgia, the privately run Irwin Detention Center was the county's top employer. As the prison population dwindled in 2009, the county teamed up with the company that ran the prison to seek a contract with ICE. Paradoxically, said a report in the *Nation*, "even as Georgia and Alabama passed harsh new immigration laws last year designed to keep out undocumented immigrants . . . politicians from both states were lobbying hard to bring immigrant detainees in. ICE succumbed to the pressure, sending hundreds of detainees to the financially unstable facility in Georgia that promised to detain immigrants cheaply."[74]

CONCLUSION

Undocumented people face a veneer of ordinary life undergirded by permanent uncertainty. In the film *El Norte*, Nacha, a more seasoned undocumented Mexican woman, tries to convince Rosa, a newly arrived Guatemalan, to sign up for English classes, free and offered by the government. Rosa worries that the school will turn her in to immigration, and Nacha reassures her that it won't. "Don't try to understand the gringos," she laughs. "It will drive you crazy." Since the situation and the policies are essentially incomprehensible, the best an undocumented person can do is try to survive day by day and hope for the best.

CHAPTER 5

Working (Part 1)

You won't have your names when you ride the big airplane
All they will call you will be "deportees"...
Is this the best way we can grow our big orchards?
Is this the best way we can grow our good fruit?

—"Plane Wreck at Los Gatos (Deportee)," 1948
Words by Woody Guthrie; music by Martin Hoffman[1]

As we have seen, work has been central to the Mexican experience in the United States since the nineteenth century, and Mexican workers have been critical to the growth of the US economy. Prior to 1965, racism and the law—including government-run guest-worker programs like the Bracero Program—enabled and justified unequal treatment for Mexican workers.

After 1965, when the Bracero Program ended and numerical restrictions were placed on Mexican immigration, new systems and rationales were needed to maintain the supply of cheap Mexican labor. Undocumentedness took on a new importance in the labor market, replacing earlier methods of legally compartmentalizing Mexican labor. The undocumented were channeled into the same types of jobs that Mexicans had long occupied. Reflecting the new significance of undocumentedness, the 1986

Immigration Reform and Control Act (IRCA) was both the first legislative attempt in the country's history to address this issue and the first immigration legislation to specifically address the issue of work, making it illegal for employers to hire workers who lacked documents.

At first glance, this may seem paradoxical. If undocumented Mexican labor was so necessary, why make it illegal? But IRCA made it illegal with a large wink. Employers were required to obtain proof of eligibility to work from new hires, but they were not required to evaluate the documents they were shown. They could be punished for knowingly hiring undocumented workers, but usually only received a small fine. IRCA, it turned out, was more for show than for changing the country's labor structure. It was a bumbling intervention that succeeded in making migrant workers more vulnerable, while actually contributing to increasing the numbers of the undocumented.

Though they comprise a small proportion of the overall workforce (about 5 percent), workers without documents continue to occupy crucial niches in the economy.[2] This chapter and the next will look at how undocumentedness became an important factor in the labor market and what kinds of jobs undocumented people fill.

MAKING WORK ILLEGAL

Although the 1965 immigration law made it illegal for many Mexicans to enter or remain in the United States, it did not specifically prohibit undocumented people from working, nor did it forbid employers to hire them. The 1952 immigration law known as the McCarran-Walter Act had made it illegal to "conceal" or "harbor" a person who was undocumented, but not to employ them. The law included the so-called "Texas Proviso"—to satisfy Texas business interests that depended on undocumented Mexican workers—stipulating that employment "shall not be deemed to constitute harboring." Thus, in the words of the Immigration and Naturalization Service general counsel, "there was no prohibition at all on employment of illegal aliens."[3]

The idea of criminalizing employment gained ground toward the end of the century. Senator Peter Rodino introduced the first national employer sanctions bill in 1973, but it failed to pass in the Senate. In 1986, though, employer sanctions were a key element of the new IRCA. Many progressive organizations including the AFL-CIO, the NAACP, and the Leadership Council on Civil Rights, a national coalition of 185 civil rights organizations and the country's "premier coordinating mechanism for civil rights advocacy before Congress and the executive branch," all supported the idea, although the Leadership Council was "sharply divided."[4] A century earlier, the AFL had openly excluded nonwhites from membership. Now it joined civil rights organizations in advocating for discrimination based on citizenship.

In 1990, the NAACP reversed its position after an acrimonious debate. The AFL-CIO did the same in 2000. Those favoring the sanctions argued that citizenship should determine rights. The presence and the hiring of undocumented people, they claimed, lowered the floor and made it harder for blacks or for American workers to obtain decent employment. If it became more difficult for the undocumented to work, they reasoned, employers would have to improve conditions and employ citizen workers. "If you withdraw those sanctions, then you open the door and you flood this state with a multitude of undocumented aliens who will take the jobs of blacks and other minorities," one NAACP branch president explained.[5]

For Latino organizations, though, employer sanctions are a civil rights issue, and discrimination based on status is both harmful to workers in general and conducive to racial discrimination. (It is notable that to be heard in the public sphere, immigrant rights advocates must often frame their arguments in terms of racial discrimination—showing, for example, that anti-immigrant policies contribute to racial profiling—since the idea that humans deserve equal rights regardless of citizenship status is practically untenable in today's climate.) Armed with a March 1990 GAO report that found a "widespread pattern of discrimination," especially against Latinos and Asians who were thought to look "foreign," Latino organizations launched a campaign to press the Leadership Council and the NAACP to withdraw their support for the sanctions. Both organizations eventually did so.[6]

Opponents reversed the argument about the sanctions protecting citizen workers from a feared flood of the undocumented. Instead, they insisted that the sanctions themselves lowered the floor for everyone. By making a large group of workers more vulnerable to exploitation—because they have little recourse under the law—sanctions enable employers to lower wages and working conditions, with little fear that workers will protest or organize. Thus, the sanctions paradoxically make undocumented immigrants a *more* desirable workforce, because the sanctions make them more desperate and more willing to accept substandard working conditions.

Nicholas De Genova argues that, while billed as "employer" sanctions, the system actually targeted the workers, not the employers. Potential workers had to purchase false documents, and a new industry emerged to produce them. Employers still hired them, but now they were triply vulnerable: to the document industry, to the employer, and to the possibility of arrest and deportation. Rather than punishing employers—who were routinely given warnings prior to inspections of their hiring records or subject to token fines, at most—the law instead placed new burdens and new penalties on the workers.[7]

During the Bush administration, workplace raids became the major public face of immigration enforcement. These were high-profile operations that let government authorities bask in the public impression they created that they were getting tough on immigration. The Michael Bianco, Inc., factory in New Bedford, Massachusetts, in March 2007; the Agriprocessors plant in Postville, Iowa, in May 2008; Swift (at multiple sites) and Smithfield (North Carolina) meatpacking plants in December 2006 and January 2007; and Howard Industries electronics plant in Laurel, Mississippi (August 2008), were the sites of just a few of the many raids. Immigration authorities would descend upon the workplace and round up workers, arresting hundreds. The largest were the Swift raids, where over twelve hundred workers were arrested in a sweep of six plants.

Barack Obama publicly criticized the raids when he was a candidate for president, proclaiming during his convention speech that "I don't know anyone who benefits when a mother is separated from her infant child." But he also defended enforcement of sanctions, continuing to decry the effects when "an employer undercuts American wages by hiring illegal workers."[8] As a senator, he pressed for E-Verify, a federal program designed to electronically detect fraudulent documents and prevent the hiring of the undocumented.

As president, Obama pursued a policy during his first term that some have termed "silent raids." Instead of descending on the workplace and making arrests, the new policy used audits. ICE would require a business to turn over employment eligibility forms for all of its workers. "Since January 2009," the *Wall Street Journal* reported in May 2012, "the Obama administration has audited at least 7,533 employers suspected of hiring illegal labor and imposed about $100 million in administrative and criminal fines—more audits and penalties than were imposed during the entire George W. Bush administration."[9] With the audits, workers are not deported. But they do lose their jobs.

UNDOCUMENTED JOBS

Most undocumented people work in three specific types of jobs, all of which tend to be low wage and low status, offer few if any benefits, have difficult or unstable schedules, and offer little job security. They may be seasonal or involve night shifts. The work is generally heavy, unpleasant, dirty, and even dangerous.

Agricultural jobs, especially in plantation and other large-scale enterprises, have always occupied a special low status and employed many legally excluded workers. As large-scale agriculture spread through the Southwest in the twentieth century, migrant Mexican workers became the primary labor force. Today, 42 percent of agricultural workers work as migrants—that is, they follow the crops. Seventy-five percent of farm workers were born in Mexico, with 2 percent born in Central America and 23 percent in the United States.[10] Only about 4 percent of undocumented immigrants work in agriculture, but they make up somewhere between 25 percent and 90 percent of all agricultural workers.[11] The National Agricultural Worker Survey conducted by the US Department of Labor has consistently found approximately 50 percent of agricultural workers as undocumented over the past twenty years.[12] Some analysts, such as Rob Williams of the Migrant Farmworker Justice Project, believe that the percentage is even higher, up to 90 percent or more, since many people when interviewed will not admit to being undocumented.[13] The seasonal and back-breaking nature of farm work, along with dangerous, often unregulated conditions and low pay, make these jobs unattractive to potential workers who have the advantage of citizenship. Most farm workers only find work for about thirty weeks of the year and earn $12,500 to $15,000 annually.[14]

Second, undocumented people work at jobs that have been in-sourced or relocated within the United States, as companies attempt to resurrect the kinds of conditions they enjoyed before unionization and government regulation began to cut into their profits. A major example is the meatpacking industry, which closed down unionized plants in major urban areas to relocate in the rural Midwest. As these jobs became more unattractive—because they were relocated to areas where workers did not want to move and because they downgraded working conditions and pay—the plants too began to recruit heavily among undocumented immigrants.

Many of these in-sourced jobs differ from agricultural work because they are year-round instead of seasonal. Their rise coincides with a growing long-term, not seasonal migration of undocumented workers and a growing shift from the historic seasonal migration areas of California and the Southwest into the Midwest and especially the South. Despite poor wages and working conditions, many immigrants consider these jobs a step up from agriculture.[15]

Another type of in-sourcing has occurred in the construction industry, which employs almost one in five undocumented immigrants—about a million in the first decade of the twenty-first century.[16] During the long construction boom between 1970 and 2006, total employment more than doubled to 7.7 million before declining sharply in the housing-led recession.[17] The thriving construction industry in urban centers like Nevada and post-Katrina New Orleans attracted large numbers of undocumented immigrants.

Third, new job categories in the service sector have emerged in recent decades. Fast-food service, newspaper delivery, and landscaping are three areas with exploding demand for low-paid, contingent workers. Changing lifestyles including increased pressure on the middle class, rising expectations for consumption, and the entry of women into the workforce have created whole new sectors of the economy that have relied heavily on undocumented workers.

Steve Striffler notes, "Latinos are becoming virtually synonymous with food preparation and cleanup in our nation's restaurants. To find a meal that has not at some point passed through the hands of Mexican immigrants is a difficult task."[18] Chicken, for example, boomed in popularity in the 1980s and

'90s, as it was transformed from a low-profit farm product that was generally sold whole or in parts to a highly processed—and highly profitable—manufactured commodity in forms like nuggets and fingers. And who does the processing in the new plants that have created our contemporary incarnation of chicken? In large numbers, and across the country, it is Mexican and Central American workers, many of them undocumented.

AGRICULTURE

As fruit and vegetable agriculture spread in California at the end of the nineteenth century, farmers sought a labor force that would be as tractable and exploitable as African slaves had been in the South, or even better, one that would be there only when needed for the labor-intensive seasons. "A California farm spokesman in 1872 observed that hiring seasonal Chinese workers who housed themselves and then 'melted away' when they were not needed made them 'more efficient . . . than negro labor in the South [because] it [Chinese labor] is only employed when actually needed, and is, therefore, less expensive' than slavery."[19]

When the Chinese Exclusion Act of 1882 eliminated that option a decade later, agriculturalists turned to Mexicans. Seasonal farm labor increased rapidly over the course of the century as farming centralized. Worker mobility, writes Don Mitchell, was built into the system. He quotes Harry Drobish of the California Relief Administration, who wrote in 1935 that "the nature of crop plantings . . . compels labor mobility."[20] However, as Mitchell argues, Drobish attributed to "nature" what was actually a result of economic structure. Human decisions and policies, not nature, underlay the development of California's agricultural system.[21]

A report to Truman's Commission on Migratory Labor in 1951 noted the shift away from small farms relying on family labor and the rapid growth of large farms making heavy use of migrant labor. Earlier, most farms used no hired workers or one or two permanent employees. By 1951, more and more were using large numbers of seasonal workers.[22]

American workers didn't want these jobs. As the commission reported, "The American farm worker is still legally and morally responsible to feed his family every day." With seasonal work, "it is almost impossible for him to meet American standards of life."[23] But employers had little use for permanent workers: "When the work is done, neither the farmer nor the community wants the wetback around."[24] Furthermore, agricultural employers preferred a kind of "feudal" relationship that they could only enjoy with migrants. They "do not care for workers who may voice complaints in regard to working conditions, housing, or sanitary facilities. They want only those people who will go quietly about their work and make no comments or objections. They want the Mexican worker who has just come across the border and is strange to our language and ways of life. They find that the Mexican who has been in this country for some time and become acquainted with our free customs is no longer suited to the economic and social status of a stoop laborer."[25]

The Bracero Program, starting in 1942, was a building block in the establishment of the California agricultural system based on a highly exploitative labor process.[26] Migratory labor was "the *essential* labor force" at the basis of this system.[27] And not only migratory labor: frequently and cyclically, these migratory workers were undocumented. As geographer Don Mitchell shows, the existence of a large pool of "officially invisible" undocumented workers was crucial to the functioning of the Bracero Program and tacitly acknowledged by those administering and benefiting from it. Farmers could request Bracero contract workers even as they enjoyed a surplus of available (but officially invisible) undocumented migrants. This permanently renewed oversupply of labor "was not a privilege big California growers wanted to relinquish lightly."[28]

As Mitchell illustrates, there was never a labor shortage in California agriculture. California agribusiness depended on workers who were cheap, temporary, and exploitable, and on government policies that ensured their continued access to these workers both as braceros and as undocumented migrants.[29]

"For growers, a productive, living landscape required that workers become more and more mere vessels of labor power . . . [and] less and less living, breathing people."[30] The Bracero system contributed simultaneously to "the destabilization of working people" and "the stabilization of the profitable landscape: *it* saved the crops—precisely *because* it destroyed lives."[31] As geographer Richard Walker points out, the enormous prosperity of California's agriculture should—or at least could—have improved the lives of workers as well. It didn't. "Low-wage labor has been systematically built into labor relations and the reproduction of capital. . . . The low wages of farm labor are an important factor in the continuing profitability of California agribusiness."[32]

With the end of the Bracero Program in 1964, undocumented workers came to the fore as the migrant agricultural labor force. The program was phased out gradually between 1965 and 1967, so that it ended completely just as the limit of 120,000 immigrants per year from the Western Hemisphere—the first numerical limit ever—went into effect.[33] As described in chapter 2, by 1965 the program was no longer necessary because the flow of undocumented workers was large enough to fulfill the needs of agribusiness.[34] Seasonal migration continued unabated, except that now even former braceros migrated without documents.[35] Some scholars termed the post-1965 system of undocumented migration a "de facto guest-worker program."[36]

The special provisions for farm workers in the Immigration Reform and Control Act (IRCA) of 1986 highlighted the special need for undocumented—"illegal"—workers in agriculture. To apply for legal status, most migrants (mostly Mexicans) had to prove that they had been in the United States continuously since 1982. This provision rested on the same rationale that previous legalizations (of Europeans) had relied upon: that length of residence could outweigh technical irregularities in means of arrival and justify legalization.

However, the provisions for agricultural workers were different: instead of requiring the four years of continuous residence, the act offered legal status to migrant farm workers who had simply been employed in agriculture for at least ninety days during the 1985–1986 season. (Or, as shown earlier, who could provide false documents stating that this was the case.) The law made this exception precisely because it acknowledged agriculture's reliance on these migrant workers.

The employer sanctions provision of IRCA contributed to a shift away from direct employment and to the use of Farm Labor Contractors. The use of FLCs increased from about one-third of farms hiring migrant labor in the mid-1980s to over half in the early 1990s.[37] This system allowed employers to evade legal responsibility for the workers they relied on. As Philip Martin concludes, "FLCs are practically a proxy for the employment of undocumented workers and egregious or subtle violations of labor laws."[38] He noted that while the US manufacturing sector shrank in the 1980s, the agricultural sector expanded, as farmers continued to be confident of their ability to rely on low-wage labor. Immigrant workers earning below poverty-level wages subsidized the expansion of an agribusiness model that increased poverty at the same time that it increased profits.[39]

The IRCA contributed to the growth of the FLC system in three ways. Employer sanctions encouraged farmers to seek third parties to take the risks of employing laborers. Many former migrant workers, now legalized under the SAW Program, took advantage of their new status to become FLCs. Finally, the rise of the FLC system coincided with the shift from Mexico's traditional sending regions to new, indigenous areas in southern

Mexico and Guatemala, in which the FLCs served as important recruiters and intermediaries.[40]

A temporary labor force that will simply move on when the work dwindles at the end of the season may seem ideal from an employer's perspective. For the workers, though, such a life is characterized by poverty, uncertainty, and long periods of unemployment. *The Economist* in 2010 noted the parallels between today's Mexican migrants and the desperate "Okies" who migrated during the Depression in their struggle to find work, comparing a contemporary Mexican migrant family, the Vegas, to the Joads in John Steinbeck's *Grapes of Wrath:*

> Often they take the same roads on which the "Okies" travelled en masse in the 1930s as they fled the depressed dust bowl of Oklahoma, Texas and Arkansas to seek a living in California. These Okies are forever etched into America's psyche. . . . Joads then and Vegas now are pushed by the same need, pulled by the same promise. Now as then, there is no clearing house for jobs in the fields, so the migrants follow tips and rumours. Often, like the Joads, they end up in the right places at the wrong times. Felix Vega and three of his group, including his wife, were dropped off in Oxnard, famous for its strawberries. But they arrived out of season, so they slept on the streets, then in a doghouse, then in somebody's car. For two months they did not bathe and barely ate. Finally, they found jobs picking strawberries and made their first money in America.[41]

In the summer of 2010, the United Farm Workers decided to confront the myth that "they [immigrants] take our jobs" directly. The union organized a campaign called "Take Our Jobs," inviting citizens and green-card holders to apply for agricultural work. The campaign got an extra publicity boost when comedian Stephen Colbert took up the challenge and then testified to Congress about the experience. Three months into the campaign, the union announced that its website, takeourjobs. org, had been visited by 3 million people; 8,600 had expressed an interest in a job in agriculture, but only 7 had actually followed through. "These numbers demonstrate that there are more politicians and finger-pointers interested in blaming undocumented farm workers for America's unemployment crisis than there are unemployed Americans who are willing to harvest and cultivate America's food," the Farm Workers concluded.[42]

In 2010 the US Department of Agriculture published an analysis of the probable impact of increased immigration enforcement on the US agricultural sector. The report cited the common figure that over half of the agricultural labor force consisted of undocumented Mexican workers.[43] A reduction in undocumented migrant labor would lead to rising labor costs, the report concluded, and different scenarios, depending on the characteristics of the crop. Where the potential existed, mechanization would spread. Where mechanization was not an option, farmers would face market loss due to higher costs. Finally, new research in mechanization and rising consumer prices would likely result. It is notable that in no case did the report foresee improved working conditions or rising employment of domestic workers in agriculture.[44]

"The US fruit and vegetable industry competes in a global economy with producers from other countries who often have much lower wages. With increasing trade, competitive pressures are greater than ever. In summer 2009, the Federal minimum wage was $7.25 per *hour* and the minimum wage in California was $8.00 per hour, while the minimum wage in Mexico ranged from $3.49 to $4.16 per *day*, depending on the region," the report explained.[45] It's no surprise that so many of the fruits and vegetables we find in the supermarket are labeled "Product of Mexico."

Labor's share made up 42 percent of the variable production costs for fruit and vegetable farms, and labor is the "single largest input cost" for many crops. Moreover, said the USDA report, "most [farm workers] will move on to nonagricultural employment within a decade of beginning to work in the fields."[46] Thus, agribusiness interests see a continuing supply of (undocumented) migrant workers as essential to their continued production and have lobbied heavily for a century to ensure that this supply continues to be available to them. As another USDA report put it bluntly: "The supply of farmworkers for the US produce industry depends on a constant influx of new, foreign-born labor attracted by wages above those in the workers' countries of origin, primarily Mexico. Immigration policy helps to determine whether the produce industry's labor force will be authorized or unauthorized."[47]

The State of Kansas sought in 2012 to develop a system of its own to legalize undocumented farm workers.[48] Georgia's farmers panicked in the summer of 2011, when a new law made it a felony for an undocumented person to apply for work. The Georgia Department of Agriculture wrote that "[n]onresident immigrant laborers, those of legal and illegal status, harvest crops, milk cows, gin cotton and maintain landscapes. Georgia farmers and agribusiness employers widely attribute the need for these workers due to the fact that local citizens do not generally possess or care to develop the specialized skills associated with agriculture and, further do not regularly demonstrate the work ethic necessary to meet the productivity requirements of the farm business."[49] A majority of Georgia farm employers hired laborers for a limited period of one to three months, another reason that citizen workers are reluctant to take these jobs.[50]

One season after the passage of Georgia's new law, 26 percent of farmers answered that they had lost income because of the lack of available labor for their farms. For some specialty crops like labor-intensive fruits and vegetables (blueberries, cabbage, cantaloupe, cucumbers, eggplant, peppers, squash, tobacco, and watermelon), over 50 percent were in that situation.[51] Fifty-six percent said they had trouble finding qualified workers.[52] "A major response theme for this question was that the work is too physically demanding and difficult for US citizens (non-immigrants). Respondents believe that only immigrant workers are willing to do the tasks needed in their operations."[53]

Productivity was also an issue. "Producers expressed great concern with the quality of work from domestic workers." According to data provided by one onion producer, "A migrant worker was twice as productive as a non-migrant worker in planting Vidalia onions."[54] As one Georgia farmer remarked, "American workers are not interested in getting dirty, bloody, sweaty, working weekends & holidays, getting to work at 4 a.m. 2 mornings a week & at 6 a.m. 5 mornings a week."[55]

Experiments with criminal offenders who are out on probation—and required to work as a condition of their probation—backed up the farmer's opinion. One crew leader "put the probationers to the test . . . assigning them to fill one truck and a Latino crew to a second truck. The Latinos picked six truckloads of cucumbers compared to one truckload and four bins for the probationers. 'It's not going to work,' [the crew leader] said. 'No way. If I'm going to depend on the probation people, I'm never going to get the crops up.'"[56]

As Philip Martin explains, most workers won't spend more than ten years working in agriculture. "As it is currently structured, fruit and vegetable agriculture requires a constant inflow of workers from abroad who are willing to accept seasonal farm jobs."[57] Farm labor is so marginal, strenuous, and low paid, that if workers achieve legal status, they quickly move into other sectors. Thus "farmers and their political allies . . . oppose simply legalizing unauthorized workers, which would enable them to get nonfarm jobs. Instead, farmers agree to legalization only in exchange for large guest-worker programs that give employers considerable control of foreign workers."[58]

Sixty years ago the folk singer–songwriter Woody Guthrie asked somewhat rhetorically, "Is this the best way we can grow our big orchards? Is this the best way we can grow our good fruit?" In the ensuing half-century, the United States has only deepened its "modern agricultural dilemma." It has devised a vast and multifaceted agricultural system that depends upon desperate workers for its survival. True, for many Mexicans— from the Bracero days to the present—low-wage, temporary, migrant labor in the United States offers a viable or even hopeful alternative to poverty at home. But this merely means that the US agricultural system depends upon the existence of a lot of extremely poor people in Mexico.[59]

While modern large-scale agricultural systems produce vast amounts of food, they have also created large-scale problems: "high capital costs; environmental deterioration of farmland through erosion, salinization, compaction, and chemical overload; pesticide and chemical fertilizer pollution of lakes, streams, and groundwater; unhealthy working conditions for farm workers, farmers, and farm families; dependence on an extremely narrow and destabilizing genetic base in major crops; dependence on nonrenewable mineral and energy resources; the destruction of rural communities; and the increasingly concentrated control of the nation's food supply."[60] Other critiques examine the consumption side: the increasing reliance on over-processed, high-sugar, and fatty foods, fast food and junk food, and the lifestyle diseases like heart disease and diabetes that have resulted.[61]

As we in the United States confront the problems in our agricultural and food production system, the problem of labor scarcity and continued reliance on impoverished, undocumented workers has to be central to the discussion. Given the way the agricultural system currently works, farm labor is so precarious and so harsh that only displaced migrants, the majority of them rendered illegal by US laws, are willing and able to carry it out. Paradoxically, most of these migrants were in fact displaced from centuries-old systems of subsistence agriculture in Mexico by precisely the same agricultural modernization that now demands their labor elsewhere. A truly comprehensive approach to immigration reform would look at these interlocking economic and structural systems, not merely make more narrow changes in immigration law.

We must recognize the basic irrationality, immorality, and unsustainability of the food production system. Farmers overwhelmingly oppose the harsh state-level immigration laws that make it more difficult for them to find the seasonal workers they need. In the short term, simply making it legal for immigrants to work in agriculture would address the needs of both farmers and immigrant farm workers who are undocumented. The larger problems await a longer-term and more profound reform of the global agricultural system. We can begin by acknowledging that our access to relatively cheap and abundant food in the United States exists because of the hard labor of poor Mexicans, in their country and in our own.

CHAPTER 6

Working (Part 2)

If the US agricultural system has relied on Mexican labor as it developed over many decades, meat processing and construction are two industries that shifted to heavy use of Mexican and Central American—and, in particular, undocumented—immigrants at the end of the twentieth century. This shift coincided with the trend of outsourcing, when manufacturing plants began to shift their labor-intensive production abroad. Manufacturing employment declined from a high of 20 million in 1979 to 11 million in 2012.[1] Meatpacking and construction couldn't exactly be moved abroad. But meatpacking could be moved out of heavily unionized urban centers like Chicago into the rural Midwest. Construction boomed in new regions, with employment doubling between 1970 and 2006 to a high of 7.7 million.[2] Both industries increasingly employed immigrant, and undocumented, workers.

CONSTRUCTION

While the manufacturing sector was shrinking in the last decades of the twentieth century, construction was expanding. But this industry was also changing profoundly. Unionization plummeted, from 40 percent in the 1970s to only 14 percent in 2011. Unions lost ground especially in the high-growth area of residential construction, which was being buoyed by low interest rates and subprime loans through the first decade of the new century. But as employment rose, working conditions and wages deteriorated. Immigrants and especially undocumented workers increased their presence in the workforce.[3] The low wages of undocumented workers helped contribute to the housing bubble by making building costs artificially cheap.[4]

In Las Vegas, the population doubled to almost 2 million between 1990 and 2007, and the share of immigrants in the city's population also doubled during the same time span from 9 percent to 19 percent. Many of the newcomers worked in hotel construction and tourism-related services in the booming city: half of the state's construction workers were Latino immigrants. By 2008, Nevada had the largest percentage of undocumented workers of any state, 12 percent.[5]

Houston's 1970s oil boom likewise spurred a jump in construction. "The record-breaking construction of office buildings, shopping centers, storage facilities, apartment projects, and suburban homes in the 1970s and early 1980s created an insatiable demand for Mexican immigrant labor. Undocumented workers from rural and urban Mexico became a preferred labor force, especially among construction employers who paid low wages and offered poor working conditions."[6] The Greater Houston Partnership estimated that 14 percent of Houston's construction workforce was undocumented in 2008, more than any other job category.[7]

In Texas as a whole, one in thirteen workers—about a million total—labored in the construction industry as of 2013. Half of them are undocumented. A study by the Workers Defense Project in Austin showed that 41 percent of Texas construction workers are subject to payroll fraud, including being illegally classified as independent contractors instead of employees. Employers use this method to evade their legal responsibilities for payroll taxes, minimum wages, working conditions, and benefits. Working conditions are so dangerous that one in five construction workers in the state will require hospitalization for job-related injuries. "More construction workers die in Texas than in any other state," the study discovered.[8]

In New Orleans, only days after Hurricane Katrina hit, the federal government waived employer sanctions provisions, allowing employers to hire workers without documents. Soon after, it waived prevailing federal wage standard requirements for contractors working on federally funded reconstruction projects. These exemptions set the stage for an influx of low-paid, undocumented workers.[9] US census figures showed that some one hundred thousand Hispanics moved into the Gulf Coast after Katrina. Hispanics made up half of the labor force working in reconstruction, and half were undocumented. Undocumented workers formed "the backbone of post-Hurricane Katrina reconstruction," reported *USA Today*.[10] Curiously, while the workers remained undocumented, it was ostensibly not illegal for them to work, at least during the first month and a half, because of the employer sanctions waiver.

Overall, undocumented workers made up a quarter of the workforce in New Orleans in the months following the hurricane.[11] Almost 90 percent were already in the United States and moved to New Orleans from other areas, primarily Texas (41 percent) and, to a lesser extent, Florida (10 percent).[12] Unsurprisingly, undocumented workers faced lower wages and poorer working and living conditions than those with documents.

When Hurricane Ike hit southeastern Texas in 2008, undocumented immigrants performed a significant portion of the cleanup work. "All across southeast Texas, roofs need repair, debris must be discarded and towns hope to rebuild. Hurricane Ike's destruction is sparking one of the largest rebuilding efforts the state has seen in decades, but at the same time is highlighting a thorny facet of the region's labor force: A lot of the recovery work will be done by illegal immigrants," reported the *Houston Chronicle.*[13]

When the housing boom went bust after 2008, strangely, statistics showed that construction wages began to rise. What was actually happening was that the lower-paid newcomers were the first to lose their jobs, so that the rise in wages was more apparent than real. Individual workers weren't receiving better wages; there were just fewer construction workers employed overall.[14]

MEATPACKING

Like construction, meatpacking is an industry that is very difficult to outsource. In some ways, the work process in meatpacking more resembles that of other large manufacturing plants than it does construction, in which most workers are employed by small companies and contractors. But while industries like textiles or electronics can transport the raw materials and the finished products over long distances to save on the costs of production, this strategy is not practical for dealing with a perishable, bulky, and sometimes cantankerous product. So like construction, meatpacking has relied on bringing immigrant workers to the point of production, rather than sending production to countries where it is cheaper.

Lance Compa summarizes how in-sourcing happened in Nebraska, in a process repeated throughout the Midwest:

> From its founding as a territory in 1854 until the late twentieth century, Nebraska was mostly populated by white Americans of European origin, joined by a minority of African-Americans. Omaha was always an important meatpacking center because of its proximity to livestock and feedlots. Immigrant workers from southern and eastern Europe made up most of the meatpacking labor force in the early twentieth century. In

the 1940s and '50s, the children of these immigrants, along with African-American coworkers in key roles, formed strong local unions of the United Packinghouse Workers. As happened in the industry generally, in the 1980s and 1990s, many meatpacking businesses closed plants that provided good wages and benefits. Following closures, company owners often relocated plants to rural areas. In Omaha, some companies later reopened closed factories employing low wage, new immigrant workforces without trade union representation.[15]

Wages in meatpacking fell 45 percent between 1980 and 2007. The downgrading of meatpacking jobs proved "devastating to the standard of living for workers in an industry that once sustained a blue-collar middle class."[16] As both wages and working conditions deteriorated, immigrant workers became the mainstay of the labor force. By the late 1990s, fully a quarter of meatpacking workers were estimated to be undocumented.[17]

In the climate of heightened calls for immigration enforcement, the meatpacking industry attracted attention. In 1999, the INS launched Operation Vanguard in Nebraska, subpoenaing the employment records of every meatpacker in the state. After reviewing all 24,000 employee records received, the agency identified 4,700 cases in which the employee's legal status was in doubt. It presented employers with the list and required all of the "suspects" to appear for interviews with the agency. It seemed clear to the meatpackers that "INS's intention was not to apprehend potentially unauthorized employees, but to 'chase off' those workers who were present in illegal status."[18]

In chasing them off, the operation succeeded. Only one thousand of the workers dared to appear for their interviews. The others simply left their jobs. Overnight, the state's meatpacking industry lost 13 percent of its workforce. Meanwhile, of the one thousand interviewed, thirty-four were determined to be unauthorized to work and were arrested and deported. "Meatpacking company officials . . . believe that a substantial number of these employees [who disappeared] were authorized to work but chose not to appear because of the intimidation inherent in any such interview (for example, from questions such as 'are you *or any members of your family* not authorized to be present in the United States?').'' The Nebraska Cattlemen's Association estimated that its members lost $5 million and the state economy as a whole lost $20 million as the result of the operation.[19]

Operation Vanguard ended in 2000, but in 2006 a new enforcement effort began, focused on workplace raids. On December 12, 2006, ICE agents descended on six Swift meatpacking plants in Iowa, Minnesota, Nebraska, Texas, Colorado, and Utah, arresting thirteen hundred of the company's seven thousand day-shift workers. Swift was also part of the industry pattern of shifting from urban to rural, and employing large numbers of new Latin American immigrants, many of them undocumented. In several Swift plants, researchers drew a direct connection to the Bracero Program. Two small communities in the Mexican states of Michoacán, Villachuato and La Huacana, which had begun to send recruits northward as braceros, had now become major sources of migrants to Swift plants. These workers were later joined by Central Americans. In Swift's Cactus, Texas, plant, most of the workers were Maya Quiche Guatemalans, many of them undocumented.[20]

In an eerie replay of previous roundups and deportations of Mexicans like Operation Wetback, ICE agents relied on appearance to determine who to detain. One American citizen of Mexican origin at Swift's Nebraska plant recounted that "when they said all the US citizens come over to this place, I went up there and I stood right by my boss. My boss showed his driver's license and then he was free to go. I showed my driver's license and my voting registration card and that was not enough. He [the ICE agent] said, no, you need either your passport or citizenship certificate."[21] Most of those arrested in the raids were charged not with the civil violation of unauthorized presence in the country, but with criminal charges of fraudulent use of Social Security numbers and/or identity theft.

The raids affected more than just those arrested, as family members and others were afraid to show up to work in the aftermath. The Center for Immigration Studies looked at what happened in the devastated plants over the following months. All managed to replace the hundreds of workers who were arrested, but none improved working conditions or wages, and none shifted back to employing US citizens. The companies scoured the United States for workers willing to accept the jobs, and most of the lost workers were eventually replaced by immigrants from Burma and different parts of Africa who held refugee status and thus had legal authorization to work.[22]

THE POSTVILLE RAID

Another devastating raid took place at the Agriprocessors plant in Postville, Iowa, in May 2008. Agriprocessors represented a cross between in-sourcing and a new industry. Although meatpacking in general was an old industry that was moving into new rural areas, kosher processing had been a local, small-scale industry before the late twentieth century. "In the 1980s, before the Postville plant had opened, almost all fresh kosher meat had been sold through local butchers. It came in raw quarters from slaughterhouses that were rented out by rabbis, and it rarely made it beyond major cities on the coasts."[23]

The Rubashkin family changed all that. Locating their new plant in the small town of Postville, Iowa, they proposed to turn kosher meat into a nationally available, mass-produced product. "The Rubashkins created a world in which it was possible to buy fresh kosher beef and poultry in ordinary supermarkets across the country, even in places that had few Jews. . . . The changes brought about by the Rubashkins did something more than expand the reach of kosher meat. They brought an entirely new customer base to kosher food: the secular Jews and even non-Jews who never would have stopped at a butcher shop. The expansion also allowed Orthodox communities in places that had never had them."[24]

Agriprocessors also differed from other meatpackers in choosing the tiny town of Postville as its location. Most meat-packers moved to medium-sized towns of thirty thousand to sixty thousand when they left the urban centers. Postville, with a population of fourteen hundred, was "a town with no stop-lights, no fast-food restaurants and a weekly newspaper that for years featured the 'Yard of the Week.'"[25] Most of the work-ers were recruited from two small villages in Guatemala. Over 75 percent of the workers were undocumented, and some were minors.[26] Working conditions at the plant were abysmal.

"One of those workers—a woman who agreed to be iden-tified by the pseudonym Juana—came to this rural corner of Iowa a year ago from Guatemala," said one newspaper account. Since then, she has worked 10-to-12-hour night shifts, six nights a week. Her cutting hand is swollen and deformed, but she has no health insurance to have it checked. She works for wages, starting at $6.25 an hour and stopping at $7, that several industry experts described as the lowest of any slaughterhouse in the nation."[27]

In May 2008, ICE agents descended on the plant and ar-rested 389 of its 900 workers, most of them Guatemalan. As their lengthy saga of incarceration and deportation began, the rest of the town's immigrant population panicked. "Within weeks, roughly 1,000 Mexican and Guatemalan residents—about a third of the town—vanished. It was as if a natural disaster had swept through, leaving no physical evidence of de-struction, just silence behind it."[28]

The Agriprocessors raid in May 2008 was "the largest single-site operation of its kind in American history."[29] Because one of the court interpreters, Erik Camayd-Freixas, wrote a detailed protest about the irregularity of the procedures, which circulated widely on the Internet and was later submitted to Congress, the public obtained access to an unusually complete picture of the process. According to Camayd-Freixas's account, "The arrest, prosecution, and conviction of 297 undocumented workers from Postville was a process marred by irregularities at every step of the way." The government charged the workers en masse, and without any evidence whatsoever, of the criminal charge of "aggravated identity theft." Prosecutors then coerced them into a plea bargain for a lesser but still criminal charge of misuse of a Social Security number.[30]

The Guatemalan workers knew that they were in the country without legal permission. But that's a civil violation, not a crime. The only punishment should have been removal. Through their own networks, most of the undocumented immigrants know that they have few rights in the immigration court system. Most of them had no idea what the criminal charges meant, and when pressured to accept a plea bargain, most of them did so. Many acquiesced out of desperation, since as the sole support for their families, they could not afford to remain in detention awaiting trial. They believed they would quickly be deported. Instead, they had signed up for a five-month prison sentence.

Camayd-Freixas described the heart-wrenching scenes as court-appointed lawyers tried to explain the criminal charges and advise those arrested. One conversation illustrates the utter disconnect between the world of the workers and the legal system they were caught in.

> The client, a Guatemalan peasant afraid for his family, spent most of that time weeping at our table, in a corner of the crowded jailhouse visiting room. How did he come here from Guatemala? "I walked." What? "I walked for a month and ten days until I crossed the river. . . . I just wanted to work a year or two, save, and then go back to my family, but it was not to

be. . . . The Good Lord knows I was just working and not doing anyone any harm." This man, like many others, was in fact
not guilty. "Knowingly" and "intent" are necessary elements of
the [criminal] charges, but most of the clients we interviewed
did not even know what a Social Security number was or what
purpose it served. This worker simply had the papers filled out
for him at the plant, since he could not read or write Spanish, let
alone English. But the lawyer still had to advise him that plead-
ing guilty was in his best interest. He was unable to make a decision. "You all do and undo," he said. "So you can do whatever
you want with me." To him we were part of the system keeping
him from being deported back to his country, where his children, wife, mother, and sister depended on him. He was their
sole support and did not know how they were going to make it
with him in jail for 5 months. None of the "options" really mat-
tered to him. Caught between despair and hopelessness, he just
wept. He had failed his family, and was devastated. I went for
some napkins, but he refused them. I offered him a cup of soda,
which he superstitiously declined, saying it could be "poisoned."
His Native American spirit was broken and he could no longer
think. He stared for a while at the signature page pretending to
read it, although I knew he was actually praying for guidance
and protection. Before he signed with a scribble, he said: "God
knows you are just doing your job to support your families, and
that job is to keep me from supporting mine."[31]

Like Swift, Agriprocessors looked to other sources of marginalized, immigrant workers in the wake of the raid. "In one
of its most desperate moves, Agri recruited 170 people from the
Micronesian island of Palau—whose status as a former US pro-
tectorate means its citizens can work legally in the United States.
In September 2008, the Palauans traveled 72 hours and 8,000
miles on planes and buses before arriving in Postville with little
more than flip-flops and brightly colored shorts and tops."[32]

Six months later, the plant closed. It was later sold and re-opened, and like other plants in the industry, implemented the E-Verify system. However, as a journalist found in 2011,

> few Iowan-born locals work there. Ridding this small community of its illegal workforce, far from freeing up jobs for American-born citizens, has resulted in closed businesses and fewer opportunities. Even nearly four years later, many homes still remain empty, and taxable retail sales are about 40 percent lower than they were in 2008.
>
> In order to staff its still low-paying jobs with legal immigrants, the new owner of the plant has recruited a hodgepodge of refugees and other immigrants, who often leave the town as soon as they find better opportunities, creating a constant churn among the population. The switch to a legal workforce has made the community feel less stable, some locals say, and it's unclear if Postville will again become a place where immigrants will put down roots, raise children, and live in relative harmony with their very different neighbors.[33]

Years later, a researcher in Guatemala met with families that had been deported, including sixteen US-born, US citizen children. The children, Aryah Somers reported, were "growing up in extreme poverty, with little schooling and scant medical care. . . . The kids are undernourished and barely literate in either Spanish or English." Their parents planned to send them back to the United States once they are ten or twelve years old and able to travel alone.[34]

While the Obama administration scaled down the Bush-era policy of workplace raids, the E-Verify system expanded rapidly. E-Verify was created in 1997 under the auspices of the 1996 Illegal Immigration Reform and Immigrant Responsibility Act (IIRIRA) and requires participating employers to check each new hire against a set of federal databases to ensure that the individual is either a citizen or an immigrant specifically authorized to work in the United States. The system was initially voluntary, but in 2007, the Office of Management and Budget required all federal government agencies to screen all new hires through the system and, in 2009, required certain federal contractors and subcontractors to use it for existing employees as well as new hires. Several states, beginning with Arizona in 2007, have mandated that all employers in the state utilize E-Verify.[35] Other states have tried to restrict its use.[36] S. 744, the comprehensive immigration reform bill supported by President Obama and passed by the Senate in June 2013, would make the system mandatory for all employers nationwide. (As this book goes to press, the bill seems to have little chance of passing in the House or becoming law.)

But the experience of the meatpacking industry shows that eliminating undocumented workers, either through workplace raids or through the use of E-Verify, has not increased employment opportunities for citizens. Instead, it has destabilized businesses and communities, created temporary flows of refugees, and brought harm to innumerable immigrants, citizens, and businesses with benefit to none. Many argue against the use of E-Verify because the GAO found it to be plagued with errors and false alarms, as amply illustrated by several GAO investigations between 2005 and 2011.[37] While it's quite true that the program has mistakenly ensnared large numbers of work-authorized immigrants and naturalized citizens, that is not the only or even the main reason to oppose it. Even if the program worked perfectly, its impact on individuals, businesses, communities, and the economy would only be to cause harm.[38]

NEW JOBS: LANDSCAPING

Other sectors that employ significant numbers of undocumented workers are the mostly unregulated, small-scale niches in the service sector like landscaping, nanny services, and newspaper delivery. The first two are sectors where employment has grown in recent decades, while in the latter it has shrunk. But all three have been refuges for undocumented workers, in part because they involve low pay; insecurity and lack of benefits; difficult hours; and isolated, heavy, and sometimes dangerous working conditions. These poor working conditions parallel the working conditions in industries that have been outsourced (manufacturing) and in-sourced (meatpacking, construction). The cheap products provided by outsourcing and in-sourcing, along with the cheap services provided by these new service industries, have contributed to rising consumption and illusions of affluence in the United States.

The landscaping industry has grown steadily since the 1970s, hand in hand with the construction industry. Newly built homes, businesses, and public buildings created a fresh demand for landscaping services. Landscaping companies responded to the increased demand by creating new products and services, which soon came to be considered essential.[39]

Two additional, interrelated changes in the past decades have contributed to the increase in demand for landscaping services. First, the ranks of the super-rich who hire landscaping companies to maintain their palatial grounds have increased. Second, middle- and upper-middle-class suburban families that once might have maintained their own yards are now too busy and are contracting out services that they or their children used to provide. As the industry grew, the new jobs were filled by immigrants, especially undocumented immigrants.

One of many companies to expand and transform in the new era belonged to Nikita Floyd. The *Washington Post* described its trajectory:

> In the early 1990s, Floyd had fewer than a dozen employees, all of them black. Today, 73 percent of the Washington area's landscaping workers are immigrants, along with 51 percent of office

cleaners and 43 percent of construction workers. . . . Floyd's 20 wintertime workers are all men from El Salvador, except for two black women who manage the office. In the summer, he employs twice as many men, all immigrants. Floyd's experience illustrates immigrants' impact. Once just a guy with a lawnmower, he runs a business with annual sales of more than $2.5 million. He credits immigrant employees for his business's growth and pays about $10 an hour, with no work and no pay in inclement weather. It's grueling labor in the winter; a man can spend the day stabbing a spade into frozen dirt or be asked to shimmy up a tree with a chainsaw in one hand and no netting below.[40]

Like the farm and meatpacking associations discussed earlier, the California Landscape Contractors Association is strongly opposed to the criminalization of immigrant work and implicitly acknowledges its industry's reliance on the undocumented. Calling for legalization, the association notes that "[t] he status quo is untenable, as it puts employers in a strange 'don't ask, don't tell' situation where they can never be sure of their workforce." The industry operates under a continuous labor shortage, the association explains:

> The landscaping industry relies heavily on an immigrant labor force. Landscaping is physically demanding work. It is performed in hot, cold, and sometimes rainy weather. Some landscaping jobs are seasonal. American-born workers increasingly are not attracted to such jobs. Because landscaping work involves outdoor manual labor, it is to some extent young person's work. Yet America has an aging workforce. At the same time, the landscape industry is growing and therefore has a need for more workers, partly because this same aging population tends to enlarge the market for landscaping services. Immigrants, who tend to be young, address this unmet need for younger workers in the landscape industry.[41]

NEW JOBS: NANNIES

Landscaping is not the only personal-service job that has proliferated with the use of undocumented immigrants in recent decades. A number of high-profile public figures have been embarrassed when reporters uncovered their use of undocumented domestic workers. Lawyer Zoe Baird, who had worked for the Carter administration and the Department of Justice, was withdrawn as President Bill Clinton's nominee for attorney general when it was revealed that she had employed undocumented workers as chauffeur and nanny. Then Clinton's second choice, Kimba Wood, was withdrawn for the same reason.[42] When Mitt Romney was running in the Republican primary in 2007, in large part on an anti-immigrant platform, the *Boston Globe* published an investigation showing that undocumented workers maintained the 2.5-acre lot around his home in Belmont, Massachusetts.[43] California Republican gubernatorial candidate and former eBay CEO Meg Whitman fired her nanny of nine years during the campaign when she allegedly first learned that she was undocumented.[44] And Bernard Kerik stepped down from his nomination as chief of the Department of Homeland Security in 2004 when it was learned that he too had hired a nanny who lacked documents.[45]

But not only the super-rich hire nannies, landscapers, and house cleaners. In 2001, sociologist Pierrette Hondagneu-Sotelo described the proliferation of services in the previous twenty years that had transformed middle-class life in heavily immigrant Los Angeles. At the time she was writing, Los Angeles was still in the vanguard; a decade later, what she described had become commonplace throughout the United States.

She writes:

> When you arrive at many a Southern California hotel or restaurant, you are likely to be first greeted by a Latino car valet. The janitors, cooks, busboys, painters, carpet cleaners, and landscape

workers who keep the office buildings, restaurants, and malls running are also likely to be Mexican or Central American immigrants, as are many of those who work behind the scenes in dry cleaners, convalescent homes, hospitals, resorts, and apartment complexes. . . . Only twenty years ago, these relatively inexpensive consumer services and products were not nearly as widely available as they are today. The Los Angeles economy, landscape, and lifestyle have been transformed in ways that rely on low-wage, Latino immigrant labor.[46]

The number of gardeners and domestic workers in Los Angeles doubled between 1980 and 1990.[47]

The inexpensive nature of these services—in part because of the often undocumented immigrant labor that provided them—helped to sustain an illusion of upward mobility for people in the working and middle classes.[48] This illusion overlays other changes in the US economy over the past fifty years, as the rapid expansion of the middle class that began in the post–World War II era slowed and then reversed in the 1970s, to be replaced by growing economic inequality. Paradoxically, Hondagneu-Sotelo found that increasing social inequality led to greater numbers of people employing domestic help. The middle class works harder to maintain its standard of living and must increasingly rely on low-cost services provided by the more impoverished.[49] Formerly, domestic workers were found mostly in the employ of upper-middle-class suburbanites. By the 1980s, employers came to include "apartment dwellers with modest incomes, single mothers, college students, and elderly people living on fixed incomes. They live in tiny bungalows and condominiums, not just sprawling houses." Even Latina domestic workers found themselves employing other immigrant women to clean, cook, and care for their children, while they provided those same services to their wealthier clients.[50]

Tellingly, Los Angeles was the vanguard. In the 1990s, "when Angelenos, accustomed to employing a full-time nanny/house-keeper for about $150 or $200 a week, move[d] to Seattle or Durham, they [were] startled to discover how 'the cost of living that way' quickly escalate[d]. Only then [did] they realize the extent to which their affluent lifestyle and smoothly running household depended on one Latina immigrant woman."[51] As the Latino immigrant population spread from the Southwest to other parts of the country, access to the services it provided also became more widespread.[52]

Business Review reported, "[N]annies [are] a growth indus-try in slow economy." With more parents working, and child care expensive or unavailable, the nanny industry fills the gap.[53] The *Arizona Republic* reported, "[U]nconventional work sched-ules, increased awareness and flexible care options have ignited growth in the nanny industry. At the same time, parents have a desire for more personalized care."[54]

The *New York Times* commented on the widespread nature of the so-called nanny problem with regard to the Zoe Baird case: "As everyone learned before a conveniently childless can-didate ended the search for an Attorney General, the hiring of illegal caregivers is an endemic labor practice, among para-legals and secretaries as well as $250,000-a-year executives, in cities like New York, Los Angeles or Miami—points of entry to the United States as well as centers of immigrant popu-lation. Cities with a baby sitter or nanny labor force tend to lack even the fragile, faint day-care networks that exist in other parts of the country."[55]

NEWSPAPER DELIVERY

Newspaper delivery, of course, has been around for a long time. But today's newspaper delivery system is something entirely new. No longer does a neighborhood kid walk or bike through the streets tossing papers into his neighbors' yards. Today, 81 percent of paper deliverers are adults, and a large proportion of them are undocumented immigrants. A look at the structure of the industry will help explain why.[56]

In many areas of the country, newspapers are delivered through a system of independent contractors—the same system construction companies use to evade their legal responsibilities as employers. The newspaper publisher works with a contracting company, which in turn hires workers who must sign a contract confirming that they are not employees but independent contractors. In Connecticut, all fourteen respondents to a survey of newspaper publishers in the state confirmed that they used this system.[57] Likewise in the Boston area, the *Wall Street Journal, New York Times*, and *Boston Globe* are all distributed by a single company, which hires contractors to deliver all three in a given area.

As independent contractors, workers may not receive the minimum wages and may not be eligible for workers' compensation or unemployment benefits. (States and courts have varied as to how they treat these cases, but newspaper publishers overwhelmingly insist that their deliverers are contractors, not employees.) In a case where independent contractors sued and appealed for class status in a class action suit, the US District Court–Southern District of California described the job in the following terms:

> Plaintiffs deliver the North County Times to the homes of subscribers. Each morning, the newspaper carriers arrive at one of several distribution centers in San Diego County. The carriers arrive at different times. Although they generally arrive between 1:00 a.m. and 4:00 a.m., some arrive earlier or later. The arrival time varies depending on the day of the week.
>
> The carriers are contractually obligated to deliver the assembled newspapers by 6:00 a.m. each weekday and 7:00 a.m. on Saturday and Sunday.

Upon arrival, the carriers are responsible for assembling the newspapers. Some assemble the papers at the distribution center—those that use the distribution center pay a rental fee—and others assemble the papers elsewhere. Assembling the newspapers may involve folding or inserting the following: newspaper inserts, sections, pre-prints, samples, supplements and other products at NCT's direction. The carriers pay for their own rubber bands and plastic bags used to assemble the papers. Some carriers buy the rubber bands and bags from Defendant, and others purchase them elsewhere. The carriers also pay for their own gas and automobile expenses they incur delivering the newspapers.[58]

Contractors sign up to deliver papers 365 days a year, starting no later than 4 a.m. every day. They cannot miss a day unless they can arrange for their own replacement, must own a car, and have a valid driver's license. They have to maintain and buy gas for the car, driving hundreds of miles a week. All for less than minimum wage. During winter weather emergencies, when public transportation is shut down and the governor of Massachusetts calls a state of emergency, closing public offices and begging residents to stay at home and businesses to remain closed until the plows can clear the streets, independent contractors receive a curt message with their newspapers. "SNOW IS EXPECTED . . . WE WILL BE WORKING. IC'S ARE EXPECTED TO DELIVER THEIR ROUTES. PLAN ACCORDINGLY: BE EARLY; DO NOT ALLOW YOUR CAR TO BE BLOCKED IN; EXPECT TO HAVE TO SHOVEL OUT."[59]

It's a job, in other words, made for an undocumented immigrant.

CONCLUSION

Overall, the rise in undocumented workers over the past several decades has gone along with a rise in the invisible, exploited labor that they perform. The generally unacknowledged work that they do is a crucial underpinning to the standard of living and consumption enjoyed by virtually everyone in the United States. But, clearly, an economic system that keeps a lot of people unemployed and another group trapped in a legal status that restricts them to the worst kinds of jobs does not really benefit everyone.

Some have argued that the influx of undocumented workers depresses the labor market, lowers wages for less educated workers, and creates more competition for jobs at the lower end of the pay scale. Labor economist George Borjas has made this argument most persuasively, and many commentators who argue that we should restrict immigration base their arguments on his work.[60]

Other economists, however, have found that the low-wage labor of undocumented immigrants actually increases the wages and employment of even low-paid citizen workers. By increasing productivity, low-paid undocumented workers can increase capital available for investment, hiring, and wages. Because undocumented workers add to the population, their consumption stimulates the economy.[61] One recent study tried to document the expected economic impact of deportation versus legalization of the undocumented population of Arizona. The study found that legalization would be far more beneficial and deportation far more costly for American citizens.

> Undocumented immigrants don't simply "fill" jobs; they create jobs. Through the work they perform, the money they spend, and the taxes they pay, undocumented immigrants sustain the jobs of many other workers in the US economy, immigrants and native-born alike. Were undocumented immigrants to suddenly vanish, the jobs of many Americans would vanish as well. In contrast, were undocumented immigrants to acquire

legal status, their wages and productivity would increase, they would spend more in our economy and pay more in taxes, and new jobs would be created.[62]

Two recent films, one a feature film and one a documentary, demonstrate this effect. *A Day without a Mexican* imagines that California awakens one morning to a strange fog, which has caused everyone of Mexican origin to vanish. Non-Mexicans stumble through their lives trying to fill in the gaps and realizing along the way how utterly dependent their economy and daily lives are on Mexican immigrants. In a moving scene at the end, after the fog lifts and the Mexicans reappear, the Border Patrol comes across a group in the wilderness at night. Flashing their lights, a patrolman asks, "Are you guys Mexican?" When the migrants confirm, the patrollers break into welcoming applause.

The film *9500 Liberty* looks at a case in which the fantasy of *A Day without a Mexican* became a reality. In Prince William County, Virginia, a local ordinance in 2007 required police to stop and question anyone they suspected of being undocumented. Although the ordinance was eventually repealed, the acrimonious anti-immigrant mobilization surrounding it as well as fear of its implementation caused many immigrants to leave. As businesses closed, schools and neighborhoods emptied, and the housing market collapsed, the white citizen majority in the county became more dubious about the supposed benefits of expelling the undocumented.

Although the current system benefits many people in the United States, we must also recognize its fundamental injustice and think seriously about how it works and what steps could make it more just. If immigrants are being exploited by the current system, and if undocumentedness is one of the concepts that sustains inequality and unjust treatment, then we need to question undocumentedness itself.

The system benefits most Americans materially, given that Americans—even poor Americans—consume an extraordinary proportion of the planet's resources. Only 4 percent of the world's children are American, but they consume 40 percent of the world's toys.[63] Despite the fact that many Americans are unemployed, in debt, and struggle to pay for health care and put food on their plates, *they still consume more than their share.* They do so because of the economic chain that links them to workers who are legally marginalized, either because they work in other countries or because they work illegally inside the United States.

Undocumentedness has everything to do with work and the economy. It is a key component of the late-twentieth-century global system. Every so-called industrialized country—or more accurately, deindustrializing country—relies on the labor of workers who are legally excluded to maintain its high levels of consumption. Like the United States, these countries rely on the legal conveniences of borders, countries, and citizenship to impose different rules for different people and maintain a legally excluded working class.

This system also creates fantastic profits for the few. But a fairer economic system would distribute the planet's resources more equally. If we can understand undocumentedness as a mechanism for creating and perpetuating economic inequality, it will be easier for us to reject it outright.

CHAPTER 7

Children and Families

Although the need to work—and the availability of work—has played a central role in the rise of both immigration and un-documentedness in the past half-century, every worker is also a human being. Like everyone else, undocumented workers have children and families. The undocumented population and those personally affected through family relations by undocumented-ness include much more than the single, working-age male. As border enforcement has increased over the past two decades and the circular, seasonal migration of workers has shifted to long-term family settlement, more and more children have been affected by issues of status.

Some children are undocumented themselves, while others live in mixed-status families, with one or both parents, siblings, or other relatives who are undocumented. Still others have temporary and unstable statuses. Some children, whether citizens or undocumented themselves, lose parents or other family members to deportation, while others cross the border illegally to reunite with parents they had lost to migration. Virtually all parents who come to the United States do so because they want better lives for their children; the US law claims to protect the best interests of children. But immigration law makes these children's lives tenuous and unpredictable.

About 17 percent of all Hispanics and 22 percent of all Hispanic youth ages sixteen to twenty-five are unauthorized immigrants, according to Pew Hispanic Center estimates in 2009.
These percentages refer to all Hispanics, whether native-born
or immigrant. Among immigrants, the numbers are, of course,
much higher. Some 41 percent of all foreign-born Hispanics
and 58 percent of foreign-born Hispanic youths are estimated
to be unauthorized immigrants.[1]

Other youth fall into in-between categories, like asylum applicants or those who have received Temporary Protected Status, wherein their presence is currently legal, but in an unstable
status that could easily be revoked—what Cecilia Menjívar
termed "liminal legality."[2] President Obama's DACA program
of 2012 created another temporary status, allowing certain undocumented youth a two-year respite from illegality, but with
no guarantee of what would occur at the end of the two years.
While immensely popular among Latinos (Romney called it a
"big gift" to Hispanic voters), DACA did little to address the
underlying problem of undocumentedness.[3]

The immigration system in general is designed to deprive
undocumented adults of most rights, but, in some cases, laws
designed to protect children transcend status and are applied
equally to all children. Laws and policies thus struggle between
two contradictory aims: to punish violations of immigration
status or to protect the rights of children and their need to be
with their parents. In the case of US citizen children of undocumented parents, the goal of keeping children together with their
parents can contradict the goal of removing the parent, and the
goal of promoting the best interests of the children conflicts
with the laws that punish their parents for their status. In some
cases, judges have ruled that a child's best interest requires that
he or she remain in the United States and have terminated parental rights of parents who are deported. In other cases, immigration laws prevent children from entering the United States

to reunite with their parents. Undocumented youth can also be deported and face legal discrimination that prevents them from working, going to college, and receiving public benefits.

From being virtually invisible in the public sphere only a decade ago, undocumented youth, especially those who have grown up in the United States, have stepped to the forefront in organizing for immigrant rights. Their activism openly challenges the anti-immigrant propaganda and may be changing the way the citizen public views the undocumented.

YOUNG AND ALONE

The past two decades have witnessed a dramatic surge of young people fleeing their homes in Mexico and Central America and attempting the treacherous border crossing alone. They may be seeking to escape violence, gangs, or abuse at home, or they may be making a desperate attempt to reunite with parents who left them to journey to the United States. They face all of the hazards that adults face, and more.

Undocumented youth, especially Central Americans fleeing civil wars, began crossing the border alone in the 1980s. At the time, the immigrant detention system had no provisions or capacity to deal specifically with detained youth: they were simply imprisoned with and treated as adults. During 1990, the INS reported that eighty-five hundred minors had been apprehended crossing the border without documents, 70 percent of them unaccompanied. Most were Mexican and were quickly returned to Mexico under an agreement with that government. Non-Mexicans, though, were detained in immigration facilities, some for lengthy periods, awaiting immigration hearings.[4]

A series of lawsuits and court decisions starting in 1985 led finally, in 1997, the then-INS to develop special policies for detained minors. Under the *Flores v. Meese* settlement of that year, the INS developed separate standards for children that took their age and needs into account. Children would be released, if possible, to a sponsor; they would be placed in the least restrictive setting possible, and the agency would implement appropriate standards for their treatment.

A US government study in 2001 explained that most juveniles the INS encountered were still of Mexican origin and generally held for only a few hours before being returned voluntarily to Mexico. The study emphasized that the Border Patrol worked to ensure that juveniles were returned to family members or to Mexican government officials rather than being "simply dropped off across the border."[5] Most of the children who ended up in US custody, therefore, were Central American. The numbers taken into custody (rather than returned) increased rapidly over the first decade of the new century, from the low thousands to up to ten thousand a year.[6] The system scrambled to keep up with the influx.

After 2002, when the INS was replaced by ICE under the new Department of Homeland Security, responsibility for detained children was transferred to the Department of Health and Human Services and the Office of Refugee Resettlement.[7] And in 2003, the ORR created the Division of Unaccompanied Children's Services (DUCS) to handle the placement of undocumented minors.[8]

The treatment of children in detention improved with the involvement of the social service agencies. Rather than being housed indefinitely with adult criminals, children were sent to special facilities where they had access to educational and social services, and most were released within weeks to family members in the United States (many of them undocumented themselves). Facilities must provide "classroom education, health care, socializing/recreation activities, vocational training, mental health services, case management, and, when possible, assist with family reunion."[9] According to the *New York Times*, "It is not unusual for youths to recall the detention shelters . . . as some of the best times in their battered lives."[10]

Still, in 2006, a study found that detained minors "fall into the bewildering inner workings of the immigration and asylum system." Despite the changes in detention provisions, immigration law did not distinguish between children and adults, and until 2004, the courts simply treated any child, no matter how young, as an adult.[11] In 2012, yet another study found that children who are detained for immigration violations "enter a disjointed, labyrinthine system in which they may interact with numerous agencies within several federal government departments, as well as with a host of government contractors."[12]

The automatic repatriation of Mexican children was challenged in 2008 when Congress passed the William Wilberforce Trafficking Victims Protection and Reauthorization Act. The act responded to concerns that US deportation policies were contributing to the exploitation and abuse of children. It stated that a child could not be repatriated if he or she was victim of human trafficking or had a viable asylum claim and did not voluntarily agree to be repatriated. This meant that rather than immediately returning Mexican children, ICE was supposed to evaluate each case individually.[13] Still, in 2009, 70 percent of children in ORR custody came from Central America, primarily El Salvador, Guatemala, and Honduras, as most Mexican children were still simply deported.[14]

The number of Mexican children crossing the border alone has remained steady or fallen over the past few years, along with crossings by Mexican adults. The number of young unaccompanied minors from Central America, in contrast, has risen dramatically, doubling from 2011 to 2012. "The rush of young illegal border crossers began last fall but picked up speed this year" reported the *New York Times* in August 2012.[15] During 2012, more than fourteen thousand youth, most of them Central American, had been taken into ORR custody. In just the first three months of 2013, seven thousand more crossed, suggesting that the record increases were continuing.[16]

Central America's political and economic crises—exacerbated by US military involvement and trade policies—virtually guarantee that children will continue to try to escape. "Almost all of the children's migration arose out of longstanding, complex problems in their home countries—problems that have no easy or short-term solutions."[17] According to the Women's Refugee Commission, which interviewed 150 young unaccompanied border-crossers, most are fleeing gangs, drug traffickers, and violence at home. "They are willing to risk the uncertain dangers of the trip north to escape certain dangers they face at home."[18]

"The conditions in Central America have deteriorated to such a point that, when the Women's Refugee Commission asked the children if they would risk the dangerous journey north through Mexico all over again now that they had direct knowledge of its risks, most replied that they would. They said that staying in their country would guarantee death, and that making the dangerous journey would at least give them a chance to survive. Many of them expressed a longing for their homelands, stating that they would not have left but for fear for their lives."[19]

The government was unprepared for the influx and was initially unable to abide by the 1997 standards. "Children were held for up to two weeks in CBP short-term hold facilities. These facilities are not designed for long-term detention or to hold children. The lights stay on 24 hours a day, and there are no showers or recreation spaces. During the influx, they were sometimes so overcrowded that children had to take turns just to lie down on the concrete floor." The ORR began to open "emergency surge centers" where it could hold detained youth.[20]

The numbers arriving at the US border reveal only part of the magnitude of the problem, since the Mexican government also reported a doubling in the numbers of detentions of Central American children traveling through that country in 2012.[21]

Perhaps only half of the children who leave Central America even make it to the US border. Along the way, they face the same hazards that older migrants face: injury or death on the train, kidnapping, rape, torture, coercion.

It is clear that conditions for children detained crossing the border have greatly improved in the past decade. It's also clear, though, that a situation in which tens of thousands of children flee their homelands in Mexico and Central America each year is a desperate one. It's not enough to suggest that those countries need to solve their own problems. The United States has a long history of military, political, and economic involvement in the region, including overthrowing and establishing governments. It continues to provide economic and military support for policies and programs that is has designed and approved. These policies and programs provide enormous profits and cheap products for US citizens and corporations, while exacerbating the very social crises that underlie the out-migration. Those of us in the United States need to seek deeper solutions that go beyond offering humane treatment and social services to these children after they cross the border.

LOSING THEIR PARENTS

Even children who are American citizens are at risk of losing undocumented parents to deportation. Although the Obama administration announced early on that immigration detention and deportation would focus on individuals who had committed crimes or were a threat to national security, deportations increased dramatically under his watch, to four hundred thousand a year. Almost all of those deported were, like most undocumented immigrants, members of communities with jobs, homes, and families. Their lives intersected every day with those of US citizens. In many cases, they were the parents of US citizens.

As with the number of children crossing the border, the number of children losing their parents to deportation has also been rising. From 1998 to 2007, some 8 percent of those removed from the country were parents of US citizens; in 2011, it was 22 percent of a much larger number of removals. During the first half of 2011, over forty-six thousand parents of US-citizen children were deported. The Applied Research Center estimated that as of 2011, there were over five thousand US citizen children living in foster care because their parents were either in immigration detention or had been deported. Some were put up for adoption as incarcerated or deported parents lacked the resources to enforce their parental rights.[22]

The term "anchor baby" is frequently thrown around in these discussions, with the implication that giving birth to a child in the United States gives the parent some special rights or privileges. It doesn't. The child, as a US citizen, has the right to all of the benefits that citizenship offers, including a US passport, freedom to remain in or leave the country, and access to work and social services. The undocumented status of the parent, however, is not ameliorated in any way by the existence of the so-called anchor baby. Parents of citizens can be, and are, deported on a regular basis.

The Obama administration's 2010 and 2011 Morton Memos on prosecutorial discretion, issued by ICE director John Morton to revise agency policy, acknowledged the hardships caused for children when their parents were detained or deported. The first memo suggested that ICE "should not expend detention resources on aliens who are known to be suffering from serious physical or mental illness, or who are disabled, elderly, pregnant, or nursing, or *demonstrate that they are primary caretakers of children* or an infirm person." Unfortunately, the new guidelines did not significantly reduce the numbers of parents separated from their children by ICE.[23] The 2011 memo went somewhat further, specifically mentioning that one factor that ICE should take into consideration when deciding whether to prosecute a case was the immigrant's relationship to US citizens. Still, this was one on a list of suggestions rather than a specific mandate.[24]

> Behind the statistics are the stories: a crying baby taken from her mother's arms and handed to social workers as the mother is handcuffed and taken away, her parental rights terminated by a U.S. judge; teenage children watching as parents are dragged from the family home; immigrant parents disappearing into a maze-like detention system where they are routinely locked up hundreds of miles from their homes, separated from their families for months and denied contact with the welfare agencies deciding their children's fate.[25]

Consider the case of Sandra Molina, an undocumented immigrant from Guatemala. She married an immigrant with legal status, who became a citizen in 2009. They had two children, both US citizens. When her husband became a citizen, they decided that Sandra should return to Guatemala so that he could sponsor her to come legally to the United States. Even in the case of the spouse of a US citizen, however, there is no guarantee that legal permission will be granted. In Sandra's case, it was denied, even though she had no criminal record or other apparent obstacle to legal entry.

She then attempted to cross the border illegally to reunite with her family, but was caught and returned to Guatemala. Now, legal entry became even more complicated. Reentry after deportation is a felony, punishable with jail time, and one of the Obama administration's priorities for deportation is those who reentered after being deported. In Mexico, Sandra "says she feels so hopeless about her life that she has thought about ending it. 'I just want to be forgiven,' she said, sobbing on the phone. 'I feel I am about to go crazy, I miss my children so much. They are all I have. I cannot go on without them.' Back home in Stamford, her children are suffering too. The youngest cried constantly, the eldest became angry and withdrawn. Though their plight is documented in thick files that include testimony from psychologists and counselors about their need for their mother, appeals for humanitarian relief were denied."[26]

The case of an undocumented Ecuadorian immigrant who was detained with her fifteen-year-old son illustrates the contradictions as different government agencies pursue conflicting goals. The mother had lived in the United States for four years and had a one-year-old daughter born here. She sent for her fifteen-year-old son, who was detained crossing the border and placed in DUCS custody. Following DUCS policy, she was called and her son was released to her. "I received a call to come pick him up," she explained from her prison cell, "so I left my daughter with my friend who lived next door, and took a bus to Arizona to get him. I picked up my son and we went straight to the bus. At the bus station, I was approached by some officers and they detained both of us. I have been here for nine months without seeing my baby girl. She was only one year old when I left her with my friend. I don't know what is happening with her."[27]

When parents disappear into the immigration system like this, they run the risk of losing custody of their children.[28] Courts may terminate parental rights after parents are deported or detained. In the criminal justice system, prisoners have guaranteed certain rights and access to services. Immigrant detainees, though, fall into a sort of constitutional and legal netherworld. The circumstances of their detention often make it impossible for them to comply with requirements for retaining custody of their children. Relatives who could care for a child in the parent's absence may be afraid to identify themselves because they too are undocumented. From the perspective of child welfare services, the system of detention and deportation can create insuperable obstacles to the goal of enabling parents to care for their children.[29] "In the child welfare system, immigrant parents are at risk of losing their children without the same constitutional due process protections in place that other parents receive."[30] An unknown number of those children are being put up for adoption against the wishes of their parents, who, once deported, are often helpless to fight when a US judge decides that their children are better off here.

In a 2007 case, an undocumented Guatemalan woman was arrested during a raid at the chicken plant where she worked in Missouri. While she was in detention, her six-month-old son was taken from her custody and put up for adoption. The judge ruled that "smuggling herself into a country illegally and committing crimes in this country is not a lifestyle that can provide any stability for a child." Her parental rights were terminated and the infant was adopted. Although the Missouri Supreme Court overturned the judge's decision in 2011, that ruling was in turn overturned by a judge who ruled that she had "effectively abandoned her son." The mother was deported, leaving the child with his adoptive parents in Missouri.[31]

LEARNING TO BE UNDOCUMENTED

Other undocumented children, some of the most politically active today, were brought or sent here by their parents at a young age. The United States is now raising a generation of children without documents, and the legal proposals to address their status, ranging from in-state tuition to the DREAM (Development, Relief, and Education for Alien Minors) Act, reveal the discomfort that their existence poses. "They are Americans in their heart, in their minds, in every single way but one: on paper," President Obama declared.[32] As one undocumented student put it, "I breathe, eat, and live in America and have done so since I can remember."[33] The president's remarks remind us that a person's birthplace is an almost entirely arbitrary fact. Should it really be used to determine his or her subsequent life chances?

Children, of course, don't usually know much about status and immigration law unless their parents choose to explain the status issue to them. Generally their main interaction with state authority is through school, and since 1982, schools have been required to treat all children equally, regardless of status. In that year, the US Supreme Court's *Plyler v. Doe* decision struck down a Texas law that allowed local school districts to deny entry to children who lacked legal documentation and withheld state funds for their education if local districts did choose to enroll them. The court ruled that to deny children access to education not only violated the Equal Protection Clause of the Fourteenth Amendment, but would impose an unwarranted, lifetime hardship on them and bring no benefit to the state.[34] Thus, children may never confront the issue of documentation in their daily lives.

Most citizens become aware of the importance of identification documents when they are teenagers and apply for a driver's license or for their first formal job. For the first time, they may be required to dig up a birth certificate or a Social Security card to prove their citizenship status. Jose Antonio Vargas, an undocumented immigrant from the Philippines, described the shock that many undocumented youth experience when they first become aware that there is something about their legal status that divides them from their peers. Vargas joined and propelled a growing movement among undocumented youth to break the silence, come out of the shadows, and openly challenge the system that excludes them.

In the summer of 2011, Vargas published a daring exposé of his own life story in the *New York Times Magazine*. He began by recounting how his mother sent him, at age twelve, to live with his grandparents in Mountain View, California, and how he struggled to learn English and excel at school.

> One day when I was 16, I rode my bike to the nearby D.M.V. office to get my driver's permit. Some of my friends already had their licenses, so I figured it was time. But when I handed the clerk my green card as proof of U.S. residency, she flipped it around, examining it. "This is fake," she whispered. "Don't come back here again."
>
> Confused and scared, I pedaled home and confronted [my grandfather] Lolo. I remember him sitting in the garage, cutting coupons. I dropped my bike and ran over to him, showing him the green card. *"Peke ba ito?"* I asked in Tagalog. ("Is this fake?") My grandparents were naturalized American citizens—he worked as a security guard, she as a food server—and they had begun supporting my mother and me financially when I was 3, after my father's wandering eye and inability to properly provide for us led to my parents' separation. Lolo was a proud man, and I saw the shame on his face as he told me he purchased the card, along with other fake documents, for me. "Don't show it to other people," he warned.[35]

The Philippines offers a particularly convoluted case of the meaning of immigration, citizenship, and documents, since it was a US colony for the first half of the twentieth century and Filipinos were unilaterally deemed to be US nationals who could travel freely to the mainland until 1934. (The category "national" was created early in the twentieth century to apply to people who lived in newly acquired US territories in the Caribbean and the Pacific. They were essentially stateless people, with no country and no citizenship.) Tens of thousands of Filipinos were recruited legally to the United States through nursing and military exchange programs after that, while the United States maintained an enormous military presence there.

Vargas's migration was a product of this history, as well as the twists and turns of US immigration law.

In the Philippines, Vargas's great aunt married a Filipino American who was serving in the US military, starting a family chain of migration. Using the family preferences built into the law, she petitioned for her brother and his wife (Vargas's grandparents), who entered the country on immigrant visas in 1984 and later became naturalized citizens. The grandfather then petitioned for his two children. Citizens, however, can only sponsor children who are unmarried. Vargas's mother was single; she and her husband had separated almost a decade earlier. But fearing that immigration would consider the petition fraudulent based on her previous marriage, the grandfather decided to withdraw it.

Then the family entered the netherworld of false documents, obtaining a doctored passport and green card (resident alien visa) and sending twelve-year-old Jose with a coyote—who, he was told, was his uncle—to live with his grandparents in 1993. The boy never knew of the extra-legal nature of these arrangements or that there was anything unauthorized about his presence in the United States.

Vargas's experience coming of age, symbolized by his rebuff at the DMV, falls within what sociologist Roberto Gonzalez describes as the "transition to adulthood" for many undocumented youth. As Gonzalez explains, becoming an adult also involves a "transition to illegality" as "public schooling and US immigration laws collide to produce a shift in the experiences and meanings of illegal status for undocumented youth at the onset of their transition to adulthood."[36] These youth, while treated equally under the law during their childhood, are excluded from the rites of passage that lead most American youth to the adult world. They are left in a "developmental limbo." The extremely low economic status of most undocumented families pushes young people to assume more financial responsibility than their documented peers, —but they are not, officially, allowed to work. At the same time, they are cut off from other stages in the transition to majority like learning to drive, registering to vote, undertaking postsecondary education, or opening a bank account.[37] It comes as a shock that the society that nurtured them suddenly closes its doors. One student wrote, "I did not think to question the pledge of allegiance or the history that was being taught to us. . . . Looking back, I should have questioned the allegiance I pledged every morning to a country that rejected me."[38]

YOUTH ACTIVISM

This generation of undocumented youth coming of age in today's United States is historically unprecedented. Most undocumented adults are individuals who were raised in another country and came here as adults. They knew life in their country of birth, and they came here of their own volition (but, of course, under historical circumstances that they did not choose). Their experience of life in the United States is that of being undocumented.

Their children, who may be undocumented as well, have a completely different life experience. They were raised and attended schools in this country, where they were repeatedly told that this is a nation of immigrants, a country that treats everybody equally. They were taught that if they worked hard, they could attend college and get a good job. They were taught that they had rights, because that's what the schools teach children in this country. They learned about Thoreau's "Civil Disobedience" and about Martin Luther King Jr. and struggles for racial justice and equality. At home, they were taught that their parents brought them here so that they could have a better life.

When Carola Suárez-Orozco, Marcelo Suárez-Orozco, and Irina Todorova studied several generations of immigrant youth and their experiences in US schools, they found that the immigrants of the first generation are the highest achievers. They are acutely aware of the sacrifices their parents made to provide more opportunities for them, and "these parental sacrifices propel many immigrant students to launch themselves wholeheartedly into their educational journey."[39]

Learning that they are undocumented and what that means is an unexpected and unacceptable shock to many of these children. They never felt or knew that they were any different from their classmates. Consider these testimonies from students: "It's almost like I am tied down to the ground with a ball and chain because I don't have citizenship"; "It's like someone giving you a car, but not putting any gas in it"; "They say you can accomplish whatever you want or set your mind to, but they don't say that it's just for some."[40]

Just as this new generation of undocumented youth was finishing high school, the 1996 Welfare Reform Act and IIRIRA made it almost impossible for them to go to college. By prohibiting them from receiving public financial aid and depriving them of state residency, the acts effectively shut the door to higher education.[41]

These youth have been at the forefront of organizing for immigrants' rights over the past decade. Access to higher education has been one focal organizing point for high-achieving students. At the state level, they fought for the right to be considered state residents and to attend public colleges and universities. At the national level, they fought for the DREAM Act, which would give them educational rights and also put them on a path to citizenship.

In Texas, Republican governor Rick Perry signed the first in-state tuition law in 2001, allowing undocumented students to be considered state residents for tuition purposes. California passed a similar law later the same year, and other states followed. As of mid-2013, fourteen states offered in-state tuition to qualified students who were undocumented.[42]

Some arguments about in-state tuition were strictly economic. Proponents explained that it would increase state revenues by allowing more individuals to enroll in state colleges and universities, while opponents feared that letting in the undocumented would reduce the seats available to citizen students. The number of students able to take advantage of these provisions has been small: as of 2005, there were 1,620 in the University of California and California State University systems and 5,100 in Texas, including the community college system, which accounted for about 80 percent of undocumented students.[43] The Massachusetts Taxpayers Foundation estimated that such a law would allow some 350 students a year to enroll in that state, again with the majority going to community colleges.[44]

In-state tuition has been a state-level struggle. Only the federal government could address the larger issue of status. The DREAM Act, proposed and defeated or abandoned numerous times at the federal level, would create a path to citizenship for certain undocumented youth. The different versions of the act vary slightly on specifics, but in general they address a population that has come to be known as the "DREAMers": young people between the ages of sixteen and thirty who were brought to the United States by their parents before they reached the age of sixteen—that is, as children—who may have crossed the border (or remained in the country) "illegally," but not through their own will or decision. The act would extend provisional legal status to such youth for six years. If they attend college or serve in the military for two years, their provisional status could be converted into a path to citizenship.[45] (Other individuals and organizations object to the military service provision, arguing that it is trying to create a de facto military draft for young Latinos, since most would not be able to afford college tuition even at in-state rates.)[46]

The Migration Policy Institute estimated in 2010 (based on 2006–2008 figures) that there were 2.1 million undocumented youth who were potential beneficiaries of the DREAM Act. Almost a million of these were under the age of eighteen.[47]

The DREAM Act was reintroduced repeatedly in both the US Senate and the House starting in 2001, and included in S. 2611, the Comprehensive Immigration Reform Act approved by the Senate in 2006 (later defeated in the House of Representatives), and S. 744, the Border Security, Economic Opportunity, and Immigration Modernization Act passed by the Senate in 2013.

Many advocates saw the rights of DREAMers as a front line in a larger struggle over the meaning of undocumentedness. By placing a sympathetic face—a high-achieving high school student—together with the term and the status of undocumented, they sought to challenge the better-known image associating the status with criminality.

Still, there was significant debate in the movement over this tactic. By emphasizing the innocence of students who were brought to the United States as young children with no choice in the matter, did the campaign tacitly accept the guilt of these students' parents, who had made the decision? Were the students being held up as exceptional, deserving, undocumented individuals, thus implying that other undocumented people were not deserving?

While some were wary of the way the DREAM Act seemed to skim off and privilege the most publicly acceptable portion of the undocumented population, most organizations believed that it was an opening to challenge the very concept of undocumentedness. Undocumented youth who grew up in the United States do not fit the profile that many citizens hold of the "illegal immigrant." Many of these youth feel motivated to take advantage of their relative privilege as English-speaking, assimilated, and educated members of US society to fight publicly against anti-immigrant and anti-undocumented sentiment.

The DREAM Act both responded to and created an outlet for a huge upsurge in organizing by undocumented youth.

Claudia Anguiano, who studied the history of undocumented student activism in depth, outlined three phases. From 2001 to 2007, "self-identification strategies were used to create a collective group identity that countered the negative dehumanizing typecast of 'illegal aliens' by identifying DREAMers as *exceptional students*." During the following two years, "self-representation strategies worked to unite undocumented youth through the creation of national coalitional organizations and through self-identification as *undocumented and unafraid*." Finally, during 2010, "activists utilized strategies of self-reliance and self-identified as *unapologetic DREAMers*. The strategies of intervention included the use of civil disobedience tactics to petition for the legislation."[48]

In 2009, DREAMers founded the organization United We Dream to coordinate nationally and use the tactic of coming out or telling their own stories as a political weapon. "Leaders realized that encouraging young people to recount the stories of their lives in hiding and of their thwarted aspirations could be liberating for them, and also compelling for skeptical Americans."[49] Taking inspiration from the gay rights movement, many have themselves and encouraged others to come out and hold public coming-out ceremonies. Jose Antonio Vargas suggested, in his defiantly titled essay "Not Legal, Not Leaving," that "we are living in the golden age of coming out."[50] Coming out can be a personal liberation, but it is also part of a larger project to insist on social and legal acceptance, which means fundamentally changing the legal structures of belonging in the country and challenging the beliefs that underlie and justify anti-immigrant sentiment.

DREAM activist Gaby Pacheco accompanied much of this process. Pacheco, like Jose Antonio Vargas and so many others, learned that she was undocumented when she went to apply for her learner's permit. She had come from Ecuador to Miami with her parents when she was about to start third grade.

She began to organize for the rights of undocumented students in 2004, founding Students for Immigrant Rights in Florida and working with the Florida Immigrant Coalition and Presente.org. "From four of us that used to meet to try to pass the DREAM Act, we now have 16 chapters throughout Florida. Students Working for Equal Rights is part of the United We Dream network, which is led by students and represents 26 states," she explained.[51]

In January 2010, Pacheco joined three other immigrant Florida students for a fifteen-hundred-mile march to Washington, DC, part of the ongoing and increasingly public campaign to press for the rights of the undocumented. "They said they had concluded that the exposure to immigration agents on the walk was not much greater than what they faced in their daily lives. 'We are aware of the risk,' [one participant] said . . . 'We are risking our future because our present is unbearable.'" ICE declined to comment on the issue.[52]

"Coming out didn't endanger me; it had protected me," wrote Vargas. "A Philippine-born, college-educated, outspoken mainstream journalist is not the face the government wants to put on its deportation program." He also wanted to use his case to publicize the arbitrary nature of immigration enforcement. "Who flies under the radar, and who becomes one of those unfortunate 396,906 [who are deported]? Who stays, who goes, and who decides?"[53]

A year after coming out, he recounted his attempt to find out what ICE planned to do about him.

> After months of waiting for something to happen, I decided that I would confront immigration officials myself. Since I live in New York City, I called the local ICE office. The phone operators I first reached were taken aback when I explained the reason for my call. Finally I was connected to an ICE officer.
>
> "Are you planning on deporting me?" I asked.

I quickly found out that even though I publicly came out about my undocumented status, I still do not exist in the eyes of ICE. Like most undocumented immigrants, I've never been arrested. Therefore, I've never been in contact with ICE.

"After checking the appropriate ICE databases, the agency has no records of ever encountering Mr. Vargas," Luis Martinez, a spokesman for the ICE office in New York, wrote me in an e-mail.

I then contacted the ICE headquarters in Washington. I hoped to get some insight into my status and that of all the others who are coming out. How does ICE view these cases? Can publicly revealing undocumented status trigger deportation proceedings, and if so, how is that decided? Is ICE planning to seek my deportation?

"We do not comment on specific cases," is all I was told.[54]

Amid increasingly visible activism and sympathetic media coverage, Congress took up the DREAM Act again at the end of 2010. Although it passed the House of Representatives, advocates could not muster enough votes to overcome a Senate filibuster.

Most Republicans opposed the DREAM Act in the 2010 vote, even some who had supported previous attempts. The House was about to be turned over to a Republican majority. For some DREAMers, it was time to shift away from a legislative strategy. "In a meeting after the vote with Senator Harry Reid of Nevada, the majority leader, Ms. [Gaby] Pacheco said she grabbed him and whispered in his ear. 'You know the president has the power to stop deporting us,' she said. 'You know you could tell him to do this.' Startled, Mr. Reid gave her a hug and walked away." In early 2011, United We Dream decided to change its focus to the president. At the National Council of La Raza meeting in Washington in July, when Obama tried to explain that he could not bypass Congress to push for immigrants' rights, DREAMers "erupted in shouts: 'Yes you can! Yes you can!'"[55]

Meanwhile, Obama's June 2011 Morton Memo specifically included DREAMers as a category meriting "prosecutorial discretion," essentially advising that ICE refrain from prosecuting them for immigration violations. (See chapter 8 for a more detailed discussion of prosecutorial discretion.) DREAMers saw this as a concession and an opening for further action.

In March 2012, Florida Republican—and potential vice presidential candidate—Marco Rubio announced that he was preparing to propose his own version of the DREAM Act. While reluctant to address specifics, Rubio emphasized that unlike previous versions of the act, his would not open a path to citizenship for undocumented youth. "I think that one of the debates that we need to begin to have is a difference between citizenship and legalization . . . You can legalize someone's status in this country with a significant amount of certainty about their future without placing them on a path toward citizenship, and I think that is something that we can find consensus on," Rubio explained. DREAM Act supporter and Democratic senator Harry Reid declared scornfully that this was a "watered-down version" that he would do "everything in his power" to oppose.[56]

Still, Democrats worried about ceding momentum—and possibly Latino votes—to the Republicans during an election year. DREAMers praised Rubio's step, and they continued to challenge Obama to take presidential action. In May, they presented the administration with a letter signed by over ninety law professors outlining legal precedents and steps that the president could take to halt deportations of undocumented youth.[57]

"[Rubio's] plan puts Obama in a box," the *Washington Post* reported. "Democrats are reluctant to see Rubio's efforts as anything other than a political gambit to repair his party's tarnished image with Hispanics and boost his own profile as a potential vice-presidential pick or future White House contender. But if Obama does not at least try to work with Rubio, he could risk losing a centerpiece of his appeal to Hispanic voters—that he is their fiercest ally in Washington and that the GOP is to blame for lack of action on fixing the country's immigration ills."[58]

In June, Obama regained the initiative for the Democrats when he announced his DACA program.

DACA

Much smaller than a comprehensive immigration reform, smaller even than the DREAM Act, DACA offered a two-year respite to young people who, Obama said, were American "in every single way but one: on paper." "We're a better nation than one that expels innocent young kids," he explained.[59] While his announcement was celebrated by many young undocumented immigrants and organizations that advocate for immigrant rights, it did not make those young people "American," and like the DREAM Act, it implicitly raised questions about the very nature of status and illegality that were uncomfortable for both DREAMers and their opponents.

DACA followed the DREAM Act in addressing people thirty and under who had arrived in the United States before age sixteen and had lived here continuously since 2007 and were in school, high school graduates, or veterans. (Vargas, who had just turned thirty-one, was thus excluded.) Unlike the DREAM Act, however, DACA did not open up a path to citizenship. It was limited to relief from deportation for two years and, during those two years, permission to work.

The Pew Hispanic Center estimated that up to 1.4 million youth would be eligible for DACA, half of them under eighteen and half eighteen to thirty and either enrolled in school or high school graduates. Seventy percent of these were from Mexico. Together, DACA candidates represented just over 10 percent of undocumented immigrants in the United States.[60]

During the first month (August 16 to September 15), US Citizen and Immigration Services (USCIS) received 82,361 applications.[61] A month later, the agency announced that 179,794 DACA applications had been received, and 4,591 approved.[62] By April 2013, the USCIS reported a total 488,782 received, and 472,004 approved. The vast majority of applicants were from Mexico (354,002), followed by El Salvador (18,949), Honduras (12,603), and Guatemala (11,817).[63]

Grace Meng from Human Rights Watch pointed out that DACA was aimed at only a certain sector of immigrant youth. "The program's idea of 'American' is unlikely to include the children who picked the oranges for your juice or the tomatoes on your hamburgers," she explained. The children of migrant farm workers, she points out, are more likely to be out of school—they drop out at four times the national average—and less likely to have the documentation of continuous presence required to qualify for DACA. It is clear, Meng writes, that

> the program of deferred action was not designed for child farmworkers who, like many immigrants throughout U.S. history, live very different lives than middle-class, suburban kids. . . . It's not surprising that the Obama administration designed a program for the best and the brightest immigrant children. But the fact that deferred action will probably exclude many farmworker children underscores how much immigration law is out of sync with the reality of an economy that depends on unauthorized immigrants.[64]

By proposing an immigration reform—whether one as far-reaching as the DREAM Act or one as limited as DACA—for this restricted group of people, policymakers and advocates suggested that this group—and, implicitly but inevitably, not other groups—deserved access to some sort of legal status. By recognizing these young people as American, the implication was that other undocumented people were not American, but rather irredeemably foreign. If these young people were defined as innocent—because they were brought to the United States by their parents before they were old enough to make an independent decision—then their parents, who made the decision and brought them, were by implication guilty.

When Senators Robert Menendez (D-New Jersey), Dick Durbin (D-Illinois), and Harry Reid (D-Nevada) introduced a recent version of the DREAM Act in May 2011, they presented it in precisely those terms. The act, Reid claimed, was for "children brought to this nation by their parents through no fault of their own." "We should not punish children for their parents' past decisions," Menendez added. Senator Ben Cardin (D-Maryland) agreed that "we should not hold innocent children responsible for the sins of their parents."[65]

Many children found it difficult to accept the logic that counterpoised their own innocence with their parents' guilt. As one DREAMer protested, "I was brought to this country by a very courageous woman. She's my hero. She's my mother. She left everyone and everything she knew behind in order for her to give me a better life. . . . I'm not going to blame her. . . . I thank her for bringing me here."[66]

Referring to the internal border that separates the undocumented from the rest of US society, another DREAMer wrote,

> Is it possible that DACA is also perpetuating this internal border? DACA passed largely due to the pressure that was being put on politicians and President Obama by DREAMers. But, I began to question, what else could have influenced the passing of DACA? The strong movement of DREAMers started getting exposure to the general public of the country and the movement made many people question why these students . . . were being punished. DREAMers began to make this internal border visible to the country. . . . In order

for the United States to keep perpetuating undocumentedness as an unwanted and illegal "thing," they chose to help us
in a way that keeps us in the same state of second-class citizenship with a nicer title and stops the general public from
continuing to ponder this question. . . . Undocumentedness
allows the country to keep its cheap labor and discriminate
against non-whites. And, with undocumented students out of
the immediate picture of undocumentedness, the continual
perpetuation of undocumented people as outsiders can continue to thrive.[67]

Many argued that DACA was a first step rather than a solu-
tion. "'By having this relief and having access to greater resources
we can begin to push harder for relief for the entire community,'
said Lorella Praeli, advocacy director of the group United We
Dream. 'This fight for DREAMers in our community has never
been about ourselves. . . . It's been about our families.'"[68] Just a
month after the 2012 election, United We Dream agreed upon a
new platform demanding "an inclusive pathway to citizenship."
A *New York Times* reporter described the meeting:

> Their decision to push for legal status for their families was in-
> tensely emotional. When they were asked at a plenary session
> how many had been separated by deportation from a parent or
> other close family member, hundreds of hands went up. They
> were critical of Mr. Obama for deporting more than 1.4 million
> people during his first term.
>
> "When Obama is deporting all these people, separating all
> of our families, I'm sick and tired of that," said Regem Corpuz,
> a 19-year-old student at the University of California, Los An-
> geles, who was born in the Philippines.
>
> "Our families' dreams were to get a better future," said
> Ulises Vasquez of Sonoma County, Calif., "but our future is
> with our families together."

At the meeting, several parents followed their children's lead and held a coming-out ceremony to tell their stories publicly for the first time.[69]

Other contradictions plagued DACA as well. Presidential candidate Mitt Romney announced that, if elected, he would immediately halt the program upon taking office, though he said he would not revoke the status of those who had already been approved. With Obama's election, the program seemed secure at least for the two years initially announced. But many of those who it was designed to help found themselves caught in the multiple contradictions of the immigration system, which DACA could not transcend.

For many young immigrants, the very documents they needed to supply to prove that they fulfilled the program's requirements were precisely those that they lacked. As the *New York Times* asked, "How do you document an undocumented life?" Particularly difficult were work records. For those who worked off the books and were paid in cash, no records documented the transactions. For those who used false Social Security numbers, submitting the evidence incriminated them in another crime. Moreover, employers were reluctant to unearth or provide records that could implicate them, too, in legal problems.[70]

Furthermore, DACA did not affect the actions of ICE, which was pursuing deportation cases against a significant number of potential recipients. Instead, it placed two branches of the Department of Homeland Security against each other: while USCIS administered DACA, ICE attorneys were still charged with pursuing deportation cases. With 325,000 cases pending in its backlogged system, ICE found itself prosecuting—and even deporting—young people, even as USCIS was reviewing or approving their applications for deferred action.[71]

Obama also disappointed many DREAMers when he announced that DACA recipients would be excluded from federal health-care programs under the Affordable Care Act (includ-

ing Medicaid and federal subsidies for purchasing private insurance), even though immigrants deemed "lawfully present"
were eligible. The *New York Times* noted ironically that "immigrants granted such relief [i.e., Deferred Action] would or-
dinarily meet the definition of 'lawfully present' residents. . . .
But the administration issued a rule in late August that specifically excluded the young immigrants from the definition of
'lawfully present.'"[72]

The Department of Homeland Security left it up to individual states to decide whether people with DACA status
could obtain a driver's license or receive state-level benefits
like in-state tuition at state colleges and universities. Arizona's governor declared that DACA youth were not eligible for
driver's licenses, while Massachusetts became the first state
to make them eligible for in-state tuition. In Michigan, the
Secretary of State's office announced that DACA youth would
not be able to obtain a driver's license. "We rely on the federal
government to tell us who is here legally; we don't determine
that," the office explained. "So far, the federal government has
not provided information to the states indicating that DACA
grants that legal status." As one Michigan DACA recipient
put it wryly, "I'm caught in this situation where I can go to
work, I can go to school, I'm legal here, but I can't go to work
and can't go to school."[73]

As President Obama celebrated his victory in the 2012
election, he highlighted immigrant youth. "We believe in a
generous America, in a compassionate America, in a tolerant
America open to the dreams of an immigrant's daughter who
studies in our schools and pledges to our flag, to the young boy
on the south side of Chicago who sees a life beyond the nearest
street corner, to the furniture worker's child in North Carolina
who wants to become a doctor or a scientist, an engineer or
an entrepreneur, a diplomat or even a president," the president
proclaimed stirringly.

"Obama was very clearly referencing the immigrant youth who he's supported with his backing of the DREAM Act and deferred action," said Julianne Hing, *Colorlines* immigration reporter. "But it should be noted that his support came largely because immigrant youth have put his feet to the fire and relentlessly demanded more humane treatment of undocumented youth and their families."[74] The Senate's comprehensive immigration reform bill (S. 744) passed in June 2013 included the most generous version yet of the DREAM Act, but as the bill subsequently stalled in the House, the future for immigrant youth remained as uncertain as ever.

CHAPTER 8

Solutions

In order to talk about solutions, we have to understand the real roots and nature of the problem. Many politicians and others who see immigration control as an issue of security and sovereignty imagine that hordes of poor people of color are seeking to appropriate the resources of this land that we now call the United States. This formulation of the problem is a precise reversal of the actual European settlement of the country, from the perspective of the Native Americans.

It is also a mirror image of the United States' relationship with the countries—primarily Mexico, Central America, and other Latin American countries—from which the undocumented come. In every case, the products and profits accumulated in the sending countries are a major source of the abundance and affluence in the United States. A quick review of any supermarket or clothing or electronics store reveals the Third World and often Latin American origins of many of the products we consume. More invisible are the mines, oil wells, multinationals, and profits behind the products. But the flow of resources is undeniable.

The history that is drummed into the heads of US schoolchildren insists that the "country of immigrants" was founded and built by Europeans. The invisible underside of this narrative is the imperial narrative of conquest and dispossession that continued until the end of the nineteenth century and upon which the new "country of [white] immigrants" was built.

The country-of-immigrants narrative is very much a narrative of race. Immigrants were conceived as white Europeans (the only people allowed to naturalize), and their presence and comfort depended upon the labor of people who were legally excluded from the polity. Throughout the nineteenth and much of the twentieth centuries, Mexicans, like African Americans prior to 1868, were accepted as a necessary evil for their labor and considered unthreatening to the white nature of the country that viewed them as exploitable workers rather than as potential citizens. The history of reliance on Mexican labor coupled with the refusal to grant rights to Mexican workers is a long one indeed.

The Treaty of Guadalupe Hidalgo and the Gadsden Purchase (La Mesilla Purchase of 1853) offered US citizenship to Mexican citizens resident in the territories newly taken. By specifying "Mexican citizens," the laws excluded the Native American population resident in the area. And by offering citizenship to Mexicans at a time when citizenship was restricted to whites, the laws implied that Mexicans would be considered white. In the midcentury, then, "it was possible . . . to be both white *and* Mexican in the United States."[1] However, as Katherine Benton-Cohn explains in her detailed study of four Arizona border towns, Mexican nationality became racialized as nonwhite during the nineteenth century through work. Where Mexicans were workers, rather than landholders, they came to be legally defined as racially Mexican and disqualified from citizenship.

"Where Mexicans owned ranches and farms, racial categories were blurry and unimportant. But in the industrial copper-mining town of Bisbee, Mexican workers were segregated economically by their lower pay ('Mexican wage') and geographically by new town-planning experiments. To most non-Mexican residents of Bisbee, Mexicans were peon workers or potential public charges, not neighbors or business partners, not co-workers or co-worshipers, and certainly not potential marriage partners." In these areas, where Mexicans became defined as racially Mexican through their laboring status, "'American' increasingly equaled 'white,' and so 'Mexican' came to mean the opposite of both."[2]

Nicolas De Genova notes the "longstanding equation of Mexican migration with a presumably temporary, disposable (finally, deportable) labor migration predominated by men (who were predominantly single or left wives and children behind)."[3] The 1911 Dillingham US Immigration Commission argued that "while [Mexicans] are not easily assimilated, this is of no very great importance as long as most of them return to their native land. In the case of the Mexican, he is less desirable as a citizen than as a laborer."[4] "One way or the other, then," De Genova concludes, "US policy would ensure that 'most of them' proved to be sojourners."[5]

The laws that restricted citizenship to whites did not restrict the right to work to whites. On the contrary, Congress has repeatedly created new categories of nonwhite people who were specifically cast as workers. (Slave laborers comprised the original worker-but-not-potential-citizen category.) Deportability became a crucial factor in cementing the association between Mexican-ness as a race and legal status as a temporary worker. The threat of deportation worked to institutionalize the fragile character of Mexicans' claims to rights in the land where they came, invited, to work. It could be used to accommodate the changing needs of employers, and it could also be used to discourage union organizing or other forms of social protest.[6] Until the 1960s, racial justifications seemed sufficient for legal discrimination against Mexicans.

MAKING IMMIGRATION ILLEGAL

After the 1960s, when race was finally rejected as a rationale for excluding people from access to public spaces, citizenship, or entry into the United States, new forms of legal and legalized exclusion took its place. The last two major immigration reforms, in 1965 and 1986, turned Mexican migrant workers into "illegal" workers and used that legal status to justify discrimination. They also, paradoxically, helped to greatly increase both the immigrant and the undocumented population.

The 1965 law is generally seen as a civil rights triumph. One typical account explains that it "ended discrimination" and "represented a significant watershed in US immigration history and particularly in its explicit reversal of decades of systematically exclusive and restrictive immigration policies." Immigration scholars agree that the climate of the civil rights movement of the 1960s set the context for the 1965 immigration reform.[7]

Despite this generous interpretation, the 1965 law was actually "distinctly and unequivocally restrictive" when it came to Mexican migrants.[8] Through the 1950s and early 1960s, hundreds of thousands of Mexicans were crossing the border as braceros or alongside the braceros each year. Then the Bracero Program was ended and Mexican immigration was suddenly capped. By 1976, a cap of twenty thousand immigrant visas a year was enforced. The seasonal, circular migration of Mexicans over many decades that had attracted little national attention suddenly became "a yearly and highly visible violation of American sovereignty by hostile aliens who were increasingly framed as invaders and criminals."[9]

If the new restrictions were intended to lower migration from Latin America, they failed miserably. Instead, all types of immigration from Latin America rose after 1965: temporary and permanent, legal and illegal. Legal immigration from Latin America grew from about 450,000 between 1950 and 1960 to over 4 million between 1990 and 2000, while the number of undocumented Latin Americans living long term in the United States grew from almost none in 1965 to close to 10 million in the first decade of the new century.[10]

Further "unintended consequences" flowed from the greatly increased border enforcement of the 1990s and 2000s. As border crossing became more difficult, more dangerous, and more expensive, seasonal migrants began to change their patterns and stay on in the United States, sometimes bringing their families as well. The undocumented population grew rapidly in those decades, not because more immigrants were arriving, but because fewer were leaving. "It was thus a sharp decline in the outflow of undocumented migrants, not an increase in the inflow of undocumented migrants, that was responsible for the acceleration of undocumented population growth during the 1990s and early 2000s, and this decline in return migration was to a great extent a product of US enforcement efforts."[11]

Starting in 1990, a series of laws made life even more difficult for noncitizens, including green-card holders (legal permanent residents). Family reunification privileges favored citizens over legal permanent residents. In 1996, legal permanent residents were barred from receiving most social services, while the Antiterrorism and Effective Death Penalty Act made noncitizens deportable for a wide range of crimes, even if they had been committed in a distant past. Then, in 2001, the USA-PATRIOT Act made deportation and arrest possible for virtually any noncitizen, based only upon the US Attorney General's decision.[12]

In response to the increasingly punitive climate for noncitizens, more immigrants chose to naturalize. As new citizens, they were now able to take advantage of the family preferences created by the 1965 law and petition for their family members, thus contributing to an increase in overall immigration.[13]

STRUCTURAL CAUSES OF INCREASED MIGRATION

While US legislative changes played a large role in increasing both documented and undocumented immigration, the enormous political and economic convulsions that wracked Latin America in the post-1965 era and the shifts in the global economy were also important. Political movements for social change were crushed as a wave of extraordinarily repressive right-wing dictatorships spread through the continent. Supply-side economics and structural adjustment programs tore apart social safety networks and spurred export-oriented extraction and production. The new policies disrupted traditional economies while creating expectations and hopes that couldn't be fulfilled at home. Meanwhile, both consumption and inequality shot up in the United States, creating massive demand for cheap immigrant workers. Globalizing technologies and migration chains transformed the possibility of migration from remote to realistic. The forces behind the rise in Latin American, especially Mexican and Central American, migration were multiple indeed.

Even as US politicians railed about illegal immigration and border control, they pursued policies that served to increase migrant flows. Policies imposed on Latin America that destroy subsistence farming and degrade agricultural work, and limit employment opportunities and social services, set the stage for out-migration. Policies at home that create demand for low-wage, immigrant workers and establish recruitment networks structure the destinations of migrant flows. These are precisely the policies that the United States has implemented.

Over the past century, the United States has consistently promoted export-oriented economies in Latin America based on foreign investment. It has opposed and overthrown Latin American governments that have tried to take control of or redistribute their countries' resources. During recent decades, US policies promoting neoliberal austerity measures and market fundamentalism have had noxious effects on Latin American society. They undermine subsistence agriculture, employment, and the social safety network, while increasing structural and individual violence in Latin America. The United States has used international institutions, military interventions, trade agreements, and corporate privilege to arrive at a situation in which it, with 4 percent of the world's population, consumes between 25 percent and 50 percent of the planet's major resources, while simultaneously creating an enormous demand for low-wage, informal, and seasonal labor. Thus, the United States continues to set the stage for large migrations from Latin America.[14]

Perhaps the advocates of border control believe that while the open border worked in the past, these structural changes have made it untenable in today's world. A focus on securing—or more accurately, militarizing—the border, though, only serves to reinforce the structural conditions behind migration. As Jacqueline Stevens argues, "Illegitimate regimes benefit from the restrictive immigration policies of their neighbors. In most countries run by tyrants, emigration is not curtailed by the regimes themselves, which often lack the resources to police wide swaths of their borders. Rather, neighboring countries fearing the incursion of political and economic refugees take care of this."[15]

In the case of the United States and Latin America, Stevens's argument must be refined. It is not pure coincidence that poor and violent countries in Latin America coexist alongside the overconsuming United States. Deliberate US policies, from invasions and occupations to military aid to loans and investments, have created the Latin American polities and economies and the disparities that are now the roots of today's migrations. Attempts to seal the border only reinforce the very inequalities that contribute to migration.

CHALLENGING DISCRIMINATION

The campaigns to strengthen immigration law and make it harsher are fairly well known and have been related to the successive punitive measures against undocumented immigrants since the 1980s. But organizations that defended the rights of immigrants and, in particular, the undocumented also grew in the last decades of the twentieth century.[16]

While nativism has been part of US society and culture since the country was founded, specifically anti-*undocumented* sentiment and movements date to the post-1965 and especially the post-1986 period. The Republican Party first mentioned immigration enforcement in its 1980 national platform and in 1984 first "affirmed the right of the United States to control its boundaries and voiced concern about illegal immigration." The Democratic Party first mentioned illegal immigration in its 1996 platform.[17] Popular movements for the defense of the rights of the undocumented also grew this period.

Mexican American rights organizations like LULAC have taken mixed stances on the undocumented and even on immigrants in general over the course of the twentieth century. Mexican Americans sought to claim their rights by demonstrating their patriotism and distancing themselves from new arrivals, even as their communities, friends, and families included both documented and undocumented new immigrants.[18] Even the United Farm Workers union, made up primarily of immigrants, was hesitant to defend the rights of the undocumented.

However, Mexican American rights, immigrant rights, and the rights of the undocumented have also been intertwined. The Chicano movement of the 1960s and '70s rejected the emphasis on patriotism and assimilation of earlier generations, and insisted on a cultural nationalism that united people of Mexican origin, regardless of status. (The movement adopted the name Chicano to emphasize the indigenous roots of Mexicans and the difference in their historical experience from that of European immigrants.) "Chicano families became the new underground railroad," explained Alma Martínez evocatively, referring to the ties that bound US-born Chicanos to new, including undocumented, immigrants.[19] Even as politicians and the media raised their voices against the undocumented, networks and organizations grew to defend their rights.

In the 1980s, growing numbers of Central American refugees joined the ranks of what had previously been primarily a Mexican phenomenon. The sanctuary movement, growing primarily out of Central American refugee organizations and Anglo religious congregations, sought to aid Salvadoran and Guatemalan refugees in the United States without legal status. Some organizations were made up of refugees themselves, like the Central American Refugee Center (CARECEN, later changed to Central American Resource Center), founded in 1983. These and other organizations concerned with the rights of Salvadoran (and to a lesser extent, Guatemalan) refugees were the first to bring the question of the rights of the undocumented into the public sphere. They also emphasized how US intervention was behind much of the violence that was causing people to flee Central America.

A series of lawsuits focused specifically on the right to asylum, reflecting these organizations' concern with the situation of Central American refugees. *Orantes-Hernandez v. Meese* and *Perez-Funes v. District Director* both required the INS to strengthen Central Americans' right to seek and obtain asylum in the mid-1980s. Finally, in 1990, *American Baptist Church v. Thornburgh* required the INS to reopen asylum cases that had been unfairly denied. The organizations pushing the lawsuits also worked to end US military aid to El Salvador. Their focus was on the Central American crisis and its victims, more than on the issue of undocumentedness per se.

THE FIRST COMPREHENSIVE REFORM

The 1986 Immigration Reform and Control Act (IRCA) was comprehensive in the same way that twenty-first-century proposals for comprehensive reform were. It combined enforcement—in the form of employer sanctions and increased border security—with legalization or amnesty. The rationale was that by legalizing some of the undocumented population, encouraging others to leave (through employer sanctions that would make it more difficult for them to work), and making it more difficult for further undocumented people to enter the country, the numbers of the undocumented should be significantly reduced.

IRCA had complicated implications for the undocumented. For those who could document presence since 1982 or eligibility for Special Agricultural Worker Status, the chance to obtain legal status was priceless. (As discussed earlier, the law also created a black market of falsified papers trying to document eligibility.) The employer sanctions provisions of the law, however, created a new system for marginalizing and discriminating against the undocumented. By offering legal status to some, but not all of the undocumented, IRCA (like the DREAM Act and DACA) invited even more pernicious racism against those it left out.

The National Network for Immigrant and Refugee Rights was established in 1986, growing out of a coalition that coalesced in 1985 to organize a National Day of Justice for Immigrants and Refugees in opposition to legislative proposals for employer sanctions for the hiring of undocumented workers, which was incorporated in the 1986 IRCA. Following the passage of the law, new organizations like the New York Immigrant Coalition and the Massachusetts Immigrant and Refugee Advocacy Coalition formed both to help undocumented immigrants gain legal status and to challenge discriminatory aspects of the enforcement of employer sanctions (and sometimes the notion of employer sanctions itself).

Despite its supposed comprehensiveness, IRCA did not live up to its claims. Around 1.7 million immigrants became legalized through IRCA provisions, which succeeded in reducing the total undocumented population by that number. However, the gradual net inflow of undocumented people did not seem to change much. As Karen Woodrow and Jeffrey Passel explain, "The entire decrease in the undocumented population from 3.1 million in 1986 to 1.9 million in 1988 is attributable to . . . formerly undocumented immigrants changing their status to legal residents under the provisions of the IRCA."[20] In other words, the law led to neither an increased outflow nor a reduced inflow of undocumented immigrants. In fact, "after this group [those who legalized] is taken into account, our research suggests that the remaining undocumented population may actually have increased between June 1986 and June 1988. . . . Thus *IRCA has not cut off the flow of new undocumented immigrants to the United States.*"[21]

The AFL-CIO supported employer sanctions in 1986. But as Jeff Stansbury wrote a few years later, "The IRCA is not a border-control law," rather, it is "a worker-control law." In the words of Asian Law Caucus staff attorney Bill Tamayo, "The new law has codified the existence of a cheap and highly exploitable class of labor, largely non-white and non-English-speaking, with little rights, if any." And employers lost no time in using the law as a weapon against workers who tried to organize unions.[22] In 2000, the AFL-CIO reversed its stance and called for a repeal of employer sanctions.[23] AFL-CIO executive vice president Linda Chavez-Thompson explained, "Employers often knowingly hire workers who are undocumented, and then when workers seek to improve working conditions employers use the law to fire or intimidate workers."[24]

Proponents of employer sanctions argued that by making it more difficult for undocumented immigrants to find work, the law would discourage them from migrating to begin with. For Mexicans contemplating migration, though, employer sanctions did not appear to loom very large. In one important study of Mexican sending communities in 1990, "Interviewees made it clear that having a job in the United States is far more important to them than any law the US Congress might pass: If they have a solid job prospect, they will migrate, with or without papers. Our field studies suggest that the robust growth in employment opportunities in the United States in the second half of the 1980s has been at least as important in fueling the current wave of emigration as the effects of Mexico's lingering economic crisis."[25]

THE ANTI-IMMIGRANT 1990S

In the 1990s, explicitly anti-undocumented or anti-illegal mobilization took off, especially in California, where Proposition 13 in 1978 had decimated state finances. Under Governor Pete Wilson, "illegal" immigrants became a convenient scapegoat.[26] Proposition 187 in 1994 was the first of many state- and nationwide efforts to impose austerity on the backs of the most vulnerable. Nicknamed "Save Our State," it sought primarily to bar the undocumented from receiving public services. The text of the proposed law began by stating: "The People of California find and declare as follows: That they have suffered and are suffering economic hardship caused by the presence of illegal aliens in this state. That they have suffered and are suffering personal injury and damage caused by the criminal conduct of illegal aliens in this state. That they have a right to the protection of their government from any person or persons entering this country unlawfully."[27] Wilson "made undocumented immigration the cornerstone of his 1994 re-election campaign."[28] Proposition 187's language and rationale became widespread in the anti-undocumented movement in subsequent years.

Many of Proposition 187's provisions were never enacted, being tied up or rejected in the courts. However, as California goes, so goes the nation. After the Democrat Bill Clinton became president in 1993, Wilson connected anti-immigrant with anti-Washington bombast, claiming that the federal government had failed to protect the country's borders. Wilson's attacks helped to push Clinton to the right on border enforcement, as Clinton sought to woo California's apparently increasingly anti-immigrant electorate.[29]

Anti-"illegal" rhetoric mirrored and intertwined with a growing anti-black, anti–civil rights backlash in multiple ways. It replaced explicitly racialized language with a two-pronged attack against people of color. First, starting with the 1980 election, conservatives "repeatedly raised the issue of welfare, subtly framing it as a context between hardworking blue-collar whites and poor blacks who refused to work."[30] Second was rhetoric about law and order.[31] "The shift to a general attitude of 'toughness' toward problems associated with communities of color began in the 1960s. . . . By the late 1980s, however, not only conservatives played leading roles in the get-tough movement, spouting the rhetoric once associated only with segregationists. Democratic politicians and policy makers were now attempting to wrest control of the crime and drug issues from Republicans by advocating stricter anti-crime and anti-drug laws—all in an effort to win back the so-called 'swing voters' who were defecting to the Republican Party."[32]

By the end of 1993, "politicians began tripping over one another to take a tough stance on boundary enforcement and unauthorized migration."[33] In 1994, President Clinton implemented Operation Gatekeeper to bring the border "under control" and undercut Pete Wilson's protagonism by taking the lead on border enforcement as the elections approached.[34] In 1996, Clinton pressed for punitive Welfare Reform and Immigration Reform laws that enacted federally much of what California had tried to do at the state level. With these laws, Clinton made both welfare reform and law and order centerpieces of the Democratic Party program, and linked the anti-black and the anti-immigrant aspects of these policies. In the panic following the 9/11 attacks, the USA-PATRIOT Act of 2001 and the subsequent creation of the Department of Homeland Security in

2003 strengthened both institutional controls against potential and current immigrants, as well as the ideological climate of anti-immigrant sentiment.

Joseph Nevins argues that the government's increasing attention to border enforcement in the 1990s actually served to *create* the supposed immigration crisis. Through its sensationalist rhetoric and justifications, as well as its ostentatious enforcement policies, the state helped to convince the population that such a crisis indeed existed.[35]

Republicans were torn between their traditional allies in the business community—who had little incentive to join the anti-"illegal" hysteria—and the new right-wing populism. Texas went the opposite direction from California in the 1990s. "In Texas, the economy was booming; the suburbs of Dallas, Houston, Austin, and San Antonio were exploding; and thousands of illegal immigrants sat astride two-by-fours, nail guns in hand, building those neighborhoods. So, then-governor Bush and his man Karl Rove crafted a different strategy from their California colleagues: Hispanic-friendly. The result? In 1998, George W. Bush crushed his Democratic opponent, getting nearly half the Hispanic vote—a triumph that placed him on the path to the presidency one year later."[36] In 2001, Texas Republican governor Rick Perry's decision to sign the nation's first in-state tuition law in 2001 represented the crest of the pro-immigrant wave.

A decade later Texas Republicans had gone the way of their California colleagues. Texas Republicans promoted a redistricting plan and voter identification law that federal courts struck down as discriminatory. As late as 2010, Perry declared that a law like Arizona's S.B. 1070 "would not be the right direction for Texas."[37] By 2012, however, he was defending Arizona. "No state should be held hostage to a federal government that refuses to enforce the laws of the land. . . . The people of Arizona took action consistent with federal law and in direct response to the failure of this administration to secure our nation's borders. The absence of federal action on immigration enforcement directly spoils the integrity of our nation's laws."[38] Moreover, Perry was pushing for a Texas version of this legislation, banning sanctuary cities that would prevent local law enforcement agencies from enforcing federal immigration law.[39]

"COMPREHENSIVE" VERSUS "ENFORCEMENT ONLY" IN THE NEW CENTURY

In January 2004, president and candidate George W. Bush had lauded the country's immigrant history in a speech whose audience included representatives of LULAC and other Hispanic organizations. Bush acknowledged the country's need for migrant workers and expressed great sympathy for the undocumented:

> Reform must begin by confronting a basic fact of life and economics: Some of the jobs being generated in America's growing economy are jobs American citizens are not filling. Yet these jobs represent a tremendous opportunity for workers from abroad who want to work and to fulfill their duties as a husband or a wife, a son or a daughter. Their search for a better life is one of the most basic desires of human beings. Many undocumented workers have walked mile after mile, through the heat of the day and the cold of the night. Some have risked their lives in dangerous desert border crossings or entrusted their lives to the brutal rings of heartless human smugglers. Workers who seek only to earn a living end up in the shadows of American life, fearful, often abused and exploited. When they're victimized by crimes they're afraid to call the police or seek recourse in the legal system. They are cut off from their families far away, fearing if they leave our country to visit relatives back home they might never be able to return to their jobs.

Thus, Bush proposed offering temporary legal status to all undocumented workers in the country. Although he emphasized that the status would be temporary—initially for three years, but renewable—he also emphasized that those who wanted to apply for citizenship should also be allowed to do so.[40]

Several congressional proposals for so-called comprehensive immigration reform were launched in the first decade of the new century: John McCain and Ted Kennedy's Secure America and Orderly Immigration Act (S. 1033) in 2005; John Cornyn and Jon Kyl's Comprehensive Enforcement and Immigration Reform Act (S. 1438), also in 2005; Arlen Specter's Comprehensive Immigration Reform Act (S. 2611), which passed the Senate in 2006; and finally the Comprehensive Immigration Reform Act or Secure Borders, Economic Opportunity and Immigration Reform Act of 2007 (S. 1348), which drew on the earlier three and was promoted by Senators McCain, Kennedy, and Kyl, as well as then-president Bush. The right-wing reaction against the concept they termed amnesty gained political traction and contributed to the failure of these measures, even though all of them incorporated strong anti-immigrant measures euphemistically called enforcement components. Rarely was it pointed out that the combination of legalization and enforcement pioneered in 1986 had been followed by a huge increase in the size of the undocumented population. The proposals were generally critiqued from the right rather than from the left. Comprehensive reform, willy-nilly, had become the rallying cry of political liberals and supporters of immigrant rights.

While these comprehensive approaches stalled, the House passed an extraordinarily punitive piece of legislation that epitomized what came to be called the enforcement-only approach, H.R. 4437, the Border Protection, Antiterrorism, and Illegal Immigration Control Act of 2005. This vote became a catalyst for a new level of immigrant rights mobilization, the huge demonstrations in the spring and especially on May 1, 2006.

NEW PROTESTS IN THE NEW CENTURY

The major academic study of the 2006 demonstrations points out that they dwarfed even the largest protest movements in the country's history, which only occasionally reached a half-million protesters. "In a short span of twelve weeks between mid-February and early May 2006, an estimated 3.7 million to 5 million people took to the streets in over 160 cities across the United States to rally for immigrant rights."[41] The protests were also unique in being carried out within the political system but primarily by people legally excluded from the polity—the undocumented.

Local activist organizations, hometown associations, and unions as well as Spanish media and the Catholic Church played important roles in disseminating publicity and motivating participants. "Radio show hosts and DJs on popular Spanish-language radio stations across the country endorsed the marches and encouraged listeners to attend. In addition, the two main Spanish-language networks, Univisión and Telemundo, pro-moted it through public service announcements broadcast during popular evening newscasts, regular reporting on the preparations for the marches and interviews with march organizers during newscasts, and frequent informal banter during talk-show and variety show formats, even incorporating the subject into the plotlines of their *telenovelas,* or soap operas."[42] National-level or-ganizations took a backseat as different coalitions mobilized in different cities.[43] The culmination of these many protests was on May 1, when a coordinated day-without-an-immigrant protest brought walkouts and business closings throughout the country to illustrate the importance of immigrants to the economy and their role in citizens' daily lives.

Another thing the immigrant and undocumented communi-ties had in their favor were the reformers in the labor movement who pushed for more pro-immigrant, and pro-undocumented positions. In the fall of 2003, the AFL-CIO, UNITE-HERE, and the SEIU sponsored the first Immigrant Workers Freedom

Ride. Undocumented immigrant workers took off from 101 cities around the United States, headed for Washington, DC, where they lobbied and demanded legislative change, and to New York, where they held public rallies.[44] One study suggests that the Immigrant Workers Freedom Ride three years earlier helped bring groups together and lay the groundwork for the 2006 mobilizations.[45]

To the extent that the protests aimed to prevent H.R. 4437 from becoming law, they succeeded: the Senate declined to consider the proposal and, in fact, passed its own, comprehensive reform bill later in May 2006 (which was then rejected by the House).

Some analysts believe that it was Bush's immigration agenda and the battles over comprehensive immigration reform that led to the Republican losses in Congress in 2006. After Obama's victory in 2008, backlash came in the form of the Tea Party movement, outflanking the Republicans to the libertarian and anti-immigrant right. The Republicans are currently torn between appealing to the fast-growing population of Hispanic voters—who have traditionally voted Democratic—and playing to the far right anti-immigrant sentiment fanned by talk radio and the Tea Party. Thirty-five percent of Hispanics voted for Bush in 2000, and over 40 percent did so in 2004, when Hispanic Republican support peaked.[46] In 2008, with Barack Obama running against John McCain and Sarah Palin, the Hispanic Republican vote sank to 31 percent. In 2012, as candidate Mitt Romney took an outspokenly anti-immigrant position, this went still lower to 27 percent. Meanwhile, the Hispanic vote rose to 10 percent of the total, up from 9 percent in 2008 and 8 percent in 2004.[47]

CONSULTING FIRMS AND THE CULTURAL BATTLE

Rinku Sen argues that despite the successes of 2006, a cultural battle for the rights of the undocumented was lost in the rise of xenophobia after 9/11. Fox News, talk radio, reality TV, and other media and entertainment sources offer the public epic battles between "criminal aliens" and beleaguered law enforcement in what Sen calls a "racialized cultural fight over the nation's identity."[48] Sen especially critiques the immigrants' rights organizations that have sought and followed the advice of consultants and "mainstreamed" their messages so as to tacitly accept, rather than challenge, common anti-immigrant sentiments. Many large organizations have relied on consulting firms like Westen Strategies that use surveys and focus groups to determine what messages will resonate with different sectors of the American public.

The firm's founder, psychologist Drew Westen, urged advocates to concede to the public's antipathy for immigrants considered illegal, rather than to challenge that stance. Advocates should aim for the center, he argued, by avoiding talk of immigrants' rights and instead relying on some key phrases that would resonate with those less sympathetic. His surveys found that the phrases "comprehensive immigration reform" and "fixing a broken immigration system" went over especially well with these centrist voters. An effective message, Westen discovered, begins with "taking tough measures to secure our borders," continues with "cracking down on illegal employers," and finally ends with "requiring those who came here without our permission to get in line, work hard, obey our laws, and learn our language."[49] His firm works with and has been commissioned by major immigrants' rights organizations like the Migration Policy Institute, the Center for American Progress, and Reform Immigration for America. Indeed, Westen's key phrases began to enter every politician's immigration proposals.

The Democratic Party also constructed its twenty-first-century agenda based on survey and focus group research about what messages would resonate with the American public. A study the party commissioned by Democracy Corps and

Greenberg Quinlan Rosner Research as the 2008 election approached argued that immigration is "especially important in Congressional battleground districts and states where views on illegal immigration are more negative. Failing to show real determination to get this problem under control costs incumbent Democrats votes."

Like Westen, the authors recommended "acknowledgment of the problem, pragmatic and tough ideas to stem the flow of illegal immigration with a path to citizenship laden with the kinds of requirements that anyone should meet if they are to attain the honor of being an American citizen." Their bullet points included the following:

> Attack [then-president] Bush for losing control of the problem; enforcement at both the border and with employers [sic]; opposition to non-essential benefits; and responsibility and a path to citizenship.
>
> A large majority of voters support a path to citizenship if we are serious about having to qualify for citizenship: expelling anyone who has committed a crime, others pay a fine and taxes, learn English, and get in the back of the queue. But if voters hear only the part about a path to citizenship without the responsibilities, they do not support this—and punish incumbent Democrats. But if Democrats "get it" and are very serious about getting the problem under control, including benefits, their leaders can get support for solving this problem.[50]

As a candidate, Obama echoed this position when he outlined what he believed comprehensive immigration reform should look like and vowed to press for its passage. "I can guarantee . . . that we will have in the first year an immigration bill that I strongly support and that I'm promoting. And I want to move that forward as quickly as possible," he stated in May 2008.[51] "We need immigration reform that will secure our borders, and punish employers who exploit immigrant labor; reform that finally brings the 12 million people who are here illegally out of the shadows by requiring them to take steps to become legal citizens," he told the National Association of Latino Elected Officials in June.[52] A large coalition of immigrant rights organizations favored this idea of a comprehensive reform, despite its punitive aspects, and supported the Obama candidacy and presidency.

Obama continued to reiterate this refrain once in office. "The way to fix our broken immigration system is through common-sense, comprehensive immigration reform," he declared at a Cinco de Mayo celebration in 2010, seeming to take his cue directly from Westen. "That means responsibility from government to secure our borders, something we have done and will continue to do. It means responsibility from businesses that break the law by undermining American workers and exploiting undocumented workers—they've got to be held accountable. It means responsibility from people who are living here illegally. They've got to admit that they broke the law and pay taxes and pay a penalty, and learn English, and get right before the law—and then get in line and earn their citizenship.'"[53]

He continued to sound the same themes after winning the 2012 election:

> When I say comprehensive immigration reform . . . I think it should include a continuation of the strong border security measures that we've taken, because we have to secure our borders. I think it should contain serious penalties for companies that are purposely hiring undocumented workers and taking advantage of them. And I do think that there should be a pathway for legal status for those who are living in this country, are not engaged in criminal activity, are here simply to work. It's important for them to pay back taxes, it's important for them to learn English, it's important for them to potentially pay a

fine, but to give them the avenue whereby they can resolve their legal status here in this country, I think is very important."[54]

A core of mainstream immigrant rights organizations linked to the Democratic Party continues to push for this kind of a comprehensive reform. Organizations like the New Democrat Network, the National Council of La Raza, National Association of Latino Elected and Appointed Officials, We Are America Alliance, Mi Familia Vota Educational Fund, and Democracia USA are sometimes identified as the inside-the-beltway organizations. They emphasize the potential of the growing Latino vote, the need to incorporate new voters into the Democratic Party, and the need of the party to reach out to its new constituency through the project of comprehensive reform.

A few advocates and organizations opposed the focus-group approach. Oscar Chacón, executive director of the National Alliance of Latin American and Caribbean Communities, or NALAAC, rejected the "comprehensive" consensus arguing that "this is oppressive language—punitive and restrictive." The 2008 Democracy Corps report was "nothing but an effort by D.C. groups to justify their views with a public opinion survey." The Democrats were "accept[ing] more and more of the premises of the anti-immigrant lobby." "We should be trying to change the way people think about the situation . . . instead of finding a way to make anti-immigrant sentiments tolerable," Chacón urged.[55]

Once Obama took office, the idea of a comprehensive reform died a quiet death. The Obama administration moved instead on the enforcement side, promoting and imposing the Secure Communities and E-Verify programs. Secure Communities, a Bush-era program that empowered local police forces to share data on arrests with ICE, grew from a small, voluntary pilot program to one Obama insisted would be imposed nationwide by 2013. E-Verify likewise grew from a small-scale, voluntary program to one required for companies holding government contracts—about 170,000 of them, employing some 4 million workers—and encouraged for all.[56]

The immigrant rights organizations that had worked for Obama were disappointed when the first years of his presidency seemed to pander to the anti-immigrant right rather than pay them back for their support of his candidacy. Finally, in 2010, a crumb was thrown to immigrant rights supporters: prosecutorial discretion.

Memoranda by Immigration Commissioner John Morton, in 2010 and 2011 (described in chapter 7), instructed agents of ICE to exercise "prosecutorial discretion" with regard to immigration violations. The term refers to law enforcement agencies' right to choose which cases to pursue and when to allow violators relief from prosecution. Acknowledging that ICE could not possibly deport all of the millions of people in the United States without authorization, Morton instructed ICE to prioritize national security, border security, and public safety in selecting its targets. Immigrants who had committed no crimes beyond immigration violations, had US citizens who were dependent upon them, and posed no risk to national security or public should, in general, be eligible for such discretion.[57]

One complicating factor in this new set of priorities was that while entry without inspection is a civil immigration violation, "re-entry after removal" is defined as a felony. The new rules defined entry without inspection as a low-priority violation, but a second attempt to enter without inspection made a person a felon and thus a high priority for removal. In fact, of 391,953 aliens removed by ICE in 2011, over half (203,571) had no criminal violations. Of the 188,382 who did have a criminal conviction, about 60 percent were guilty of either minor drug offenses, driving offenses, or immigration offenses.[58] For fiscal year 2012, ICE proudly announced that it had hit a new record with 409,849 removals. Slightly over half of those removed (225,000) had been convicted of felonies or misdemeanors, though the vast majority of these, as usual, were for immigration or traffic offenses. Only about 7,000 were guilty of violent crimes.[59]

Toward the end of 2011, ICE began a case-by-case review of over three hundred thousand pending removal cases in order to determine which ones merited dismissal under the new guidelines. As 2012 progressed, however, immigrant advocates became concerned at the small and diminishing numbers of cases that were determined to be eligible for dismissal. By the middle of 2012, only a few thousand of the tens of thousands of cases reviewed had been approved for dismissal.[60] Prosecutorial discretion seemed to be delivering much less than it had promised.

With the 2012 campaign in full swing, Obama finally offered his signature DACA program. DACA opened some important doors, as discussed in chapter 7, and may have contributed to the return of comprehensive immigration reform to the 2013 Congressional agenda. The reforms being debated in 2013, though, continued to follow the consulting firms' emphasis on enforcement followed by a punitive path to citizenship or perhaps even something less than citizenship.

CAN WE ABANDON "ENFORCEMENT"?

The more that US authorities have tried to control or stop Mexican border crossing over the course of the twentieth century, the more people have come. Absolute numbers have increased despite the illegalizing of many border crossings. Despite increasingly harsh measures aimed at reducing or eliminating illegal crossings, these too have increased and sometimes decreased, as with those by Mexicans in recent years, due to factors unrelated to measures aimed explicitly at border control.

The past few decades have demonstrated that the more the United States tries to militarily control the border, the more out of control it gets. The huge growth in organized crime, drug smuggling, drug and smuggling cartels, kidnappings, and violent and unnecessary death at the border is the *result* of misguided policies attempting to impose control.

Supporters of the idea of border control often argue that without draconian measures to deter migrants, floods of Mexicans and other Latin Americans would overwhelm the border and the country. They forget, perhaps, that during the many decades in which the border was relatively open, there were no floods. The number of undocumented immigrants in the United States began its precipitous rise *after* the country began to try to seal the border, in large part because instead of leaving after a season of work, migrants felt compelled to stay, since they realized that returning would be difficult.

Recent trends demonstrate the extent to which structural factors still govern migrant flows. The slowing and even reversal of migration from Mexico and the concomitant rise in numbers migrating from Central America, particularly from Honduras, suggest that factors other than border policies are the ones that really affect migrant streams. Border policies can shape *where* people try to cross, how much it will cost, and how many will die in the process, but they seem to have little effect on the numbers of people crossing.

DEEPER QUESTIONS

If the United States can't close the border, and if comprehensive immigration reform is such a flawed approach, what can we do?

By now, we have become accustomed to the notion that controlling the border is a basic prerequisite for security, safety, and sovereignty. So accustomed, that we rarely question this idea.

The drive for so-called enforcement—through militarizing the border, criminalizing the undocumented, detention, deportation, and a punitive path to citizenship based on paying society back for some supposed wrong inflicted—grows from some of the beliefs outlined in the first chapter of this book. The entire immigration apparatus is based on the presumption that we know where people belong and we need to legislate their mobility.

It's also based on some unquestioned assumptions about *countries*. It is not OK for a public park, a town, a county, or a state to discriminate regarding who is allowed to enter its space. But it's OK for a country to do that. It's not OK to treat people differently based on their religion, race, gender, or many other characteristics. But it's OK to treat people differently based on where they were born or their nationality (which is generally determined by where a person is born). US immigration laws do just that: discriminate, on the basis of nationality, regarding who is allowed to be where.

If we really want to address the problem of undocumented-ness, or so-called "illegal" immigration, we need to look more in depth at why the United States made some immigration illegal to begin with. I hope that I have shown that the drive to illegalize immigration was wrongheaded from the start. It's just the latest stage in a centuries-long process of legislated inequality, a process both global and domestic.

Rather than what currently passes for comprehensive reform, some organizations are pushing for what they call a "cultural strategy" that challenges the nationalist—and racist—underpinnings of popular views of immigrants. The new generation of undocumented youth—the DREAMers discussed in chapter 7—has taken this approach. Rinku Sen emphasizes that their goal goes beyond gaining their own access to citizenship: the bigger aim is to challenge the anti-immigrant culture. "Young, savvy with social media, and artistically inclined, DREAMers have compensated for their lack of political power by telling their stories in many forms and venues." With their stories, they sought to reframe the entire debate.[61]

The Applied Research Center launched its Drop-the-I-Word (i.e., illegal) campaign in 2010 in another attempt to challenge the terms of the mainstream debate about immigration that directly contradicted Westen's advice. Arguing that the very term "illegal" (or "illegal immigrant") "opens the door to racial profiling and violence and prevents truthful, respectful debate on immigration," and that "no human being is illegal," supporters challenged politicians, the media, and others to stop using it.[62] By 2013, numerous mainstream news outlets had shifted their usage. "Illegal immigrant isn't always accurate because it implies that somebody illegally immigrated when it fact a lot of people who are here illegally are here because their documentation expired after they came," the Associated Press explained when its new style guide recommended against using the term.[63] The *New York Times* and *Los Angeles Times* soon followed suit.[64]

In December 2012, Mexican American columnist Ruben Navarrette penned a controversial column in which he chastised DREAMers—and implicitly, others who are explicitly challenging the official terms of the debate—for acting "like spoiled brats." "They don't ask, they demand," Navarrette complained. "These kids want it all . . . what some seem to really want is the golden ticket: US citizenship." They are "drunk on entitlement," he wrote, and will "alienate supporters."[65]

At my own university, Salem State, in Massachusetts, a group supporting undocumented students engaged in a similar debate a few years ago. Should the university openly admit and support students who were undocumented? Or should it quietly open some back doors? One local high school guidance counselor cautioned us that the anti-immigrant climate at her school was so virulent that she preferred to counsel students individually and would not recommend that we hold a public event at her school. A faculty member worried that if we raised the issue publicly, it would imperil our undocumented students. Another retorted: "Do you know of any historical example where social change has come about by people keeping quiet?"

That question has stayed with me over the years and seems to surface again and again, as in Navarrette's column. There are those who truly believe that the best way to help the undocumented is through backroom deals that may bring some benefits for some people without addressing the larger structural issues of unequal international relations, an economy based on the use of labor kept cheap through legal marginalization, restrictive immigration policies, discrimination, and inequality before the law. History shows, though, that whether we are trying to change foreign policy, domestic and global economic structures, or laws that discriminate, Frederick Douglass was closer to the truth when he argued that change "must be a struggle. Power concedes nothing without a demand. It never did and it never will."[66]

Although the cultural strategy is a very important way to raise awareness and open a real debate about immigration policy, we also need to address the root global and economic factors that have contributed to today's problems. In the most immediate terms, we as a society created illegal immigration by making immigration illegal. In larger terms, we created illegal immigration by fostering a global system that bases the prosperity for the few on the exploitation of the many and enforcing it, in the modern era, through borders and exclusive citizenship. It's up to us to change it.

Acknowledgments

Many people contributed their ideas and feedback, and offered me spaces to present and discuss the material in this book. The idea was born at a café in Philadelphia, where Sandi Aritza helped me think through the outline. Gayatri Patnaik at Beacon Press supported the project enthusiastically. Andy Klatt at Tufts University, Gus Cochran and Juan Allende at Agnes Scott College, María Cruz-Saco at Connecticut College, Rob Young at the University of Oregon, and Victor Silverman at Pomona College gave me the opportunity to present and get feedback on my work in progress. Gustavo Remedi at the Universidad de la República in Montevideo and Victor Silverman at Pomona College in California each offered me the immense privilege of teaching a course related to the topic of the book while I was working on it. My students in both institutions moved and inspired me with their responses and with their own stories about migrations. Pomona proved to be the ideal place to finish writing this book. I am especially grateful to Carolyn Angius, Daniella Barraza, David Baxter, Felipe Cárdenas, Monica Dreitcer, Ahtziri Fonseca, Isaac Levy-Rubinett, Morgan Mayer-Jochimsen, Diana Ortiz, Alejandra Rishton, Jeremiah Rishton, Cristina Saldana, and Nidia Tapia for their careful reading of the manuscript and helpful comments.

Notes

INTRODUCTION

1. Douglas S. Massey and Karen A. Pren, "Unintended Consequences of US Immigration Policy: Explaining the Post-1965 Surge from Latin America," *Population and Development Review* 38, no. 1 (March 2012): 6–7, http://wws.princeton .edu/coverstories/Massey_LatinAmericaImmigrationSurge/Unintended -Consequences.pdf.

2. See Thomas L. Friedman, *The World Is Flat: A Brief History of the Twenty-first Century* (New York: Farrar, Strauss and Giroux, 2005); reissued as *The World Is Flat 3.0: A Brief History of the Twenty-first Century* (New York: Picador, 2007).

3. This concept has been suggested by a number of authors and organizations; see, for example, Joseph Nevins, *Dying to Live: A Story of US Immigration in an Age of Global Apartheid* (San Francisco: City Lights Publishers, 2008).

4. Evan Pellegrino, "Factory Justice? An Effort to Prosecute Illegal Immigrants Is Expensive and Time-Consuming—but Proponents Say It's Worthwhile," *Tucson Weekly*, February 11, 2010.

5. The differential was sometimes enforced by paying Mexicans in silver and "white men" in more valuable gold currency. See Rachel St. John, *Line in the Sand: A History of the Western US-Mexico Border* (Princeton, NJ: Princeton University Press, 2012), 72.

6. Charles C. Teague, "A Statement on Mexican Immigration," *Saturday Evening Post* (March 10, 1928), reproduced in Francisco E. Balderrama and Raymond Rodríguez, *Decade of Betrayal: Mexican Repatriation in the 1930s* (Albuquerque: University of New Mexico Press, 2006), 26.

7. Massey and Pren, "Unintended Consequences," 18.

8. See Frank Bardacke, *Trampling Out the Vintage: Cesar Chavez and the Two Souls of the United Farm Workers* (New York: Verso, 2012), chap. 24, "The Wet Line."

9. "California's 1971 Employer Sanctions Law," *Rural Migration News* 1, no. 3 (July 1995), http://migration.ucdavis.edu/rmn/more.php?id=62_0_4_0.

10. Peter Brownell, "The Declining Enforcement of Employer Sanctions," Migration Information Source, September 2005, http://www.migrationinformation .org/usfocus/display.cfm?ID=332.

11. Elizabeth Llorente, "Immigration Summit: Are Undocumented Workers Really Taking 'American' Jobs?" Fox News Latino, June 12, 2012, http://latino .foxnews.com/latino/politics/2012/06/12/immigration-summit-are-undoc-workers -really-taking-american-jobs/.

12. United States Sentencing Commission, "Overview of Federal Criminal Cases: Fiscal Year 2011," September 2012, 4, http://www.ussc.gov/Research/Research _Publications/2012/FY11_Overview_Federal_Criminal_Cases.pdf. The federal government and most other official sources use the term Hispanic to categorize peoples of Latin American or Spanish descent. Many Latin Americans find the term awkward or offensive, since it erases the indigenous and African populations of Latin America and creates a meaningless sociological category that lumps Spanish-speaking Latin Americans with European Spaniards. Many Latino activists prefer the term Latino as more inclusive of Latin Americans of all ethnicities. In this book, I use the term "Hispanic" when referring to government or other sources that use that term; otherwise, I use "Latino."

13. Michelle Alexander, *The New Jim Crow: Mass Incarceration in the Age of Colorblindness* (New York: New Press, 2010), 2.

14. Ibid., 13.

15. Ibid., 4.

16. See ibid., 148. Alexander is quoting Bruce Western, *Punishment and Inequality in America* (New York: Russell Sage Foundation, 2006), 90.

17. Alexander, *The New Jim Crow*, 139. She is quoting Webb Hubbell, "The Mark of Cain," *San Francisco Chronicle*, June 10, 2001; Nora Demleitner, "Preventing Internal Exile: The Need for Restrictions on Collateral Sentencing and Consequences," *Stanford Law and Policy Review* 11, no.1 (1999): 153–63.

18. Alexander, *The New Jim Crow*, 194.

19. See Eric Schlosser, "The Prison-Industrial Complex," *Atlantic*, December 1998.

20. Manuel D. Vargas, "Immigration Consequences of New York Criminal Convictions," November 8, 2011, citing Padilla v. Kentucky, 130 S. Ct. 1473, 1478 (2010). http://blogs.law.columbia.edu/4cs/immigration/.

21. Nicholas De Genova, *Working the Boundaries: Race, Space, and "Illegality" in Mexican Chicago* (Durham, NC: Duke University Press, 2005), 214.

CHAPTER 1: WHERE DID ILLEGALITY COME FROM?

1. Anatole France, *The Red Lily* (Winifred Stephens, trans.), in Anatole France, *Works, in an English Translation*, ed. Frederic Chapman (London: John Lane, Bodley Head, 1916), 95.

2. "In European eyes most non-Europeans, and nearly all non-Christians, including such 'advanced' peoples as the Turks, were classified as 'barbarians,'" writes Anthony Pagden in *The Fall of Natural Man: The American Indian and the Origins of Comparative Ethnology* (Cambridge, UK: Cambridge University Press, 1982), 13–14.

3. Quoted in Steven Stoll, *The Great Delusion: A Mad Inventor, Death in the Tropics, and the Utopian Origins of Economic Growth* (New York: Hill and Wang, 2008), 113.

4. Karl Jacoby, *Shadows at Dawn: An Apache Massacre and the Violence of History* (New York: Penguin, 2008), 109.

5. Speech at Columbia University, April 15, 1907. Quoted in Howard Zinn, *A People's History of the United States, 1492–Present* (New York: HarperCollins, 2003), 362.

6. Teemu Ruskola, "Canton Is Not Boston: The Invention of American Imperial Sovereignty," *American Quarterly* 57, no. 3 (September 2005): 860. On the general relationship between US expansion, citizenship, and sovereignty during

this period, see also Matthew Frye Jacobson, *Barbarian Virtues: The United States Encounters Foreign Peoples at Home and Abroad* (New York: Hill and Wang, 2000).

7. Jared Diamond, *The World Until Yesterday: What Can We Learn from Traditional Societies?* (New York: Viking, 2012), 37.

8. See María Elena Martínez, *Genealogical Fictions: Limpieza de Sangre, Religion, and Gender in Colonial Mexico* (Palo Alto, CA: Stanford University Press, 2008).

9. See Margaret R. Greer, Walter D. Mignolo, and Maureen Quilligan, eds., *Rereading the Black Legend: The Discourses of Religious and Racial Difference in the Renaissance Empires* (Chicago: University of Chicago Press, 2007).

10. Aziz Rana, *The Two Faces of American Freedom* (Cambridge, MA: Harvard University Press, 2010), 30.

11. See Jill Lepore, *The Name of War: King Philip's War and the Origins of American Identity* (New York: Vintage, 1999), 167.

12. Rana, *The Two Faces of American Freedom*, 47.

13. Anderson argues, as others have, that "in Western Europe the eighteenth century marks not only the dawn of the age of nationalism but the dusk of religious modes of thought." Benedict Anderson, *Imagined Communities: Reflections on the Origin and Spread of Nationalism*, new ed. (New York: Verso, 2006), 11.

14. John Torpey, *The Invention of the Passport: Surveillance, Citizenship and the State* (Cambridge, UK: Cambridge University Press, 2000), 1, 3. He was playing with sociologist Max Weber's oft-quoted definition of a state as having a "monopoly on the use of violence."

15. See James Loewen, *Sundown Towns: A Hidden Dimension of American Racism* (New York: New Press, 2005).

16. "Under the 1802 Naturalization Act, which remained in force for most of the nineteenth century, to gain formal citizenship foreigners merely had to reside in the country for five years, declare their intent to be naturalized at least three years before admission to citizenship (but at any point after residence), pledge an oath of allegiance to the federal Constitution, and give minimal proof of good character. Critically, this process was available only to 'free white persons'" (Rana, *The Two Faces of American Freedom*, 115–16). Women, too, were nonvoting citizens. "Rather than a right that attended to all subjects of a sovereign power, suffrage was granted only to specific categories of citizens" (229).

17. Ibid., 237.

18. Ibid., 239.

19. Mae Ngai, *Impossible Subjects: Illegal Aliens and the Making of Modern America* (Princeton, NJ: Princeton University Press, 2004), 9.

20. Ibid., 7–8.

21. Helen B. Marrow, *New Destination Dreaming: Immigration, Race, and Legal Status in the Rural American South* (Palo Alto, CA: Stanford University Press, 2011), 253.

22. Ibid., 244.

23. Jacqueline Stevens, *States without Nations: Citizenship for Mortals* (New York: Columbia University Press, 2010), 52–53.

24. Ibid., 51. See also Joseph Nevins, *Dying to Live: A Story of US Immigration in an Age of Global Apartheid* (San Francisco: City Lights Publishers, 2008).

25. See James C. Scott, *The Art of Not Being Governed: An Anarchist History of Upland Southeast Asia* (New Haven, CT: Yale University Press, 2009).

26. Rana, *The Two Faces of American Freedom*, 188.

27. Alexander, *The New Jim Crow*, 207. She is citing Loïc Wacquant, "From Slavery to Mass Incarceration: Rethinking the 'Race Question' in the United States," *New Left Review*, 2nd series, no. 13 (February 2002): 53.

28. Nicolas De Genova, *Working the Boundaries: Race, Space, and "Illegality" in Mexican Chicago* (Duke University Press, 2005), 123.

CHAPTER 2: CHOOSING TO BE UNDOCUMENTED

1. The admonition that the undocumented should "do it the right way" is extraordinarily common in anti-immigrant discourse. See, for example, Mike Huckabee's statement at *On the Issues*, http://www.ontheissues.org/celeb/Mike _Huckabee_Immigration.htm.

2. See Kelly Lytle Hernández, *Migra! A History of the US Border Patrol* (Berkeley: University of California Press, 2010), 26–27.

3. US, Bureau of Immigration and Naturalization, *Immigration Laws and Regulations of July 1, 1907*, 14.

4. Marian L. Smith, "INS-US Immigration and Naturalization Service History," *United States Citizenship*, http://www.uscitizenship.info/ins-usimmigration-insoverview.html. See also Mae Ngai, "The Strange Career of the Illegal Alien: Immigration Restriction and Deportation Policy in the United States, 1921–1965," *Law and History Review* 21, no. 1 (Spring 2003): 69–107.

5. US Bureau of Labor Statistics, *Handbook of Labor Statistics* (September 1931), 281.

6. Daniel Kanstroom, *Deportation Nation: Outsiders in American History* (Cambridge, MA: Harvard University Press, 2007), 165.

7. US Bureau of Labor Statistics, *Handbook of Labor Statistics*, 249.

8. His story is recounted on the National Park Service Ellis Island website, http://www.nps.gov/elis/historyculture/upload/Irving-Berlin.pdf.

9. Mae Ngai, "How Grandma Got Legal," *Los Angeles Times*, May 16, 2006.

10. Ngai, "The Strange Career of the Illegal Alien."

11. Ibid., 107.

12. Ngai, "How Grandma Got Legal."

13. Donna Gabaccia, "Great Migration Debates: Keywords in Historical Perspective," in Social Science Research Council, *Border Battles: The US Immigration Debates*, 2006, http://borderbattles.ssrc.org/Gabaccia/index1.html.

14. Michael Hoefer, Nancy Rytina, and Bryan Baker, "Estimates of the Unauthorized Immigrant Population Residing in the United States: January 2011," Department of Homeland Security, Office of Immigration Statistics, Population Estimates, March 2012.

15. Ibid.

16. Douglas S. Massey and Karen A. Pren, "Unintended Consequences of US Immigration Policy: Explaining the Post-1965 Surge from Latin America," *Population and Development Review* 38, no. 1 (March 2012): 25, 23, http://wws.princeton .edu/coverstories/Massey_LatinAmericaImmigrationSurge/Unintended -Consequences.pdf.

17. Ibid., 17. See also Hoefer, Rytina, and Baker, "Estimates of the Unauthorized Immigrant Population Residing in the United States."

18. Massey and Pren, "Unintended Consequences," 24.

19. Jeffrey Passel and D'Vera Cohn, "Unauthorized Immigrant Population: National and State Trends, 2010," part II, Pew Hispanic Center, February 1, 2011, http://www.pewhispanic.org/2011/02/01/ii-current-estimates-and-trends/.

20. Jeffrey Passel, D'Vera Cohn, and Ana Gonzalez-Barrera, "Net Migration from Mexico Falls to Zero—and Perhaps Less," Pew Hispanic Center, April 23, 2012, http://www.pewhispanic.org/2012/04/23/vi-characteristics-of-mexican-born-immigrants-living-in-the-u-s/.

21. Jennifer Cairns, Francis Smart, William Kandel, and Steven Zahniser, "Agricultural Employment Patterns of Immigrant Workers in the United States," Selected paper prepared for presentation at the Agricultural & Applied Economics Association 2010, AAEA, CAES, and WAEA Joint Annual Meeting, Denver, July 25–27, 2010, http://ageconsearch.umn.edu/bitstream/61327/2/5_2_2010.pdf.

22. Victor S. Clark, "Mexican Labor in the United States," in US Bureau of Labor, *Bulletin of the Bureau of Labor* (1908): 466.

23. Ibid., 485.

24. Gilbert G. Gonzalez, "Mexican Labor Migration, 1876–1924," in *Beyond La Frontera: The History of Mexico-US Migration*, ed. Mark Overmyer-Velázquez (New York: Oxford University Press, 2011), 31. A few decades later, railroads would similarly structure the Great Migration of African Americans to the North. Rail lines led blacks from "Tennessee, Alabama, western Georgia, or the Florida panhandle" to Detroit. The Illinois Central took "upward of a million colored people from the Deep South up the country's central artery . . . and into a new world called the Midwest . . . along with the Atlantic Coast line and Seaboard Air Line railroads, running between Florida and New York, and the Southern Pacific, connecting Texas and California," they became "the historic means of escape, the Overground Railroad for slavery's grandchildren." After the Civil War, "the railroad laid or acquired tracks into the more isolated precincts of Mississippi, Arkansas, Tennessee, and Louisiana and unwittingly made the North a more accessible prospect for black southerners desperate to escape." See also Isabel Wilkerson, *The Warmth of Other Suns: The Epic Story of America's Great Migration* (New York: Vintage, 2010), 178, 190, 191.

25. Gonzalez, "Mexican Labor Migration," 33.

26. Eric V. Meeks, *Border Citizens: The Making of Indians, Mexicans, and Anglos in Arizona* (Austin: University of Texas Press, 2007), 27.

27. Clark, "Mexican Labor in the United States," 469–70.

28. Ibid., 471.

29. Paul S. Taylor, *A Spanish-Mexican Peasant Community: Arandas in Jalisco, Mexico* (Berkeley: University of California Press, 1933), 13.

30. Ibid., 35.

31. Ibid., 36.

32. Ibid., 45.

33. Gonzalez, "Mexican Labor Migration," 39.

34. Taylor, *A Spanish-Mexican Peasant Community*, 36, 40.

35. United States Bureau of Labor, *Handbook of Labor Statistics* (1931), 281.

36. Taylor, *A Spanish-Mexican Peasant Community*, 41.

37. Ibid., 43.

38. Ibid., 45–46.

39. Aristide Zolberg, "A Century of Informality on the US-Mexico Border," in Social Science Research Council, *Border Battles: The US Immigration Debates*, August 17, 2006, http://borderbattles.ssrc.org/Zolberg/.

40. Lytle-Hernandez, *Migra! A History of the US Border Patrol*, 3.

41. Francisco E. Balderrama and Raymond Rodríguez, *Decade of Betrayal: Mexican Repatriation in the 1930s* (Albuquerque: University of New Mexico Press, 2006), 11.

42. Gonzalez, "Mexican Labor Migration," 34.

43. Ibid., 38–39.

44. Ibid., 46.

45. Balderrama and Rodríguez, *Decade of Betrayal*, 1.

46. See Deborah Cohen, *Braceros: Migrant Citizens and Transnational Subjects in the Postwar United States* (Chapel Hill: University of North Carolina Press, 2011), 2.

47. Michael Snodgrass, "Patronage and Progress: The Bracero Program from the Perspective of Mexico," in *Workers across the Americas: The Transnational Turn in Labor History*, ed. Leon Fink (New York: Oxford University Press, 2011), 252. See also Taylor, *A Spanish-Mexican Peasant Community*.

48. Ibid., 254.

49. Zolberg, "A Century of Informality."

50. Snodgrass, "Patronage and Progress," 254–55.

51. Ibid., 257, 260.

52. Ibid., 261.

53. Michael Snodgrass, "The Bracero Program, 1942–1964," in Overmyer-Velázquez, *Beyond La Frontera*, 91.

54. Mark Overmyer-Velázquez, "Introduction: Histories and Historiographies of Greater Mexico," in Overmyer-Velázquez, *Beyond La Frontera*, xxxvii.

55. Cited in Kanstroom, *Deportation Nation*, 219.

56. Ibid., 222.

57. *Wetbacks* is a derogatory term referring to the idea that Mexicans entered the country by crossing the Rio Grande river and avoiding official entry points.

58. Cindy Hahamovitch, *No Man's Land: Jamaican Guestworkers in America and the Global History of Deportable Labor* (Princeton, NJ: Princeton University Press, 2011), 124–25.

59. Don Mitchell, *They Saved the Crops: Labor, Landscape, and the Struggle over Industrial Farming in Bracero-Era California* (Athens: University of Georgia Press, 2012), 223.

60. Mae Ngai, *Impossible Subjects: Illegal Aliens and the Making of Modern America* (Princeton, NJ: Princeton University Press, 2004), 153.

61. Kanstroom, *Deportation Nation*, 224.

62. Snodgrass, "The Bracero Program," 91.

63. See Kanstroom, *Deportation Nation*, 161.

64. David G. Gutiérrez, *Walls and Mirrors: Mexican Americans, Mexican Immigrants, and the Politics of Ethnicity* (Berkeley: University of California Press, 1995), 154. See also Lorena Oropeza, *¡Raza Sí, Guerra No! Chicano Protest and Patriotism during the Viet Nam War Era* (Berkeley: University of California Press, 2005), for an analysis of Mexican American organizations' aspirations toward acceptance as white in the midcentury.

65. Massey and Pren, "Unintended Consequences," 22.

66. Overmyer-Velázquez, "Introduction," xxxviii.

67. Oscar J. Martínez, "Migration and the Border, 1965–1985," in Overmyer-Velázquez, *Beyond La Frontera*, 110.

68. Ibid., 106.

69. Ibid., 111.

70. Jorge Durand and Douglas S. Massey, "What We Learned from the Mexican Migration Project," in *Crossing the Border: Research from the Mexican Migration Project*, ed. Jorge Durand and Douglas S. Massey (New York: Russell Sage Foundation, 2007), 6.

71. Overmyer-Velázquez, "Introduction," xlii.

72. Helen B. Marrow, "Race and the New Southern Migration, 1986 to the Present," in Overmyer-Velázquez, *Beyond La Frontera*, 130.

73. Philip L. Martin, "Good Intentions Gone Awry: IRCA and US Agriculture," *Annals of the Academy of Political and Social Science* 534 (July 1994): 50–51.

74. See Roberto Suro, "False Migrant Claims: Fraud on a Huge Scale," *New York Times*, November 12, 1989.

75. See ibid.

76. Martin, "Good Intentions Gone Awry," 52.

77. Nicholas De Genova, *Working the Boundaries: Race, Space, and "Illegality" in Mexican Chicago* (Durham, NC: Duke University Press, 2005), 237–381.

78. Durand and Massey, "What We Learned from the Mexican Migration Project," 11–12.

79. The Mexican governments identifies four regions of out-migration: The Traditional region, encompassing Aguascalientes, Colima, Durango, Guanajuato, Jalisco, Michoacán, Nayarit, San Luis Potosí and Zacatecas; the Northern region, comprised of Baja California, Baja California Sur, Coahuila, Chihuahua, Nuevo León, Sinaloa, Sonora and Tamaulipas; the Central region: Distrito Federal, Hidalgo, México, Morelos, Puebla, Querétaro and Tlaxcala; and the South-Southeast region: Campeche, Chiapas, Guerrero, Oaxaca, Quintana Roo, Tabasco, Veracruz y Yucatán. See Consejo Nacional de Población, "Flujos Migratorios EMIF Norte," http://conapo.gob.mx/es/CONAPO/flujos_Migratorios_EMIF_NORTE.

80. In Mexico, *mestizos* generally refers to people of mixed Spanish and indigenous origin.

81. See Overmyer-Velázquez, "Introduction," xxxii; Angus Wright, *The Death of Ramón González: The Modern Agricultural Dilemma* (Austin: University of Texas Press, 1990; rev. ed., 2005), 138, 309; Jeffrey Harris Cohen, *The Culture of Migration in Southern Mexico* (Austin: University of Texas Press, 2004); David Bacon, *Illegal People: How Globalization Creates Migration and Criminalizes Immigrants* (Boston: Beacon Press, 2008), especially chap. 2.

82. Lynnaire M. Sheridan, *"I Know It's Dangerous": Why Mexicans Risk Their Lives to Cross the Border* (Tucson: University of Arizona Press, 2009), 56.

83. Ibid., 57.

84. De Genova argues that today's "illegality" is something "produced" by the law, rather than by the actions of individual Mexicans (*Working the Boundaries*, chap. 6, esp. p. 244).

85. For a historical summary of Mayan migration, see Christopher H. Lutz and W. George Lovell, "Survivors on the Move: Maya Migration in Time and Space," in *The Maya Diaspora: Guatemalan Roots, New American Lives*, ed. James Loucky and Marilyn M. Moors (Philadelphia: Temple University Press, 2000), 11–34.

86. See David McCreery, *Rural Guatemala, 1760–1940* (Palo Alto, CA: Stanford University Press, 1994); Julio C. Cambranes, *Café y campesinos en Guatemala, 1853–1897* (Guatemala: Editorial Universitaria, 1985); Lutz and Lovell, "Survivors on the Move," 32.

87. Lutz and Lovell, "Survivors on the Move," 32.

88. Rigoberta Menchu, with Elisabeth Debray, *I, Rigoberta Menchu: An Indian Woman from Guatemala* (New York: Verso, 1987), 21–23.

89. Ibid., 23.

90. Daniel Wilkinson, *Silence on the Mountain: Stories of Terror, Betrayal, and Forgetting in Guatemala* (Durham, NC: Duke University Press, 2004), 43.

91. Patricia Foxen, *In Search of Providence: Transnational Mayan Identities* (Nashville, TN: Vanderbilt University Press, 2007), 63.

92. Ibid., 78.

93. Ibid., 99.

94. Ibid., 100. David Stoll describes a similar phenomenon in another Guatemalan town, where labor contractors have been using force, debt, or landlessness and need to recruit indigenous workers for migrant labor for over a century. Today's coyotes and contractors simply recruit them to work in another country. David Stoll, *El Norte or Bust! How Migration Fever and Microcredit Produced a Financial Crash in a Latin American Town* (Lanham, MD: Rowman & Littlefield, 2013), 198.

95. Stoll describes this process in *El Norte or Bust!*, 89.

96. Lutz and Lovell, "Survivors on the Move," 33.

97. Foxen, *In Search of Providence*, 149.

98. Ibid., 115.

99. Ibid., 115; Sarah J. Mahler, *American Dreaming: Immigrant Life on the Margins* (Princeton, NJ: Princeton University Press, 1995), 141.

100. Erik Camayd-Freixas, *US Immigration Reform and its Global Impact: Lessons from the Postville Raid* (New York: Palgrave Macmillan, 2013), 100.

101. Randal C. Archibold, "In Trek North, First Lure Is Mexico's Other Line," *New York Times*, April 26, 2013.

CHAPTER 3: BECOMING ILLEGAL

1. Ruth Ellen Wasem, *Nonimmigrant Overstays: Brief Synthesis of the Issue*, Congressional Research Service Report for Congress, May 22, 2006, http://trac .syr.edu/immigration/library/P735.pdf.

2. Department of Homeland Security, Office of Immigration Statistics, "2010 Yearbook of Immigration Statistics," table 26, http://www.dhs.gov/xlibrary/assets /statistics/yearbook/2010/ois_yb_2010.pdf.

3. Randall Monger, "Non-Immigrant Admissions to the United States, 2011," Homeland Security, Office of Immigration Statistics, July 2012, http://www.dhs .gov/xlibrary/assets/statistics/publications/ni_fr_2011.pdf; Department of State, "Non-Immigrant Visas Issued, 2007–2011," http://www.travel.state.gov/pdf /NIVClassIssued-DetailedFY2007–2011.pdf; Department of State, "Nonimmigrant Visa Issuance by Visa Class and Nationality, FY 2011," http://www .travel.state.gov/pdf/FY11NIVDetailTable.pdf. The Visa Waiver Program applies to thirty-seven mostly European countries and allows would-be visitors to be processed at the border without obtaining a visa prior to departure.

4. In 2009, 126.8 million of 163 million total entries were Border Crossing Cards rather than nonimmigrant visa entries. See Ruth Ellen Wasem, *US Immigration Policy on Temporary Admissions*, Congressional Research Service, February 8, 2011, 15–16, http://www.fas.org/sgp/crs/homesec/RL31381.pdf.

5. Pew Hispanic Center, "Modes of Entry for the Unauthorized Migrant Population," May 22, 2006, http://pewhispanic.org/files/factsheets/19.pdf.

6. Lynnaire M. Sheridan, *"I Know It's Dangerous": Why Mexicans Risk Their Lives to Cross the Border* (Tucson: University of Arizona Press, 2009), 66.

7. Ibid., 61.

8. Ibid., 79.

9. See Florida Fruit and Vegetable Association, "Who Will Harvest the Food?" November 2011, http://www.ffva.com/imispublic/Content/NavigationMenu2 /NewsCenter/HarvesterOnline/Mainfeature1111/default.htm.

10. United States Government Accountability Office, "Report to the Chairman, Committee on Education and Labor, House of Representatives: H-2B VISA PROGRAM Closed Civil and Criminal Cases Illustrate Instances of H-2B Workers Being Targets of Fraud and Abuse," September 2010, 4, http://www.gao .gov/assets/320/310640.pdf.

11. Gardenia Mendoza Aguilar, "A merced de fraudes con visas," *Impremedia*, May 11, 2011, http://www.impre.com/noticias/2011/5/11/a-merced-de-fraudes-con -visas-255317–1.html.

12. Gardenia Mendoza Aguilar, "El botín de los coyotes: Miles deben pagar para tramitar trabajo temporal en EEUU," *Impremedia*, May 9, 2011, http://www .impre.com/noticias/2011/5/9/el-botin-de-los-coyotes-legale-254910–2.html.

13. Dan LaBotz, "Farm Labor Organizer Murdered in Mexico, Labor Contractors Suspected," *CounterPunch*, April 14–16, 2007, http://www.counterpunch .org/labotz04142007.html.

14. Mendoza Aguilar, "A merced de fraudes con visas."

15. Southern Poverty Law Center, *Close to Slavery: Guestworker Programs in the United States*, April 2007, http://www.splcenter.org/get-informed/publications /close-to-slavery-guestworker-programs-in-the-united-states#.UaIQ-cokSSo.

16. Jeffrey Passel, D'Vera Cohn, and Ana Gonzalez-Barrera, "Net Migration from Mexico Falls to Zero—and Perhaps Less," Pew Hispanic Center, April 23, 2012, http://www.pewhispanic.org/2012/04/23/vi-characteristics-of-mexican-born -immigrants-living-in-the-u-s/.

17. Comisión Nacional de Derechos Humanos (CNDH), "Informe especial sobre secuestro de migrantes en México," February 22, 2011, 5, http://www.cndh .org.mx/sites/all/fuentes/documentos/informes/especiales/2011_secmigrante.pdf.

18. Randal C. Archibold, "In Trek North, First Lure Is Mexico's Other Line," *New York Times*, April 26, 2013.

19. Olga R. Rodríguez, "Central American Migrants Flood North Through Mexico to US," *Huffington Post*, July 13, 2012, http://www.huffingtonpost.com /2012/07/13/central-americans-in-the-united-states_n_1671551.html.

20. Abril Trigo, *Memorias migrantes: Testimonios y ensayos sobre la diáspora uruguaya* (Rosario, Argentina: Beatriz Viterbo Editora, 2003), 190.

21. Maxine L. Margolis, *Little Brazil: An Ethnography of Brazilian Immigrants in New York City* (Princeton, NJ: Princeton University Press, 1993), 49–50.

22. Samuel Martinez, "Migration from the Caribbean: Economic and Political Factors versus Legal and Illegal Status," in *Illegal Immigration in America: A Reference Handbook*, ed. David W. Haines and Karen E. Rosenblum (Westport, CT: Greenwood Press, 1999), 278–79.

23. Margolis, *Little Brazil*, 51.

24. Kurt Birson, "Mexico: Abuses against US Bound Migrant Workers," *NACLA Report*, September 23, 2010, https://nacla.org/node/6753.

25. Centro de Derechos Humanos Miguel Agustín Pro Juárez, A.C. (Centro ProDH) et al., "Secuestros a personas migrantes en tránsito por México," 7–8, http:// www2.ohchr.org/english/bodies/cmw/docs/ngos/prodh_Mexico_CAT47.pdf.

26. Sebastian Rotella, "The New Border: Illegal Immigration's Shifting Frontier," *ProPublica*, December 6, 2012, http://www.propublica.org/article/the-new -border-illegal-immigrations-shifting-frontier.

27. Paul Imison, "The Freight Train That Runs to the Heart of Mexico's 'Drugs War': Riding 'La Bestia' to Freedom or Death," *Independent*, February 3, 2013; Archibold, "In Trek North"; Karl Penhaul, "'Train of Death' Drives Migrant American Dreamers," CNN, June 25, 2010, http://www.cnn.com/2010/WORLD /americas/06/23/mexico.train.death/index.html. See also Sonia Nazario, *Enrique's Journey* (New York: Random House, 2007).

28. CNDH, "Informe especial," 12.

29. Ibid., 26–27.

30. Ibid., 28–29.

31. Centro ProDH, "Secuestros a personas migrantes," 1.

32. Ibid., 9.

33. Ibid., 9.

34. CNDH, "Informe especial," 37.

35. La Redacción, "Capturan al responsable de la masacre de indocumentados en San Fernando," *Proceso*, June 17, 2011, http://www.proceso.com.mx/?p=273018; Voz de América, "Detenido por masacre en México," June 16, 2011, http://www .voanoticias.com/content/detenido-masacre-indocumentados-mexico-124079179 /100610.html.

36. El Salvador Noticias.net, "Masacre de 49 supuestos migrantes en Nuevo León, México," May 13, 2012, http://www.elsalvadornoticias.net/2012/05/13/masacre -de-49-supuestos-migrantes-en-nuevo-leon-mexico/.

37. Centro ProDH, "Secuestros a personas migrantes," 10.

38. Ibid., 13.

39. Univision.com, "A dos años de masacre de migrantes en San Fernando, Tamaulipas," August 22, 2012, http://noticias.univision.com/narcotrafico/reportajes /article/2012-08-22/dos-anio-masacre-san-fernando-tamaulipas#ixzz2BPEzSZg9.

40. See Joseph Nevins, *Operation Gatekeeper and Beyond: The War on "Illegals" and the Remaking of the US–Mexico Boundary*, 2nd ed. (New York: Routledge, 2010), chap. 5, for a detailed discussion of how California politicians, led by Governor Pete Wilson, created and manipulated the so-called "crisis" of "illegal immigration."

41. Ibid., 111.

42. Office of the Inspector General, "Background to the Office of the Inspector General Investigation," July 1998, http://www.justice.gov/oig/special/9807 /gkp01.htm.

43. Maria Jimenez, "Humanitarian Crisis: Migrant Deaths at the US-Mexico Border," American Civil Liberties Union, October 1, 2009, 7, http://www.aclu.org /files/pdfs/immigrants/humanitariancrisisreport.pdf.

44. Ibid., 21.

45. Coalición de Derechos Humanos, "Arizona Recovered Bodies Project," http://derechoshumanosaz.net/projects/arizona-recovered-bodies-project/.

46. US Government Accountability Office, "Illegal Immigration: Border-Crossing Deaths Have Doubled since 1995," August 2006, 4, http://www.gao.gov /new.items/d06770.pdf.

47. Stephen Dinan, "Figures Point to Securer Border, But Risk of Death for Illegals Still High," *Washington Times*, March 22, 2012, http://www.washingtontimes .com/news/2012/mar/22/figures-point-to-securer-border-but-risk-of-death -/?page=all.

48. US Border Patrol, Southwest Border Sectors, "Southwest Border Deaths by Fiscal Year (October 1 through September 30)," http://www.cbp.gov/linkhandler /cgov/border_security/border_patrol/usbp_statistics/usbp_fy12_stats/border _patrol_fy.ctt/border_patrol_fy.pdf.

49. Brady McCombs, "No Signs of Letup in Entrant Deaths," *Arizona Daily Star*, December 27, 2009, http://azstarnet.com/news/local/border/article_faf5b437 -b728-527b-9eb8-77977d0cdf84.html.

50. Jimenez, "Humanitarian Crisis," 33.

51. Las Americas Premium Outlets, San Ysidro, CA, Yelp.com, http://www .yelp.com/biz/las-americas-premium-outlets-san-ysidro.

CHAPTER 4: WHAT PART OF "ILLEGAL" DO YOU UNDERSTAND?

1. Jose Antonio Vargas, "Not Legal Not Leaving," *Time*, June 25, 2012, http:// www.time.com/time/magazine/article/0,9171,2117243,00.html#ixzz27acH8fKJ.

2. Twenty-nine percent arrived between 2000 and 2004, and 26 percent between 1995–1999, with another 14 percent arriving between 1990 and 1994 and 17 percent arriving in the 1980s. Michael Hoefer, Nancy Rytina, and Bryan Baker, "Estimates of the Unauthorized Immigrant Population Residing in the United States: January 2011," Department of Homeland Security, Office of Immigration Statistics, Population Estimates, March 2012.

3. Jeffrey Passel and D'Vera Cohn, "Unauthorized Immigrant Population: National and State Trends, 2010," part II, 10–11, February 1, 2011, http://www .pewhispanic.org/2011/02/01/ii-current-estimates-and-trends/.

4. Sarah Gammage, "El Salvador: Despite End to Civil War, Emigration Continues," Migration Information Source, July 2007, http://www.migrationinformation .org/Profiles/display.cfm?ID=636; Hemispheric Migration Project, *Central Americans in Mexico and the United States*, Center for Immigration Policy and Refugee Assistance (Washington, DC: Georgetown University, 1988), 29.

5. "Salvadoran TPS to Expire," *Migration News* 2, no.1 (January 1995), http:// migration.ucdavis.edu/mn/more.php?id=512_0_2_0.

6. Cecilia Menjívar and Leisy Abrego, "Parents and Children across Borders: Legal Instability and Intergenerational Relations in Guatemalan and Salvadoran Families," in *Across Generations: Immigrant Families in America*, ed. Nancy Foner (New York: New York University Press, 2009), 165.

7. Ester E. Hernandez, "Relief Dollars: US Policies toward Central Americans, 1980s to Present," in *Immigration, Incorporation and Transnationalism*, ed. Elliott Robert Barkan (Piscataway, NJ: Transaction Publishers, 2007), 216.

8. Ibid., 217.

9. Menjívar and Abrego, "Parents and Children across Borders," 164.

10. Cecilia Menjívar, "Liminal Legality: Salvadoran and Guatemalan Immigrants' Lives in the United States," *American Journal of Sociology* 111, no. 4 (January 2006): 1000–1001.

11. US Code, 2011 Edition, Title 8—ALIENS AND NATIONALITY. CHAPTER 14—RESTRICTING WELFARE AND PUBLIC BENEFITS FOR ALIENS. SUBCHAPTER IV—GENERAL PROVISIONS. Sec. 1641— Definitions, http://www.gpo.gov/fdsys/pkg/USCODE-2011-title8/html/USCODE -2011-title8-chap14-subchapIV-sec1641.htm.

12. Steve A. Camarota, *The High Cost of Cheap Labor: Illegal Immigration and the Federal Budget*, Center for Immigration Studies, August 2004, http://www.cis .org/High-Cost-of-Cheap-Labor.

13. See Edmund H. Mahony, "Fifty Indicted in Identity Theft Ring," *Hartford Courant*, January 11, 2012.

14. See Marianne McCune, "Puerto Rican Birth Certificates Will Be Null and Void," National Public Radio, March 18, 2010, http://www.npr.org/templates /story/story.php?storyId=124827546.

15. In fact, these payments subsidize the Social Security system, since undocumented immigrants using false numbers will never receive the benefits that they are paying into. The Social Security Administration estimated these payments came to about $12 billion a year in 2007, adding up to somewhere between $120 billion and $240 billion over the years. See Edward Schumacher-Matos, "How Illegal Immigrants Are Helping Social Security," *Washington Post*, September 3, 2010.

16. Susan Carroll, "Immigrant Drivers in US Now Face an Uncertain Road," *Houston Chronicle*, January 11, 2011.

17. Julia Preston and Robert Gebeloff, "Some Unlicensed Drivers Risk More Than a Fine," *New York Times*, December 9, 2010.

18. Ibid.

19. Dennis Romero, "Illegal Immigrants Can Now Drive in L.A. Without Fear of Having Cars Taken by Police," *LA Weekly Blog*, February 28, 2012, http:// blogs.laweekly.com/informer/2012/02/illegal_impound_tow_lapd_police_policy .php.

20. Maria Sacchetti, "Framingham, Barnstable No Longer Enforcing US Immigration Laws," *Boston Globe*, October 1, 2009.

21. Mary MacDonald, "Local Officials Disappointed by Governor's 'No' on Secure Communities," *Milford (MA) Patch*, June 8, 2011, http://milford-ma.patch .com/articles/local-officials-disappointed-by-governors-no-on-secure-communities.

22. Michael John Garcia, *Criminalizing Unlawful Presence: Selected Issues*, CRS Report for Congress, May 3, 2006, http://trac.syr.edu/immigration/library/ P585.pdf.

23. US Citizenship and Immigration Service, "Voluntary Departure," http:// www.uscis.gov/. See also Michael A. Pearson, Executive Associate Commissioner, Field Operations, Immigration and Naturalization Service, Statement before the Committee on Governmental Affairs Permanent Subcommittee on Investigations United States Senate Regarding Processing Persons Arrested for Illegal Entry into the United States Between Ports of Entry, November 13, 2001, http://www .aila.org/content/default.aspx?docid=6549.

24. US Citizenship and Immigration Service, "Deportation," http://www .uscis.gov/portal/.

25. US Department of Homeland Security (DHS), Office of Immigration Statistics (OIS), "2011 Yearbook of Immigration Statistics," table 39, p. 102, http:// www.dhs.gov/sites/default/files/publications/immigration-statistics/yearbook/2011 /ois_yb_2011.pdf.

26. Spencer H. Hsu, "Arrests on US-Mexico Border Decline 27%," *Washington Post*, May 21, 2009; Lourdes Medrano, "Bullets vs. Rocks? Border Patrol Under Fire for Use of Deadly Force," *Christian Science Monitor*, December 3, 2012; US Department of Homeland Security, "About Customs and Border Protection: Organization," http://www.cbp.gov/xp/cgov/about/organization/assist_comm_off/.

27. US Department of Homeland Security, OIS, "2011 Yearbook," table 35.

28. Encuesta sobre la Migración en la Frontera Norte de México, *Boletín EMIF Norte 2011*, http://www.colef.mx/emif/resultados/boletines/Boletin%20NTE %202011.pdf.

29. Andrew Becker, "Rebranding at ICE Meant to Soften Immigration Enforcement Agency's Image," *Washington Post*, June 17, 2010.

30. CNBC, "Billions Behind Bars: Inside America's Prison Industry," 2011, http://www.cnbc.com/id/44762286/Billions_Behind_Bars_Inside_America039s _Prison_Industry; United States Bureau of Justice, "Direct Expenditures by Justice Function, 1982–2007 (Billions of Dollars)," http://bjs.ojp.usdoj.gov/content /glance/tables/exptyptab.cfm. The $74 billion figure comes from 2007 and is the most recent data available.

31. Leo Ralph Chavez, *The Latino Threat: Constructing Immigrants, Citizens, and the Nation*, 2nd ed. (Palo Alto, CA: Stanford University Press, 2013), 24.

32. Ibid., 25.

33. American Civil Liberties Union, "Immigration Detention," http://www .aclu.org/immigrants-rights/detention; Chris Kirkham, "Private Prisons Profit From Immigration Crackdown, Federal And Local Law Enforcement Partnerships," *Huffington Post*, June 7, 2012, http://www.huffingtonpost.com/2012/06/07 /private-prisons-immigration-federal-law-enforcement_n_1569219.html.

34. Kirkham, "Private Prisons Profit."

35. Amnesty International, "USA: Jailed Without Justice," March 25, 2009, 1, http://www.amnestyusa.org/pdfs/JailedWithoutJustice.pdf.

36. Human Rights First, *Jails and Jumpsuits: Transforming the US Immigration Detention System, a Two-Year Review*, 2011, iv, http://www.humanrightsfirst.org /wp-content/uploads/pdf/HRF-Jails-and-Jumpsuits-report.pdf.

37. See the long history of Rodriguez v. Robbins compiled by the ACLU at http://www.aclu-sc.org/rodriguez/.

38. Amnesty International, "USA: Jailed without Justice," 6.

39. Alistair Graham Robertson, Rachel Beaty, Jane Atkinson, and Bob Libal, *Operation Streamline: Costs and Consequences*, Grassroots Leadership, September 2012, 2, http://grassrootsleadership.org/files/GRL_Sept2012_Report%20final.pdf.

40. Ibid., 5.

41. Ibid., 6.

42. Ibid., 7.

43. US Sentencing Commission, "Overview of Federal Criminal Cases: Fiscal Year 2011," 1–2, 9; TRAC Immigration, "Illegal Reentry Becomes Top Criminal Charge," http://trac.syr.edu/immigration/reports/251/.

44. Ibid.

45. Ibid., 3.

46. Jacob Chin, Katherine Fennelly, Kathleen Moccio, Charles Miles, and José D. Pacas, "Attorneys' Perspectives on the Rights of Detained Immigrants in Minnesota," AILA InfoNet Doc. No. 09111064 (posted 11/10/09), emphasis in original, http://www.aila.org/Content/default.aspx?docid=30514.

47. James M. Chaparro to Field Office Directors, "Keep Up the Good Work on Criminal Alien Removals," memo, *Washington Post*, February 22, 2010, http:// media.washingtonpost.com/wp-srv/politics/documents/ICEdocument032710 .pdf?sid=ST2010032700037.

48. Ibid.

49. See John Morton to Field Office Directors, "National Fugitive Operations Program," December 2009, http://www.ice.gov/doclib/detention-reform/pdf/nfop _priorities_goals_expectations.pdf.

50. US Immigration and Customs Enforcement, "Secure Communities: A Modernized Approach to Identifying and Removing Criminal Aliens," January 2010, http://www.ice.gov/doclib/secure-communities/pdf/sc-brochure.pdf.

51. Aarti Kohli, Peter L. Markowitz, and Lisa Chavez, "Secure Communities by the Numbers: An Analysis of Demographics and Due Process," Chief Justice Earl Warren Institute on Law and Social Policy, University of California, Berkeley, School of Law, October 2011, http://www.law.berkeley.edu/files/Secure_Communities _by_the_Numbers.pdf.

52. Douglas C. McDonald, "Private Penal Institutions," *Crime and Justice* 16 (1992): 382.

53. See Alfredo Blumstein and Allen J. Beck, "Population Growth in US Prisons, 1980–1996," *Crime and Justice* 26 (1999). Incarceration rates for immigration offenses rose from 0.6 per 100,000 in 1980 to 2.7 per 100,000 in 1996, an increase of 350 percent (45–46). For federal commitment rates for convicted offenders, "the largest upward trend is for immigration offenses, which had a fairly steady growth in commitment rate from 46 percent to 82 percent" (48).

54. Kirkham, "Private Prisons Profit."

55. Llewellyn Hinkes-Jones, "Privatized Prisons: A Human Marketplace," *Los Angeles Review of Books*, January 10, 2013.

56. "Incarceration, Inc.," *Phoenix Magazine*, March, 2012, http://www .phoenixmag.com/lifestyle/valley-news/201203/incarceration—inc-/1/.

57. Associated Press, "Private Prison Companies Making Big Bucks on Locking Up Undocumented Immigrants," *New York Daily News*, August 2, 2012, http:// www.nydailynews.com/news/national/private-prison-companies-making-big -bucks-locking-undocumented-immigrants-article-1.1127465#ixzz2PQbUHM9a.

58. The Geo Group, http://www.geogroup.com/; Management & Training Corporation, http://www.mtctrains.com/corrections/corrections-overview.

59. Corrections Corporation of America, http://www.cca.com/about/.

60. Justice Policy Institute, "Gaming the System: How the Political Strategies of Private Prison Companies Promote Ineffective Incarceration Policies," June 2011, 12, http://www.justicepolicy.org/uploads/justicepolicy/documents/gaming _the_system.pdf.

61. "Incarceration, Inc." In the last decade, the CCA spent $23 million in lobbying. See Kirkham, "Private Prisons Profit."

62. US Securities and Exchange Commission, Corrections Corporation of America, Form 10K for the fiscal year ended December 31, 2005, cited in Michelle Alexander, *The New Jim Crow: Mass Incarceration in the Age of Colorblindness* (New York: New Press, 2010), 218–19. The company's 2010 Annual Report used virtually identical language. See excerpt from the report in Justice Policy Institute, "Gaming the System," 3. The reports themselves are online at http://ir.correctionscorp .com/phoenix.zhtml?c=117983&p=irol-reportsannual.

63. Laura Sullivan, "Prison Economics Help Drive Ariz. Immigration Law," National Public Radio, October 28, 2010, http://www.npr.org/2010/10/28/130833741 /prison-economics-help-drive-ariz-immigration-law.

64. Justice Policy Institute, "Gaming the System," 3.

65. Sullivan, "Prison Economics Help Drive Ariz. Immigration Law."

66. Laura Sullivan, "Shaping State Laws with Little Scrutiny," National Public Radio, October 29, 2010, http://www.npr.org/2010/10/29/130891396/shaping -state-laws-with-little-scrutiny.

67. Ibid.

68. Sullivan, "Prison Economics Help Drive Ariz. Immigration Law."

69. Ibid.

70. Ibid.

71. Kirkham, "Private Prisons Profit."

72. Ibid.

73. Ibid.

74. Hannah Rappleye and Lisa Riordan Seville, "How One Georgia Town Gambled Its Future on Immigration Detention," *Nation*, April 10, 2012.

CHAPTER 5: WORKING (PART 1)

1. WGP/TRO-© Copyright 1961 (Renewed), 1963 (Renewed) Woody Guthrie Publications, Inc. & Ludlow Music, Inc., New York, NY. Administered by Ludlow Music, Inc. Used by Permission.

2. Jeffrey Passel, *Size and Characteristics of the Unauthorized Migrant Population in the US*, Pew Research Hispanic Center, March 7, 2006, part IV, "Unauthorized Migrants: The Workforce," http://www.pewhispanic.org/2006/03/07/iv -unauthorized-migrants-the-workforce/.

3. Robert Pear, "Judge's Hiring of Illegal Alien in 1980s Did Not Violate Immigration Law," *New York Times*, February 6, 1993.

4. William R. Tamayo, "Immigration and the Civil Rights Movement," in *Double Exposure: Poverty and Race in America*, ed. Chester W. Hartman (Armonk, NY: M. E. Sharpe, 1997), 115.

5. Charles B. Johnson, president of the Pasadena branch, quoted in Hector Tobar, "NAACP Calls for End to Employer Sanctions," *Los Angeles Times*, July 12, 1990.

6. See Edward R. Roybal, "If You Look 'Foreign,' It's 'No Help Wanted,'" *Los Angeles Times*, April 15, 1990; Tobar, "NAACP Calls for End to Employer Sanctions."

7. Nicholas De Genova, *Working the Boundaries: Race, Space, and "Illegality" in Mexican Chicago* (Durham, NC: Duke University Press, 2005), 235–36.

8. "Remarks of Senator Barack Obama: The American Promise," Democratic Convention, Denver, *Huffington Post*, August 8, 2008, http://www.huffingtonpost .com/2008/08/28/barack-obama-democratic-c_n_122224.html.

9. Miriam Jordan, "Fresh Raids Target Illegal Hiring," *Wall Street Journal*, May 2, 2012. See also Julia Preston, "Obama Administration Cracks Down on Illegal Immigrants' Employers," *New York Times*, May 29, 2011.

10. US Department of Labor, *Findings from the National Agricultural Workers Survey (NAWS) 2001–2002: A Demographic and Employment Profile of United States Farm Workers*, Research Report 9, March 2005, 11, http://www.doleta.gov/agworker /report9/naws_rpt9.pdf.

11. Passel, *Size and Characteristics of the Unauthorized Migrant Population*, estimates 24 percent, based on the 2005 Current Population Survey. Other estimates are much higher.

12. In 2001–2002, the National Agricultural Worker Survey estimated that 53 percent lacked authorization to work in the United States. See US Department of Labor, "Findings from the National Agricultural Workers Survey," 11. Although this is the most recent report that is fully available to the public, Daniel Carroll of the Department of Labor has summarized the results through 2009 and shows the percentage of farm workers who are undocumented falling only slightly, to around 50 percent, in subsequent years. See Daniel Carroll, "Changing Characteristics of US Farmworkers: 21 Years of Findings from the National Agricultural Workers Survey," May 12, 2011, http://migration.ucdavis.edu/cf/files/2011-may/carroll-changing -characteristics.pdf.

13. "Migrant Farm Workers: Fields of Tears," *Economist*, December 16, 2010, http://www.economist.com/node/17722932.

14. Carroll, "Changing Characteristics of US Farmworkers."

15. See Helen B. Marrow, *New Destination Dreaming: Immigration, Race, and Legal Status in the Rural American South* (Palo Alto, CA: Stanford University Press, 2011), for a discussion of this phenomenon in North Carolina.

16. Passel, *Size and Characteristics of the Unauthorized Migrant Population.*

17. Philip Martin, "Migration and Competitiveness in US Construction and Meatpacking," April 2012, http://migration.ucdavis.edu/rs/files/2012/9/ciip/martin -us-construction-and-meatpacking.pdf.

18. Steve Striffler, *Chicken: The Dangerous Transformation of America's Favorite Food* (New Haven, CT: Yale University Press, 2005), 5.

19. Philip L. Martin, "Good Intentions Gone Awry: IRCA and US Agriculture," *Annals of the Academy of Political and Social Science* 534 (July 1994): 45. He is quoting Varden Fuller in *The Supply of Agricultural Labor as a Factor in the Evolution of Farm Organization in California*, Congressional Committee on Education and Labor (LaFollette Committee), 1940, pt. 54, p. 19809.

20. Don Mitchell, *They Saved the Crops: Labor, Landscape, and the Struggle over Industrial Farming in Bracero-Era California* (Athens: University of Georgia Press, 2012), 11.

21. Ibid.

22. Truman Library, "The Migratory Worker in the American Agricultural Labor Force," ca. November 1950, Subject File, Record Group 220: President's Commission on Migratory Labor, 1, http://www.trumanlibrary.org/whistlestop/study _collections/migratorylabor/documents/index.php?pagenumber=1&documentdate =1950–11–00&documentid=16–2.

23. Ibid., 3.

24. Quoted in Daniel Kanstroom, *Deportation Nation: Outsiders in American History* (Cambridge, MA: Harvard University Press, 2007), 223.

25. Truman Library, "The Migratory Worker," 15.

26. Mitchell, *They Saved the Crops*, 6.

27. Ibid., 13.

28. Ibid., 242.

29. Ibid, 419.

30. Ibid., 420.

31. Ibid., 422.

32. Richard A. Walker, *The Conquest of Bread: 150 Years of Agribusiness in California* (New York: New Press, 2004), 74–75.

33. Douglas S. Massey and Karen A. Pren, "Unintended Consequences of US Immigration Policy: Explaining the Post-1965 Surge from Latin America," *Population and Development Review* 38, no.1 (March 2012): 3, http://wws.princeton .edu/coverstories/Massey_LatinAmericaImmigrationSurge/Unintended -Consequences.pdf.

34. Mark Overmyer-Velázquez, ed., "Introduction," *Beyond La Frontera: The History of Mexico–US Migration* (New York: Oxford University Press, 2011), xxxvii.

35. Massey and Pren, "Unintended Consequences," 5.

36. Douglas S. Massey, Jorge Duran, and Nolan J. Malone, *Beyond Smoke and Mirrors: Mexican Immigration in an Era of Economic Integration* (New York: Russell Sage Foundation, 2002), 45.

37. Martin, "Good Intentions Gone Awry," 53.

38. Ibid., 55.

39. Ibid., 53, 54, 57.

40. Ibid., 56. David Stoll cites a study of twenty-four labor contractors in the 1990s, all of whom were former migrant farm workers who had obtained legal status through the IRCA. "The ultimate in profitability is to turn one's co-ethnics or co-nationals into a captive labor force," he writes in *El Norte or Bust! How Migration Fever and Microcredit Produced a Financial Crash in a Latin American Town* (Lanham, MD: Rowman & Littlefield, 2013), 197.

41. "Migrant Farm Workers: Fields of Tears," *Economist.*

42. United Farm Workers' Take Our Jobs Update, September 24, 2010, http://www.ufw.org/_board.php?mode=view&b_code=news_press&b_no=7812&page=7&field=&key=&n=680.

43. Linda Calvin and Philip Martin, *The US Produce Industry and Labor: Facing the Future in a Global Economy,* US Department of Agriculture, Economic Research Service, Economic Research Report 106, November 2010, 1, http://www.ers.usda.gov/media/135123/err106.pdf.

44. Ibid., iii–iv.

45. Ibid., 1.

46. Ibid., 1.

47. Linda Calvin and Philip Martin, "Labor-Intensive US Fruits and Vegetables Industry Competes in a Global Market, *Amber Waves,* December 2010, http://webarchives.cdlib.org/sw1vh5dg3r/http://ers.usda.gov/AmberWaves/December10/Features/LaborIntensive.htm.

48. "Kansas Seeks Waiver for Undocumented Workers to Solve Farm Crisis," Fox News Latino, January 30, 2012, http://latino.foxnews.com/latino/politics/2012/01/30/kansas-seeks-waiver-for-undocumented-workers-to-solve-farm-crisis/.

49. Georgia Department of Agriculture, "Report on Agricultural Labor, as Required by House Bill 87," January 2012, 2, http://agr.georgia.gov/Data/Sites/1/media/ag_administration/legislation/AgLaborReport.pdf.

50. Ibid., 21.

51. Ibid., 41–43.

52. Ibid., 46.

53. Ibid., 50.

54. Ibid., 63.

55. Ibid., 100.

56. "Georgia Immigration Law Forces State to Replace Migrant Farm Workers with Criminals," *Huffington Post,* June 22, 2011, http://www.huffingtonpost.com/2011/06/22/georgia-immigration-law-f_n_882050.html.

57. Philip Martin, *Importing Poverty? The Changing Face of Rural America* (New Haven, CT: Yale University Press, 2009), xiii.

58. Ray Marshall, "Foreword," in ibid., ix.

59. Wright argues that the creation of rural poverty in Mexico's south is a result of the same economic and agricultural policies that created the export plantations of the North. Angus Wright, *The Death of Ramón González: The Modern Agricultural Dilemma* (Austin: University of Texas Press, 1990; rev. ed., 2005).

60. Ibid., xvi.

61. See, for example, Eric Schlosser, *Fast Food Nation: The Dark Side of the All-American Meal* (Boston: Houghton Mifflin, 2001/2012).

CHAPTER 6: WORKING (PART 2)

1. The decline in employment was due to increased efficiency and increased imports as well as outsourcing. See Philip Martin, "Migration and Competitiveness in US Construction and Meatpacking," conference paper, April 24, 2012, http://migration.ucdavis.edu/rs/files/2012/9/ciip/martin-us-construction-and-meatpacking.pdf.1.

2. Ibid., 1.

3. Ibid., 5–6, 7.

4. Ibid., 16.

5. Ibid., 8.

6. Joan W. Moore, *In the Barrios: Latinos and the Underclass Debate* (New York: Russell Sage Foundation, 1993), 116.

7. Patrick Jankowski, "Potential Tax Revenues from Unauthorized Workers in Houston's Economy," Greater Houston Partnership, January 2012, http://www.houston.org/pdf/research/whitepapers/taxrevenuesundocumentedworkers.pdf. His estimate was based on Pew Hispanic Foundation estimates for the national level.

8. Workers Defense Project, *Build a Better Texas: Construction Working Conditions in the Lone Star State*, January 2013, http://www.workersdefense.org/Build%20a%20Better%20Texas_FINAL.pdf; Wade Goodwyn, "Construction Booming in Texas, But Many Workers Pay Dearly," National Public Radio, April 10, 2013, http://www.npr.org/2013/04/10/176677299/construction-booming-in-texas-but-many-workers-pay-dearly.

9. Laurel E. Fletcher, Phuong Pham, Eric Stover, and Patrick Vinck, "Rebuilding After Katrina: A Population-Based Study of Labor and Human Rights in New Orleans," International Human Rights Law Clinic, Boalt Hall School of Law, University of California Berkeley; Human Rights Center, University of California, Berkeley; and Payson Center for International Development and Technology Transfer, Tulane University, June 2006, 5, http://www.law.berkeley.edu/files/rebuilding_after_katrina.pdf.

10. Associated Press, "Study: Immigrant Workers Endure Hazardous Conditions, Abuse Post-Katrina," *USA Today*, June 7, 2006.

11. Fletcher et al., "Rebuilding After Katrina," 12.

12. Ibid., 14.

13. Susan Carroll, "Undocumented Workers Will Be Linchpin of Ike Cleanup," *Houston Chronicle*, September 25, 2008, http://www.chron.com/news/hurricanes/article/Undocumented-workers-will-be-linchpin-in-Ike-1766107.php.

14. Martin, "Migration and Competitiveness," 8–9.

15. Lance A. Compa, *Blood, Sweat, and Fear: Workers' Rights in US Meat and Poultry Plants* (New York: Human Rights Watch, 2004), 7.

16. Jerry Kammer, "The 2006 Swift Raids: Assessing the Impact of Immigration Enforcement Actions at Six Facilities," Center for Immigration Studies, March 2009, 5, http://www.cis.org/articles/2009/back309.pdf.

17. Martin, "Migration and Competitiveness," 3.

18. See Sherry L. Edwards, director of Legislative and Regulatory Affairs, American Meat Institute, "Operation Vanguard," prepared for the USDA Agricultural Outlook Forum, February, 2000, 1, http://ageconsearch.umn.edu/bitstream/33429/1/fo00ed01.pdf.

19. Ibid., 1.

20. Kammer, "2006 Swift Raids," 3.

21. United Food and Commercial Workers, "Raids on Workers: Destroying Our Rights," n.d., 18, http://www.icemisconduct.org/.

22. Kammer, "2006 Swift Raids," 3.

23. Nathanial Popper, "How the Rubashkins Changed the Way Jews Eat in America," *Jewish Daily Forward*, December 11, 2008, http://forward.com/articles /14716/how-the-rubashkins-changed-the-way-jews-eat-in-ame-/.

24. Ibid.

25. Maggie Jones, "Postville, Iowa Is Up for Grabs," *New York Times Magazine*, July 11, 2012.

26. Ibid.

27. Nathanial Popper, "In Iowa Meat Plant, Kosher 'Jungle' Breeds Fear, Injury, Short Pay," *Jewish Daily Forward*, May 26, 2006, http://forward.com/articles/1006 /in-iowa-meat-plant-kosher-ejunglee-breeds-fea/.

28. Jones, "Postville Iowa Is Up for Grabs."

29. Times Wire Reports, "Guilty Plea in Postville Raid," *Los Angeles Times*, August 21, 2008, http://articles.latimes.com/2008/aug/21/nation/na-briefs21.S2.

30. US House of Representatives, "Statement of Dr. Erik Camayd-Freixas, Federally Certified Interpreter at the US District Court for the Northern District of Iowa, Regarding a Hearing on 'The Arrest, Prosecution, and Conviction of 297 Undocumented Workers in Postville, Iowa, from May 12 to 22, 2008,'" before the Subcommittee on Immigration, Citizenship, Refugees, Border Security, and International Law, July 24, 2008, http://judiciary.house.gov/hearings/pdf /Camayd-Freixas080724.pdf.

31. Ibid., 10–11.

32. Jones, "Postville, Iowa Is Up for Grabs."

33. Liz Goodwin, "Years after Immigration Raid, Iowa Town Feels Poorer and Less Stable," Yahoo News/The Lookout, December 7, 2011, http://news .yahoo.com/blogs/lookout/years-immigration-raid-iowa-town-feels-poorer-less -133035414.html.

34. Helen O'Neill, "Parents Deported, What Happens to US-Born Kids?" Associated Press, August 25, 2012, http://m.yahoo.com/.

35. Richard M. Stana, "Employment Verification: Federal Agencies Have Taken Steps to Improve E-Verify, But Significant Challenges Remain," United States Government Accountability Office (GAO), December 2010, http://www .gao.gov/new.items/d11146.pdf.

36. California and Illinois prohibited states and localities from requiring employers to use the program. Illinois also tried to prohibit the use of E-Verify in the state, but that law was overturned in court. See National Conference of State Legislatures, "E-Verify," http://www.ncsl.org/issues-research/immig/e-verify -faq.aspx.

37. Stana, "Employment Verification"; GAO, *Immigration Enforcement: Weaknesses Hinder Employment Verification and Worksite Enforcement Efforts*, GAO-05-813 (Washington, DC: August 31, 2005); GAO, *Employment Verification: Challenges Exist in Implementing a Mandatory Electronic Employment Verification System*, GAO-08-895T (Washington, DC: June 10, 2008).

38. See Frank Sharry, "The Truth about E-Verify," *Huffington Post*, May 25, 2011, http://www.huffingtonpost.com/frank-sharry/the-truth-about-everify_b _865649.html.

39. John J. Haydu, Alan W. Hodges, and Charles R. Hall, "Economic Impacts of the Turfgrass and Lawncare Industry in the United States," University of

Florida, Institute of Food and Agricultural Sciences, FE 632 (2006), 5, http://www
.fred.ifas.ufl.edu/economic-impact-analysis/pdf/FE632oo.pdf.

40. Krissah Williams, "Lawn Care Entrepreneur Faces a Changing Racial
Landscape," *Washington Post*, February 5, 2007, http://www.washingtonpost.com
/wp-dyn/content/article/2007/02/04/AR2007020401088.html.

41. California Landscape Contractors Association, Immigration Reform Center, updated July 2010, http://www.clca.us/immigration/view.html#pt8.

42. In the case of Kimba Wood, the employment took place before the 1986
Immigration Reform and Control Act made it illegal to hire an undocumented
person. See Robert Pear, "Judge's Hiring of Illegal Alien in 1980s Did Not Violate
Immigration Law," *New York Times*, February 6, 1993.

43. Maria Cramer and Maria Sacchetti, "More Immigrant Woes for Romney,"
Boston Globe, December 5, 2007.

44. Michael Falcone, "Housekeeper Nicky Diaz: Meg Whitman Treated Me
Like a Piece of Garbage," ABC News, September 29, 2010, http://abcnews.go
.com/Politics/meg-whitmans-housekeeper-treated-piece-garbage/story?id=
11758365#.UX65GKJ9uCg.

45. Mike Allen and Jim VandeHei, "Homeland Security Nominee Kerik Pulls
Out," *Washington Post*, December 11, 2004.

46. Pierrette Hondagneu-Sotelo, *Doméstica: Immigrant Workers Cleaning and
Caring in the Shadows of Affluence* (Berkeley: University of California Press, 2001), 3.

47. Ibid., 7.

48. Ibid., 3.

49. Ibid., 6.

50. Ibid., 9.

51. Ibid., 3–4.

52. For a general discussion of the "new destinations" for Latino immigration, see Douglas Massey, ed., *New Faces in New Places: The Changing Geography
of American Immigration* (New York: Russell Sage Foundation, 2008). One new
destination that stands out is North Carolina, where the Hispanic population rose
by 111 percent between 2000 and 2010, reaching 8.4 percent of the state's population. Sixty-one percent of these were Mexicans. North Carolina had the eleventh
largest Latino population in the country. See North Carolina Department of
Health and Human Services, "The Hispanic or Latino Population, 2011," http://
www.ncdhhs.gov/aging/cprofile/Hispanic_Latino2010.pdf. Washington State's
Hispanic population also grew, by 71 percent, to 755,790. See Sharon R. Ennis,
Merarys Ríos-Vargas, and Nora G. Albert, "The Hispanic Population: 2010," 2010
Census Brief, May 2011, http://www.census.gov/prod/cen2010/briefs/c2010br
-04.pdf.

53. Michael De Masi, "Nannies a Growth Industry in Slow Economy," *Business Review*, July 15, 2011, http://www.bizjournals.com/albany/print-edition/2011
/07/15/nannies-a-growth-industry-in-slow.html?page=all.

54. "More Parents Opting for Nannies over Day Care," *Arizona Republic*,
September 10, 2007, http://tucsoncitizen.com/morgue/2007/09/10/62548-more
-parents-opting-for-nannies-over-day-care/.

55. Barbara Presley Noble, "At Work: Solving the Zoe Baird Problem, *New
York Times*, July 3, 1994.

56. For the 81 percent figure, see Associated Press, "While You Were Sleeping,
the Paper Boy Grew Up," April 25, 2006, http://www.msnbc.msn.com/id/12485231
/#.UA7VVvXF-So.

57. See John Moran, "Newspaper Carriers as Independent Contractors," Connecticut Office of Legislative Research, April 13, 2006, http://www.cga.ct.gov /2006/rpt/2006-R-0288.htm.

58. "S. D. California Certifies 23(b)(3) Class of Newspaper Home Delivery Carriers," August 4, 2010, California Wage and Hour Law, Archive for the "Employee/Independent Contractor" Category, http://calwages.com/category /employeeindependent-contractor/.

59. Flyer in author's possession, from January 2011.

60. See George J. Borjas, Jeffrey Grogger, and Gordon H. Hanson, "Immigration and the Economic Status of African-American Men," *Economica* 77 (2010): 255–82, http://www.hks.harvard.edu/fs/gborjas/publications/journal /Economica2010.pdf.

61. See, for example, Julie L. Hotchkiss, Myriam Quispe-Agnoli, and Fernando Rios-Avila, "The Wage Impact of Undocumented Workers," Federal Reserve Bank of Georgia, Working Paper 2012–4, March 2012; Giovanni Peri, "Immigrants, Skills, and Wages: Measuring the Economic Gains from Immigration," Immigration Policy Center, March 2006; David Card, "Is the New Immigration Really So Bad?," University of California, Berkeley, January 2005.

62. Raúl Hinojosa-Ojeda and Marshall Fitz, "A Rising Tide or a Shrinking Pie: The Economic Impact of Legalization Versus Deportation in Arizona," Center for American Progress, March 24, 2011, http://www.americanprogress.org /issues/2011/03/rising_tide.html.

63. Eric Clark, introduction, *The Real Toy Story: The Ruthless Battle for Today's Youngest Consumers* (New York: Simon & Schuster/Free Press, 2007).

CHAPTER 7: CHILDREN AND FAMILIES

1. Pew Hispanic Center, "Between Two Worlds: How Young Latinos Come of Age in America," December 2009, 7, http://pewhispanic.org/files/reports/117.pdf.

2. Cecilia Menjívar, "Liminal Legality: Salvadoran and Guatemalan Immigrants' Lives in the United States," *American Journal of Sociology* 111, no. 4 (January 2006).

3. John Santucci, Chris Good, and Shushannah Walshe, "Everything Romney Said to Explain Away Loss," ABC News, November 15, 2012, http://abcnews .go.com/Politics/OTUS/obamas-gifts-small-campaign-bill-clintons -thoughtsromneys-parting/story?id=17727179#.ULPLkYZ62So.

4. Human Rights Watch, "Slipping Through the Cracks: Unaccompanied Children Detained by the US Immigration and Naturalization Service" (Human Rights Watch Children's Project, 1997), 2 and note 3, http://www.hrw.org/reports /1997/04/01/slipping-through-cracks.

5. US Department of Justice, Office of the Inspector General, "Unaccompanied Juveniles in INS Custody," September 28, 2001, chap. 1, http://www.justice .gov/oig/reports/INS/e0109/chapter1.htm.

6. Jacqueline Bhabha and Susan Schmidt, "Seeking Asylum Alone: Unaccompanied and Separated Children and Refugee Protection in the US," Harvard University Committee on Human Rights Studies, 2006, 6; Women's Refugee Commission and Orrick, Herrington & Sutcliffe LLP, "Halfway Home: Unaccompanied Children in Immigration Custody," February 2009, 4, http:// womensrefugeecommission.org/press-room/716-unaccompanied?q=halfway+home; Amy Thompson, "A Child Alone and Without Papers: A Report on the Return and Repatriation of Unaccompanied Undocumented Children by the United States," Center for Public Policy Priorities, September 2008, 7, http://www.aecf.org/;

Department of Health and Human Services, Office of the Inspector General, "Division of Unaccompanied Children's Services: Efforts to Serve Children," March 2008, https://oig.hhs.gov/oei/reports/oei-07-06-00290.pdf.

7. Olga Byrne and Elise Miller, "The Flow of Unaccompanied Children through the Immigration System," Vera Institute of Justice, Center for Immigration and Justice, March 2012, 6, http://www.vera.org/sites/default/files/resources/downloads/the-flow-of-unaccompanied-children-through-the-immigration-system.pdf.

8. Women's Refugee Commission et al., "Halfway Home," 4.

9. Byrne and Miller, "The Flow of Unaccompanied Children," 14.

10. Julia Preston, "Young and Alone, Facing Court and Deportation," *New York Times*, August 25, 2012.

11. Bhabha and Schmidt, "Seeking Asylum Alone," 7.

12. Byrne and Miller, "The Flow of Unaccompanied Children," 5.

13. Betsy Cavendish and Maru Cortazar, "Children at the Border: The Screening, Protection, and Repatriation of Unaccompanied Mexican Minors," Appleseed, 2001, 1, http://appleseednetwork.org/wp-content/uploads/2012/05/Children-At-The-Border1.pdf.

14. Byrne and Miller, "The Flow of Unaccompanied Children," 31.

15. Preston, "Young and Alone."

16. Terry Greene Sterling, "Undocumented Kids Crossing the US Border Alone in Increasing Numbers," *Daily Beast*, March 23, 2013, http://www.thedailybeast.com/articles/2013/03/23/undocumented-kids-crossing-the-u-s-border-alone-in-increasing-numbers.html.

17. Jessica Jones and Jennifer Podkul, "Forced from Home: The Lost Boys and Girls of Central America," Women's Refugee Commission, October 2012, 1–2, http://wrc.ms/WuG8lM.

18. Ibid., 8.

19. Ibid., 7.

20. Ibid., 1.

21. Ibid., 13.

22. Seth Freed Wessler, "Shattered Families: The Perilous Intersection of Immigration Enforcement and the Child Welfare System," Applied Research Center, November, 2011, 5, http://arc.org/shatteredfamilies; Seth Freed Wessler, "US Deports 46K Parents with Citizen Kids in Just Six Months," *Colorlines*, November 3, 2011, http://colorlines.com/archives/2011/11/shocking_data_on_parents_deported_with_citizen_children.html.

23. Nina Rabin, "Disappearing Parents: A Report on Immigration Enforcement and the Child Welfare System," University of Arizona, Southwest Institute for Research on Women, College of Social and Behavioral Sciences, Bacon Immigration Law and Policy Program, James E. Rogers College of Law, May 2011, 31, http://www.law.arizona.edu/depts/bacon_program/pdf/disappearing_parents_report_final.pdf.

24. John Morton, "Memorandum," June 17, 2011, http://www.ice.gov/doclib/secure-communities/pdf/prosecutorial-discretion-memo.pdf.

25. Helen O'Neill, "Parents Deported," Associated Press, August 25, 2012. See also Rabin, "Disappearing Parents."

26. Helen O'Neill, "U.S.-Born Kids of Deported Parents Struggle as Family Life is 'Destroyed,'" *Huffington Post*, August 25, 2012, http://www.huffingtonpost.com/2012/08/25/us-born-kids-deported-parents_n_1830496.html?utm_hp_ref=immigrants.

27. Women's Refugee Commission et al., "Halfway Home," 9.

28. Rabin, "Disappearing Parents," 10.

29. Ibid.

30. Ibid., 28.

31. O'Neill, "US-Born Kids of Deported Parents."

32. Julia Preston and John H. Cushman Jr., "Obama Permits Young Migrants to Remain in US," *New York Times*, June 15, 2012.

33. Nidia Tapia, "A Take on the Internal US-Mexico Border by an Undocumented Student," unpublished undergraduate seminar paper, Pomona College, May 2013.

34. The Court's decision and other relevant documents are available through the Cornell University Law School Legal Information Institute, http://www.law.cornell.edu/supct/html/historics/USSC_CR_0457_0202_ZS.html.

35. Jose Antonio Vargas, "My Life as an Undocumented Immigrant," *New York Times Magazine*, June 22, 2011.

36. Roberto G. Gonzalez, "Learning to Be Illegal: Undocumented Youth and Shifting Legal Contexts in the Transition to Adulthood," *American Sociological Review* 76, no. 4 (2011): 603.

37. Ibid., 605.

38. Tapia, "A Take on the Internal US-Mexico Border."

39. Carola Suárez-Orozco, Marcelo M. Suárez-Orozco, and Irina Todorova, *Learning a New Land: Immigrant Students in American Society* (Cambridge, MA: Harvard University Press, 2008), 31. See also Angela Valenzuela, *Subtractive Schooling: US-Mexican Youth and the Politics of Caring* (Albany: State University of New York Press, 1999). "The record of achievement among . . . immigrant youth is significantly higher than that of their US-born, second- and third+-generation counterparts," 8.

40. William Pérez, *We Are Americans: Undocumented Students Pursuing the American Dream* (Sterling, VA: Stylus Publishing, 2009), vii–viii.

41. Michael A. Olivas, *No Undocumented Child Left Behind: Plyler v. Doe and the Education of Undocumented Schoolchildren* (New York: New York University Press, 2012), 66; National Conference of State Legislatures, "Undocumented Student Tuition: Federal Action," May 2011, http://www.ncsl.org/issues-research/educ/undocumented-student-tuition-federal-action.aspx; William Pérez, *Americans By Heart: Undocumented Latino Students and the Promise of Higher Education* (New York: Teachers College Press, 2011), 6.

42. National Immigration Law Center, "Basic Facts about In-State Tuition," May 2013, http://www.nilc.org/basic-facts-instate.html.

43. Pérez, *We Are Americans*, xxvi.

44. Massachusetts Taxpayers Foundation, "Revenues from Undocumented Immigrants Paying In-State Rates," July 18, 2011, http://www.masstaxpayers.org/sites/masstaxpayers.org/files/In-state%20tuition.pdf.

45. The various versions of the act are posted online at http://www.dreamactivist.org/text-of-dream-act-legislation/.

46. See Vamos Unidos Youth, "Latino Youth Defines Dream Act as De Facto Military Draft," WESPAC Foundation, http://wespac.org/2010/09/21/dream-act-as-military-draft/.

47. Jean Batalova and Margie McHugh, "DREAM vs. Reality: An Analysis of Potential DREAM Act Beneficiaries," Migration Policy Institute, July 2010, http://www.migrationpolicy.org/pubs/DREAM-Insight-July2010.pdf.

48. Claudia Anguiano, "Undocumented, Unapologetic, and Unafraid: Discursive Strategies of the Immigrant Youth DREAM Social Movement," PhD diss., University of New Mexico, 2011, xi.

49. Julia Preston, "Young Immigrants Say It's Obama's Time to Act," *New York Times*, November 30, 2012.

50. Jose Antonio Vargas, "Not Legal, Not Leaving," *Time,* June 25, 2012, http://www.time.com/time/magazine/article/0,9171,2117243–7,00.html.

51. Daniel Altschuler, "DREAMing of Citizenship: An Interview with Gaby Pacheco," *Huffington Post*, December 15, 2010, http://www.huffingtonpost.com /daniel-altschuler/dreaming-of-citizenship-a_b_797391.html.

52. Julia Preston, "Advocates of Immigration Overhaul Alter Tactics in New Push," *New York Times*, January 1, 2010.

53. Vargas, "Not Legal, Not Leaving," 2.

54. Ibid., 9.

55. Preston, "Young Immigrants Say It's Obama's Time to Act."

56. Alexander Bolton, "Republicans Seeking Out Hispanics," *Hill*, March 27, 2012, http://thehill.com/homenews/senate/218307-republicans-seeking-out-hispanics.

57. Preston, "Young Immigrants Say It's Obama's Time to Act."

58. Peter Wallsten, "Marco Rubio's Dream Act Alternative a Challenge for Obama on Immigration," *Washington Post*, April 25, 2012.

59. "Full Transcript of Obama's Speech on His New Immigration Policy," *Washington Post*, June 15, 2012.

60. Pew Hispanic Center, "Up to 1.4 Million Unauthorized Immigrants Could Benefit from New Deportation Policy," June 15, 2012, http://www .pewhispanic.org/2012/06/15/up-to-1-4-million-unauthorized-immigrants -could-benefit-from-new-deportation-policy/.

61. US Citizenship and Immigration Service, "Deferred Action for Childhood Arrivals Process," August 16–September 13, 2012, http://www.uscis.gov.

62. US Citizenship and Immigration Service, "Deferred Action for Childhood Arrivals Process," August 16–October 10, 2012, http://www.uscis.gov.

63. US Citizenship and Immigration Service, "Deferred Action for Childhood Arrivals Process," August 15, 2012 to March 31, 2013, http://www.uscis.gov.

64. Grace Meng, "Immigration Waivers Leave Migrant Children Behind," *USA Today*, August 28, 2012.

65. Robert Menendez Press Office, "Menendez, Durbin, Reid, 30 Others Introduce the DREAM Act," May 11, 2011, http://www.menendez.senate.gov /newsroom/press/release/?id=6e1282d4–4ec2–468b-8004–3370ba94a438.

66. Julianne Hing, "Michelle Rhee Joins Parent Blame Game in DREAM Act Support," *Colorlines*, July 7, 2011, http://colorlines.com/archives/2011/07 /michelle_rhee_supports_the_dream_act.html.

67. Tapia, "A Take on the Internal US-Mexico Border."

68. Seth Freed Wessler, "Dust Off Those Old Immigration Reform Deals? Not So Fast," *Colorlines*, November 13, 2012, http://colorlines.com/archives/2012/11 /republicans_back_immigration_reform_but_advocates_keep_pressure_on_white _house.html.

69. Julia Preston, "Young Leaders Cast a Wider Net for Immigration Reform," *New York Times*, December 2, 2012.

70. Kirk Semple, "Undocumented Life Is a Hurdle as Immigrants Seek a Reprieve," *New York Times*, October 3, 2012.

71. Susan Carroll, "Hope Turns to Despair for Many Trying To Stay in US," *Houston Chronicle*, November 26, 2012.

72. Robert Pear, "Limits Placed on Immigrants in Health Care," *New York Times*, September 17, 2012.

73. Serena Maria Daniels, "Michigan's Immigrant Youths Put in Legal Limbo," *Detroit News*, December 3, 2012, http://www.detroitnews.com/article /20121203/METRO/212030340#ixzz2E38J3Bv5.

74. Jorge Rivas, "Did Obama's Victory Speech Include Nod to Dreamers?" *Colorlines*, November 7, 2012, http://colorlines.com/archives/2012/11/did_obamas _victory_speech_ include_nod_to_dreamers.html.

CHAPTER 8: SOLUTIONS

1. Katherine Benton-Cohen, *Borderline Americans: Racial Division and Labor War in the Arizona Borderlands* (Cambridge, MA: Harvard University Press, 2009), 7.

2. Ibid., 8–9.

3. Nicholas De Genova, *Working the Boundaries: Race, Space, and "Illegality" in Mexican Chicago* (Durham, NC: Duke University Press, 2005), 91–92.

4. Ibid., 92, quoting Kitty Calavita, *Inside the State: The Bracero Program, Immigration, and the I.N.S.* (New York: Routledge, 1992), 180.

5. De Genova, *Working the Boundaries*, 93.

6. Ibid., 224.

7. Marc Georges Pufong, "Immigration and Nationality Act Amendments of 1965," in *The Encyclopedia of American Civil Liberties*, vol. 1, ed. Paul Finkelman (New York: Taylor and Francis, 2006), 796–97.

8. De Genova, *Working the Boundaries,* 230.

9. Douglas S. Massey and Karen A. Pren, "Unintended Consequences of US Immigration Policy: Explaining the Post-1965 Surge from Latin America," *Population and Development Review* 38, no. 1 (March 2012): 4, http://www.princeton .edu/coverstories/Massey_LatinAmericaImmigrationSurge/Unintended= Consequences.pdf.

10. Ibid., 2.

11. Ibid., 17–18.

12. Ibid., 19–20.

13. Ibid., 20.

14. See David Bacon, *Illegal People: How Globalization Creates Migration and Criminalizes Immigrants* (Boston: Beacon Press, 2008), and David Bacon, *The Right to Stay Home* (Boston: Beacon Press, 2013), for further discussion of how US policies foster out-migration. For US policy in Latin America more generally, see Greg Grandin, *Empire's Workshop: Latin America, the United States, and the Rise of the New Imperialism* (New York: Henry Holt, 2006).

15. Jacqueline Stevens, *States without Nations: Citizenship for Mortals* (New York: Columbia University Press, 2010), 45.

16. I would like to thank Oscar Chacón of NALAAC for sharing his thoughts on the history of these various immigration reform agendas and allowing me to incorporate his ideas in this section.

17. Joseph Nevins, *Operation Gatekeeper and Beyond: The War on "Illegals" and the Remaking of the US–Mexico Boundary*, 2nd ed. (New York: Routledge, 2010), 140.

18. David G. Gutiérrez, *Walls and Mirrors: Mexican Americans, Mexican Immigrants, and the Politics of Ethnicity* (Berkeley: University of California Press, 1995).

19. Alma Martínez, "Pancho Villa's Head: The Mexican Revolution and the Chicano Dramatic Imagination," Pomona College Oldenborg Lunch Series, April 25, 2013.

20. Karen Woodrow and Jeffrey Passel, "Post-IRCA Undocumented Immigration to the United States: An Assessment Based on the June, 1988 CPS," in *Undocumented Migration to the United States: IRCA and the Experience of the 1980s*, ed. Frank D. Bean, Barry Edmonston, and Jeffrey S. Passel (Washington, DC: Urban Institute Press, 1990), 51. They point out that because of inconsistencies in how Seasonal Agricultural Workers are counted in the Census and the Community Population Survey, the numbers don't correspond perfectly. Some 1.3 million were legalized under the SAW provisions.

21. Woodrow and Passel, "Post-IRCA Undocumented Immigration," 66. Emphasis in original.

22. Jeff Stansbury, "L.A. Labor and the New Immigrants," *Labor Research Review* 1, no. 13 (1989): 22.

23. See Nancy Cleeland, "AFL-CIO Calls for Amnesty for Illegal US Workers," *Los Angeles Times*, February 17, 2000.

24. "AFL-CIO: End Sanctions," *Migration News* 7, no. 3 (March 2000), http://migration.ucdavis.edu/mn/more.php?id=2037_0_2_0.

25. Wayne A. Cornelius, "Impacts of the 1986 US Immigration Law on Emigration from Rural Mexican Sending Communities," in Bean, Edmonston, and Passel, *Undocumented Migration*, 243.

26. See Nevins, *Operation Gatekeeper and Beyond*, 105.

27. Proposition 187: Text of proposed law, http://www.americanpatrol.com/REFERENCE/prop187text.html.

28. Ruben J. Garcia, "Critical Race Theory and Proposition 187: The Racial Politics of Immigration Law," *Chicano-Latino Law Review* 17, no. 118 (1995): 130.

29. Nevins, *Operation Gatekeeper and Beyond*, 108.

30. Michelle Alexander, *The New Jim Crow: Mass Incarceration in the Age of Colorblindness* (New York: New Press, 2010), 47.

31. Ibid., 42.

32. Ibid., 54.

33. Nevins, *Operation Gatekeeper and Beyond*, 110.

34. Ibid., 4, quoting US Border Patrol, "Border Patrol Strategic Plan: 1994 and Beyond," 1994, 114.

35. Nevins, *Operation Gatekeeper and Beyond*, 12.

36. Wade Goodwyn, "Texas Republicans Take Harder Line on Immigration," National Public Radio, March 29, 2011, http://www.npr.org/2011/03/29/134956690/texas-republicans-take-harder-line-on-immigration.

37. "Statement by Gov. Rick Perry on Immigration and Border Security," press release, April 29, 2010, http://governor.state.tx.us/news/press-release/14574/.

38. "Statement by Gov. Perry Regarding SCOTUS Decision on Arizona Law," press release, June 25, 2012, http://governor.state.tx.us/news/press-release/17373/.

39. Tim Eaton, "Perry Blasts Arizona Ruling But Ready to Push Sanctuary City Bill Again," *Austin Statesman*, June 25, 2012.

40. Text of Bush immigration speech, January 7, 2004, available on a number of websites, including PBS, http://www.pbs.org/newshour/bb/law/jan-june04/workers_bg_01–07.html.ye.

41. Irene Bloemraad, Kim Voss, and Taeku Lee, "The Protests of 2006: What They Were, How Do We Understand Them, Where Do They Go?," in *Rallying for*

Immigrant Rights: The Fight for Inclusion in 21st Century America, ed. Kim Voss and Irene Bloemraad (Berkeley: University of California Press, 2011), 3–4.

42. Beth Baker-Cristales, "Mediated Resistance: The Construction of Neoliberal Citizenship in the Immigrant Rights Movement," *Latino Studies* 7, no. 1 (Spring 2009): 61.

43. Bloemraad, Voss, and Lee, "The Protests of 2006," 23.

44. See Sarah Anne Wright, "'Freedom Ride' Focuses Attention on Immigrants' Rights," *Seattle Times*, September 21, 2003. See also Randy Shaw, "Building the Labor-Clergy-Immigrant Alliance," in *Rallying for Immigrant Rights*, ed. Voss and Bloemraad, 82–100.

45. Shaw, "Building the Labor-Clergy-Immigrant Alliance."

46. John F. Harris, "Bush's Hispanic Vote Dissected," *Washington Post*, December 26, 2004.

47. Mark Hugo Lopez, "The Hispanic Vote in the 2008 Election," Pew Hispanic Center, November 8, 2008, http://www.pewhispanic.org/2008/11/05/the-hispanic-vote-in-the-2008-election/; Donna St. George and Brady Dennis, "Growing Share of Hispanic Voters Helped Push Obama to Victory," *Washington Post*, November 7, 2012.

48. Rinku Sen, "Immigrants Are Losing the Policy Fight. But That's Beside the Point," *Colorlines*, September 17, 2012, http://colorlines.com/archives/2012/09/immigrants_are_losing_the_political_fight_but_thats_beside_the_point.html.

49. Drew Westen, "Immigrating from Facts to Values: Political Rhetoric in the US Immigration Debate," Migration Policy Institute, 2009, http://www.migrationpolicy.org/pubs/TCM-politicalrhetoric-Westen.pdf.

50. Stan Greenberg, James Carville, Mark Feierstein, and Al Quinlan, "Winning the Immigration Issue: A Report on New National Survey on Immigration," December 18, 2007, Greenberg Quinlan Rosner Research, http://www.gqrr.com/articles/2120/4038_Democracy_Corps_December_18_2007_Immigration_Memo.pdf.

51. Jorge Ramos interview with then-candidate Barack Obama, May 28, 2008, *This Week*, ABC, July 4, 2010, Politifact.com, http://www.politifact.com/truth-o-meter/promises/obameter/promise/525/introduce-comprehensive-immigration-bill-first-yea/.

52. "Obama's Remarks to NALEO," June 28, 2008, *Real Clear Politics*, http://www.realclearpolitics.com/articles/2008/06/obamas_remarks_to_naleo.html.

53. Carrie Budoff Brown, "Dems' Tough New Immigration Pitch," *Politico*, June 10, 2010, http://www.politico.com/news/stories/0610/38342.html.

54. "Transcript of President Obama's Press Conference," *New York Times*, November 14, 2012, http://www.nytimes.com/2012/11/14/us/politics/running-transcript-of-president-obamas-press-conference.html.

55. Gabriel Thompson, "How the Right Made Racism Sound Fair—and Changed Immigration Politics," *Colorlines*, September 13, 2011, http://colorlines.com/archives/2011/09/how_the_right_made_racist_rhetoric_sound_neutral—and_shaped_immigration_politics.html.

56. Spencer S. Hsu, "Obama Revives Bush Idea of Using E-Verify to Catch Illegal Contract Workers," *Washington Post*, July 9, 2009.

57. John Morton, "Civil Immigration Enforcement: Priorities for the Apprehension, Detention, and Removal of Aliens," June 30, 2010, http://www.ice.gov/doclib/detention-reform/pdf/civil_enforcement_priorities.pdf; John Morton,

"Memorandum," June 17, 2011, http://www.ice.gov/doclib/secure-communities /pdf/prosecutorial-discretion-memo.pdf.

58. John Simanski and Lesley M. Sapp, "Immigration Enforcement Actions: 2011," US Department of Homeland Security, Office of Immigration Statistics, September 2012, http://www.dhs.gov/sites/default/files/publications/immigration -statistics/enforcement_ar_2011.pdf.

59. US Department of Homeland Security, Immigration and Customs Enforcement, "FY 2012: ICE announces year-end removal numbers," December 21, 2012, http://www.ice.gov/news/releases/1212/121221washingtondc2.htm.

60. Ben Winograd, "ICE Numbers on Prosecutorial Discretion Keep Sliding Downward," Immigration Impact, July 30, 2012, http://immigrationimpact .com/2012/07/30/ice-numbers-on-prosecutorial-discretion-sliding-downward/; "ICE Prosecutorial Discretion Program: Latest Details as of June 28, 2012," Syracuse University Transactional Records Access Clearinghouse (TRAC) Immigration, http://trac.syr.edu/immigration/reports/287/.

61. Sen, "Immigrants Are Losing the Policy Fight."

62. The campaign is described on the *Colorlines* website, http://colorlines .com/droptheiword/.

63. Craig Kopp, "Associated Press Recommends Media Stop Using 'Illegal Immigrant,'" WUSF News, April 12, 2013, http://wusfnews.wusf.usf.edu/post /associated-press-recommends-media-stop-using-illegal-immigrant.

64. Adam Clark Estes, "*L.A. Times* Ban on 'Illegal Immigrant' Puts Everybody Else on the Spot," *Atlantic Wire*, May 1, 2013, http://www.theatlanticwire.com /politics/2013/05/new-la-times-ban-illegal-immigrant-puts-everybody-else -spot/64795/.

65. Ruben Navarrette, "DREAMers Are Pushing Their Luck," CNN *Opinion*, December 19, 2012, http://www.cnn.com/2012/12/19/opinion/navarette-dreamers /index.html.

66. Frederick Douglass, "West India Emancipation," August 3, 1857. Reproduced at http://www.blackpast.org/?q=1857-frederick-douglass-if-there-no -struggle-there-no-progress.

Index